REMEMBERED A

Peter Metcalfe was born in the Holway Estate, near Holywell, in 1956 and attended the Carmel County Primary and Holywell High schools.

He moved to Flint in 1969 and, in 1972, began a four-year apprenticeship as a plumber/lead burner at Courtaulds Greenfield factory near Holywell. In 1979, a work colleague introduced Peter to the fascinating hobby of genealogy.

Since then he has traced his family tree back hundreds of years, spending hundreds of hours at the Flintshire Record Office, Hawarden, and visiting record offices throughout the country. He has researched family trees for many other people, too, over the past 20 years or so.

He has been a member of the Clwyd Family History Society (CFHS) since its inception in 1980, and has written a number of articles for the Society's quarterly magazine, 'Hel Achau'. As a volunteer for the CFHS Parish Register project, he helped to transcribe, ready for publication, some of the baptism, marriage and burial registers in the counties of Flintshire and Denbighshire, up to 1812. In addition, Peter has recorded the Monumental Inscriptions for the Old London Road Cemetery and the burial register for the Northop Road Cemetery, which have also been published by the CFHS.

His personal research has produced transcriptions of the Holywell Workhouse births and deaths register, the 1912, 1918 and 1938 electoral registers for Flint, and the Flint 1901 census. Further transcriptions include the complete Flint Parish Church registers of baptisms, marriages and burials (1813–1999), and Peter has details on every Flint man who fought in the Great War, as this book attests.

His interest in the history of Flint and its people was kindled in the 1980s, and he has since collected hundreds of photos and documents relating to the town. He is a founder member, and an archivist, of the Flint Local History Society. He is also a volunteer for the Flintshire War Memorial Project and the War Graves Photographic Project.

It is because of this 'addiction', as he likes to call it, that we have this book today.

Remembered Again

Recalling Flint's fallen heroes of the First World War
Volume I (A–H)

Peter Metcalfe

Peter Metcalfe

www.browncowpublishing.com

First published by Brown Cow, 2014
Printed by Gomer Press, Llandysul, Ceredigion

www.browncowpublishing.com

This paperback edition 2014
1

© Jaffa Design Limited, 2014

A catalogue record for this book
is available from the British Library

ISBN: 978-0-9567031-2-5

All rights reserved—No part of this publication
may be reproduced, stored in a retrieval system,
or transmitted, in any form or by any means, electronic, mechanical,
photocopying, recording, scanning or otherwise, without the
prior permission of the publishers.

This book is sold subject to the condition that it shall not, by way of trade or otherwise, be lent, re-sold, hired out or otherwise circulated without the publisher's prior consent in any form of binding or cover other than that in which it is published and without a similar condition including this condition being imposed on the subsequent purchaser.

I dedicate these two volumes to the 162 men within their pages who all had hopes and dreams for the future but whose lives were cruelly cut short in what was considered by many to be "the war to end war."

Sadly, it soon became apparent that it was just another war and, 100 years after that war began, there is still no peace in the world.

Peter Metcalfe, 2014

ACKNOWLEDGEMENTS

The research for this book has been a long and pleasurable task but without the generosity and donation of photographs, documents and stories from the following people this book would have been far less interesting.

First, I wish to thank my parents, Doris and Walter Metcalfe, for buying me a laptop to use at the Record Office, which made the task so much easier.

Mr Tony Aldridge, Buckley
Mr John Bithell, Flint
Ms Rose Marie Dennan, Flint (Secretary of St Mary's Catholic Church, Flint)
Mr David Baran, Scratby, Great Yarmouth (SS Dundalk)
Mr Graham Barker, Nantwich (Sergeant William Davies)
Mr Alan Bevan, London (Private Robert Bevan)
Mr Glyn Bithell, Flint (Corporal Harold Bithell MM)
Mr Terry Bithell, Halkyn (Corporal Harold Bithell MM)
Ms Eileen Bowen, Flint (Sergeant Fred William Bowen)
Mr Philip J Broadstock, Walsall (Private Amos Broadstock)
Mr John Burke [deceased], Flint (Lance Corporal Henry Conway and Private James Conway)
Mr & Mrs Claire and David Carrington, Flint (Corporal John Bellis and Private Thomas Bellis)
Mr David Cartwright, Wrexham (Lance Corporal Henry Conway and Private James Conway)
Ms Alison Davies, Flint (Private Thomas John Hughes)
Mrs Julia Cowley, Flint (Lance Corporal Henry Conway and Private James Conway)
Mr Malcolm Dean, Coventry (Private John Joseph Dean)
Mr John Michael Denton, Rickmansworth (Sergeant George Robert Denton)
Mrs Sandra Evans, Flint (Private Thomas Humphreys)
Mrs Vivienne Evans, Babell (Company Sergeant Major John Clark)
Mr Charles Fair, Folkestone (Private Thomas John Hughes)
Ms Helen Fairhurst (Private Thomas Abrams)
Mr Andrew Gregory, Connah's Quay (Private John Campbell)
Mr Charles Evans-Gunther, Flint (Private Archie Gunther and Donkeyman Robert Henry Gunther)
Mr & Mrs Eric Gunther, Goole, Yorkshire (Donkeyman Robert Henry Gunther)
Mr Paul Hancock, Ellesmere Port (Sergeant Trevor Owen Hughes)
Mrs Marjorie Hickman [deceased], Flint (Private Charles Bennett)
Ms Anne Howard, Dublin (Mr Samuel John Cocks)
Mr & Mrs Harold and Ceridwen Hughes, Flint (Company Sergeant Major John Clark)
Mr Robert Hughes, Flint (Private Robert Bevan)
Mrs Sheila Hughes [deceased], Bagillt (Private John Dodd)
Mrs Pat Kilmore (Gunner William Hunt)
Mr Graham Knight, Solihull (Sergeant Fred Bowen)
Mrs Julie Knowles, Liverpool (Corporal John Bellis, Private Thomas Bellis and
    Private Joseph Albert Hulley)

Mrs Maddy Morgan, Trelawnydd (Private Peter Patrick Costello, Private William Costello, Private Peter Evans and Private Thomas Evans)
Mrs Marjorie Murray, Flint Mountain (Private Geoffrey George)
Mr David Shepherd, Flint (Private Edward Thomas Hughes)
Mr Kenneth Smith, Walsall (Private Amos Broadstock)
Mrs Shula Smith, Flint (Private Daniel Davies DCM)
Mr R Neville Stapely, Flint (Private Daniel Davies DCM)
Ms Margaret Walker (Gunner William Hunt)
Mr Vic Williams [deceased], Connah's Quay (Lieutenant Thomas Bate – "Kelsterton Hall and the Bate Family")
Mrs Lilian Young, Flint (Private Frank Brown [W496])
Mrs Geri Zervoudis [deceased], Ontario, Canada (Private Archie Gunther & Donkeyman Robert Henry Gunther)

I would also like to thank Mr David Hanson, MP for Delyn, for his support and for writing the introduction.

I am also deeply indebted to the following organisations for its financial help in the publication of this book:

THE JACK TIMOTHY TRUST

FLINT LOCAL HISTORY SOCIETY

SCA HYGIENE PRODUCTS UK LTD, OAKENHOLT

WALES AND WEST HOUSING, FLINT

FOREWORD

I have often been asked what prompted me to write this book and the answer is thus . . .

I had been a family historian since 1979 and my interest in local history started a few years later. Then, in the mid- 1990s, I decided I wanted to use my experience as a researcher on a major project but, for many years, no specific topic engaged my interest. Until 2005, when I was on one of my regular visits to the Flintshire Record Office, Hawarden. I stumbled across a booklet about the names on the First World War memorial in Bagillt, which was written by Mr M A Aldridge, nephew of our town's former mayor and councillor Mrs Vicky Perfect. Without giving it another thought I knew that I must do the same for Flint.

It has been an extraordinarily fascinating adventure and tremendous fun—and I've met many pleasant and generous people along the way. Generous in that they welcomed me into their homes, shared family stories and allowed me to copy photographs and documents.

I am first and foremost a family historian and not a military historian so I haven't focused too much on the military aspect. Nevertheless, I feel sure you will find the human story just as interesting, if not more so.

Each story was made up from reliable source texts, woven together to create each man's tale. This book was never intended to be an academic exercise, more a labour of love. Although I was thorough in my attention to detail, I have chosen not to provide citations for every single piece of sourced material and hope that the reader appreciates my attempt to tell each soldier's story in as colourful a way as possible, without filling the pages with intrusive footnotes and links. To view the sources I used to compile the text, see the general reference at the back of the book on page XXXIII.

The pedantic amongst us may be quick to point out some sometimes larger than life spelling or grammatical errors scattered through the pages of this book. Please note that the vast majority of these will be wholly intentional. Letters that were written by troops to those back home are used throughout and, as a mark of of respect, these have been faithfully transcribed as they were written, in their own style, retaining spelling mistakes and all. My advice would be to suspend any analytical tendencies and enjoy the letters for what they are, the uncomplicated, heartfelt writings of those a long way from home and the replies of their loved ones.

There are also clerical errors, where names are misspelt on official letters, documents and monuments, and the back-room errors of newspaper reports. All have been left exactly as the source material had them. Again, these could have been cited, but would have made for a very cluttered page, littered with the standard Latin adverb 'sic' meaning 'intentionally quoted verbatim', usually placed after each mistake. Worse still I could have guessed a correction and compounded the matter. As it is, I have chosen to trust the reader's good will and intelligence on this matter and let the stories flow.

A number of people have asked me why 31st July, 1921 is the cut-off date assigned to a Commonwealth War Graves Commission (CWGC) war death. The answer is very simple: that was the official date of the end of the war, with 11th November, 1918 being an armistice (after WW2, a similar time period was chosen by the CWGC).

This volume includes three men whose names are not recorded on any of the Flint war memorials but whom I believe are worthy of mention. They are: Samuel John Cox (a civilian), Robert Henry Gunther and William Hodgson.

If you enjoy reading this book even half as much as I have researching it, then my task will have been worthwhile.

Peter Metcalfe, Flint, North Wales

September, 2014

INTRODUCTION

HOUSE OF COMMONS

LONDON SW1A 0AA

All of us know about the history of the First World War, through film, books, TV or the personal experience of relatives who fought or knew people who had experienced the horrors of that conflict. Even in my early days as Member of Parliament for Delyn constituency, I can recall meeting Flintshire World War One veterans and sharing with them their memories of their time in uniform.

I recall, with some pride, my own grandfather vividly telling me of his experiences in that conflict in France and the Middle East. It is a war that still today has made an impact on the world in which we live.

For the people in this book, however, the Great War impacted on their lives, those of their family, and the community of Flint, in a way that few of us today could imagine.

This book brings to life those people, from the town of Flint, who gave their lives during that conflict.

Each of them was a son, a brother, a father or a friend.

Each of them had hopes and dreams of the future.

Each of them gave their lives in the service of their country.

It is fitting that, 100 years on from the commencement of the First World War, this book records their lives and their sacrifice. It tells their stories, who they were, and where they lived so that once again they are no longer just names on a memorial. They are again living people of whom today's generation of Flint can be truly proud.

David Hanson MP

Delyn

CONTENTS

	Page
Dedication	V
Acknowledgements	VII
Foreword	IX
Introduction	XI
Contents	XIII
"The war to end war" How it all began	XVII
Flint's Fallen Heroes of the First World War, Volume 1, (A-H)	1
Thomas Abrams	3
Samuel Amos	4
Thomas Bate	5
Joseph Beard	10
Henry Bellis	13
John Bellis	15
Samuel Bellis	25
Thomas Bellis	25
Charles Bennett	30
John James Bentham	32
Benjamin Bevan	35
Robert Bevan	37
Harold Bithell	39
Frederick William Bowen	42
Patrick Joseph Bradley	46
John James Bramfield	46
Patrick Brett	48
Amos Broadstock	50
Joseph Broderick	51
Frank Brown (240643)	53
Frank Brown (W496)	54
Peter Burke	55
John Campbell	57
George Carr	61
James Carroll	65

John Carroll	65
Robert Cartwright	67
John Clark	69
Thomas Pierce Clark	77
Joseph Clews	81
Samuel John Cocks	82
Henry Francis Conway	85
James Conway	87
Peter Patrick Costello	88
William Costello	90
Evelyn Napier Craven	90
Richard Craven	93
Alfred Davies	94
Benjamin Davies	96
Daniel Davies	99
William Davies	103
John Joseph Dean	105
Samuel Dean	108
George Robert Denton	111
John Dodd	115
John William Eccles	116
Robert Thomas Edwards	117
Arthur Ellis	119
Arthur Leslie Evans	122
John Evans	127
Peter Evans	127
Thomas Evans	128
William Arthur Evans	131
Thomas Ferguson	132
William Forrester	135
Peter Fox	137
Geoffrey George	138

Albert Lowther Gillott	140
Harry Gloyne	141
Herbert Hayes Gunning	142
Archibald Gunther	145
Robert Henry Gunther	151
David Hammond	153
Thomas Harris	155
John Hayes	156
Thomas Hewitt	157
Willam Hewitt	159
Joseph Walter Hill	161
William Hodgson	163
Edward Hughes	165
Edward Thomas Hughes	167
John Hughes	170
John Edward Hughes	172
Thomas Hughes	174
Thomas John Hughes	177
Trevor Owen Hughes	185
William Hughes	188
W T Hughes	192
Joseph Albert Hulley	192
Thomas Humphreys	195
William Thomas Humphreys	198
William Hunt	199
John Andrew Hyde	201
First World War Memorials in Flint	XXI
Campaign Medals mentioned in this book	XXV
War Poetry	XXVIII
References	XXXIII

"THE WAR TO END WAR"
HOW IT ALL BEGAN

The cause of the war is all rather complicated but the trigger was the assassination of the Austrian Archduke Franz Ferdinand and his wife at Sarajevo on 28th June, 1914 at the hands of Serbian Nationalist Gavrilo Princip.

On 4th August, at 11:00 pm, Britain declared war on Germany, and the 7th August edition of the County Herald reported the following:

"Not since the South African Campaign a few years ago has there been witnessed in the Borough of Flint such a spirit of militarism and patriotism as has been evidenced in the course of the present week. The serious trend which events assumed intentionally necessitated an alternation at the encampment of the 5th Battalion of the Royal Welsh Fusiliers (Territorials) near Aberystwyth. The Flint Company left the Borough last Sunday week for the camp, and were under the command of Major E J H Williams, with other officers. On Sunday last communications were flashed about the country, and the result was that early on Monday throughout Great Britain all the Territorial Camps were "struck" by special Government Orders. This dismantling occupied some few hours, together with the preparations for the returning home; and later in the day the Flintshire Companies left Aberystwyth, and travelling through the night reached Flint, and their other destinations on the coast, soon after 6 o'clock. At Flint Station the "home" men were lined up on the platform, and Major Williams, presuming that each man knew the Order for Mobilisation of the Regular and Territorial Forces, briefly addressed them, informing them that they could return to their respective homes there to be in readiness to await further Orders which might be received. Notwithstanding the long railway journey and the great tension experienced by the rumours of war intelligence the men appeared cheerful under all the conditions. It was reported they would be leaving towards the end of the week to take up a position at the headquarters at Preston.

Archduke Franz Ferdinand with his wife Sophie, Duchess of Hohenberg

Serbian Nationalist Gavrilo Princip

In the course of Monday, in consequence of information having been circulated in the town, a considerable number of women and children proceeded to the Railway Station, where they occupied some of the chief waiting rooms, in the hope they would be present to accord a greeting to their Territorial friends. Hours were devoted to weary watching for the train, but all in vain. The people were causing some inconvenience to the travelling public, as well as holiday passengers, and it was, therefore, found necessary to order them peremptorily to leave the station premises. Therefore, as the night wore on, extra railway officials were placed on duty, and the station premises were permitted only to be entered by the passengers, and others who had important business transactions. The holiday passengers had the unique experience, and one which was endured with much forbearance, of having to wait longer than three hours for a "local" train from Rhyl to Chester. After the arrival about seven o'clock of the train which was due soon after three o'clock in the afternoon, another batch of passengers numbering over one hundred arrived from the Flint districts to proceed to Chester, etc., and they also had the "distinguished" inconvenience of waiting until nearly ten o'clock for the next "local."

It transpired upon enquiries that the prolonged delays and dislocation of the "up service" was caused by the Orders received at the Military Camps along the North Wales Coast for the troops to leave immediately for their home destinations. The "troop trains" were numerous, and it was not until late in the evening that this extra pressure upon the "top" of the Bank Holiday traffic, was relieved. However, at the Flint Railway Station, Mr J C Shone, officiating as the Stationmaster, was continuously on duty for several hours, and every possible assistance was rendered the travelling public to depart by the first available trains. A number

G. R.

Young Men of Flintshire!

JOIN YOUR COUNTY REGIMENT

5th Battalion Royal Welsh Fusiliers.

TERMS OF SERVICE:

1.--Age on enlistment 19 to 38, Ex-soldiers up to 45. Certain selected Ex-Non-commissioned Officers up to 50.

2.--General Service for the duration of the War.

3.--Height, 5ft. 3ins. and upwards. Chest, 34ins. Medically fit.

4.--Pay at Army Rates. Married men or widowers with children will be accepted and will draw Separation Allowance under Army conditions. Men will be enabled to secure their discharge with all convenient speed on the conclusion of the War.

God Save the King.

A Flintshire Observer recruitment poster

The Drill Hall by Flint Castle where the 5th Battalion RWF had their Headquarters and enlistment took place

Royal Welsh Fusiliers on parade by the castle in c.1914

of youthful exuberates, and others who were satiated with the "war fever" continued their weary vigil for the home-coming of the Territorials until nearly five o'clock in the morning, when they retired, but a number who remained cheered the men as the train steamed into the station."

The majority of the Flint men joined the Royal Welsh Fusiliers and the others joined various other regiments. Two joined the Royal Navy, one the Merchant Navy and there was one civilian. Most were killed in action and some died of wounds received in action. Some died of illness and accidents, and others were victims of the so-called 'Spanish flu' pandemic of 1918–19 which claimed the lives of an estimated 50 million people worldwide, more than three times the number that died in the war.

The Armistice – an agreement to stop fighting – was signed between France, Britain and Germany on 11th November, 1918 at 11:00 am – the eleventh hour of the eleventh day of the eleventh month – bringing four years of fighting to an end. The Armistice itself was agreed 6 hours earlier at 5:00 am, with the first term being that fighting would end at 11:00 am.

When news of the Armistice reached Flint, a holiday was taken at works and elsewhere; shops were closed, and in a few minutes the place fluttered with flags and bunting. The steam whistles and hooters at the neighbouring works announced the joyful news, and townspeople promptly showed the feelings uppermost in their minds – of thankfulness at the successful termination of hostilities.

Flint's fallen heroes of the First World War (A–H)

PRIVATE
THOMAS ABRAMS

35003, 4th Battalion Alexandra, Princess of Wales's Own Yorkshire Regiment aka The Green Howards

Thomas Abrams was born in 1888, at Runcorn, Cheshire, the eldest of seven children to Thomas Abrams and Mary (Garner). As a child he lived with his family at 79, Shaw Street, Runcorn, and by the time he was 13 they had moved to 87, Shaw Street. The 1911 census revealed he was working as a packer at the Shotton Ironworks and lodging at 4, Hawarden Terrace, Shotton. He was unmarried.

On 23rd April, 1912 his father died, aged 50, at the Accident Hospital, West Bank, Widnes, Cheshire following an accident at the Alkali Works, which also caused an horrific fire that claimed the lives of five other men. He was buried in Widnes Cemetery.

Before his army service Thomas junior was residing at 88, Church Street, Flint, with his brother John William.

He died on 8th November, 1918, of chronic colitis, at Langensalza, Germany, where he was a prisoner of war since May 1918. He was buried in the Niederzwehren Cemetery, Kassel, Hessen, Germany (Plot VI, Row J, Grave 17).

He was awarded the British War Medal and Victory Medal, and is remembered on four war memorials: Flint Town, St Mary's Parish Church, Flint, Victoria Park, Widnes, and on the North Wales Heroes' Memorial Arch, Bangor and at St Ethelwold's Parish Church, Shotton. He is also remembered on his parents' headstone at Widnes Cemetery (Section C, Row 7, Grave 2997).

His mother, Mary, died on 4th February, 1934, aged 66, and is buried with her husband.

The grave of Private Thomas Abrams in the Niederzwehren Cemetery, Kassel, Hessen, Germany, in Plot VI, Row J, Grave 17

Mr and Mrs Abrams' grave in Widnes Cemetery

LANCE CORPORAL
SAMUEL AMOS

12695, 8th (Service) Battalion Royal Welsh Fusiliers

His full name was Samuel Ernest Victor Amos and he was born in 1890 in Bristol, Gloucestershire. He was the third of four children to William Henry Amos and Ruth (Whitlock) and they lived at 3, Talbot Street, Bedminster, Bristol. The 1901 census revealed that the family had moved to 26, Brook Road, Shotton, Flintshire and that William Henry was working as a sheet iron roller at the Hawarden Bridge Ironworks. By the 1911 census they had moved to 51, Brook Road and Samuel was now also employed as an ironworker.

On 21st October, 1911 Samuel married Mary Elizabeth Taylor at St Deiniol's Parish Church, Hawarden, and they lived at 26, Brook Road, Shotton. They had two children, William John (1912–80) and Samuel Ernest (1914–68).

Lance Corporal Amos was killed in action at Mesopotamia on 9th April, 1916. He has no known grave but is commemorated on the Basra memorial, Iraq, on Panel 15. He is also remembered on the following war memorials: St Mary's Parish Church, Flint, Connah's Quay Town, St Mark's Parish Church, Connah's Quay, and Hawarden Village. His name was also recorded in the Book of Remembrance at St Deiniol's Parish Church, Hawarden and his parents' headstone in Hawarden Churchyard, North Extension, West Side, in Plot A21. He is also commemorated on the North Wales Heroes' Memorial Arch, Bangor.

He was awarded 1914–15 Star, British War Medal and Victory Medal.

Lance Corporal Amos was a member of the Shotton Conservative Club and in their Minute Book dated 9th October, 1916, it was recorded that 16 widows (including Mrs Amos) of men killed in action were to be sent five shillings each.

Samuel's widow, Mary Elizabeth, re-married at St Ethelwold's Parish Church, Shotton, 4th August, 1919, to William Walton (1876–1951), an ironworker, and they resided at 17, Brook Road, Shotton. She died in March 1956 and lies on her own in an unmarked grave in Connah's Quay Cemetery.

His father died on 10th May, 1923, aged 59, and his mother Ruth died on 26th April, 1927, aged 62. They are buried together in Hawarden Churchyard (pictured right).

LIEUTENANT
THOMAS BATE

1/5th (Flintshire) Battalion Royal Welsh Fusiliers

Thomas (Tommy) Bate was born 1st July, 1889 at Kelsterton, near Flint, and baptised 4th August, 1889 at St Mark's Parish Church, Connah's Quay. He was the sixth of seven children to Thomas Bate and Perenna (Owen) and resided at Kelsterton Hall.

Thomas Bate senior was Landed Proprietor of the Kelsterton Estate, High Sheriff of Flintshire, Captain of 'K' Troop of the Flintshire and Denbigh Hussars, proprietor of the Kelsterton Brewery Company, a Justice of the Peace and President of the Flint Conservative Club.

His wife, Perenna, was born in Blessington, County Wicklow, Ireland and a daughter of William Owen, whose family were famous for breeding superb hunter horses.

Tommy was educated at Fonthill Public School in East Grinstead, East Sussex and Shrewsbury Public School, where he was a sergeant in the Cadet Corps.

In November 1908 he was abroad travelling in Australia and British Columbia, and while he was away, on 13th December, 1910, his father passed away. In his will Mr Bate had left "my Kelsterton Hall Estate" to "my son, the said Thomas Bate". Tommy returned home on 23rd November, 1912, but it wasn't until July 1914 he officially took over as landlord of the Estate, which until then had been in the care of a trustee, namely his maternal uncle Thomas Owen, Esquire. An 'at home' party took place at the Hall on 17th July, when he was the recipient of a handsome present from the tenantry of the Estate to commemorate his practical work as landlord. It was a large silver salver bought from Lowes, goldsmiths of Chester, engraved with the words "Presented to Thomas Bate by his tenants on his succession to the Kelsterton Estate, July 1st, 1914". About 60 guests and the house party (the Bate family and trustees) assembled in two marquees erected in the grounds, where an excellent meat tea was enjoyed by all. After the meal there was an informal walkabout, affording the opportunities for private communications between Mr Bate and his tenants.

Alderman Joseph Wood Massey Evans, of Flint, whose son Private Arthur Leslie Evans also died in the war, proposed the health of their landlord Mr Bate, in the most felicitous terms. He was very pleased to hear the extremely kind and generous remarks made by Mr Bate in reference to the good feeling, for he was of the opinion that all the tenants were a thoroughly loyal class and honoured their landlord. Mr Evans said that no doubt all present had recently read the report of the presentation, which had appeared in the County Herald. That presentation would show to the public what excellent feeling existed between the members of the Kelsterton Hall family and the tenants. There was a capital esprit de corps, and the landlord was thoughtful of the interest of the tenant; and that was proved by the kindly manner in which he associated himself with them. He expressed the hope that long might those good relations be experienced and long might Mr Bate live to enjoy the privileges of landlord.

Finally, amusing entertainment was provided by two artists, Mr Rogers and Mr Gilbert, from Chester. The memorable proceedings finished at 8pm; all having spent a very delightful afternoon and evening. It was idyllic; Kelsterton's future was once again secure and bright.

Mr Bate was hailed with much satisfaction by the members of the agricultural tenantry and was extremely respected by all who had pleasure of his acquaintance, and he was well known amongst the oarsmen of the River Dee at Chester.

He was commissioned as a 2nd Lieutenant in the Royal Welsh Fusiliers (Territorial Force) on 8th September, 1913. The war began on 4th August, 1914 and he enlisted the very same day with the 1/5th Battalion Royal Welsh Fusiliers, and with them trained in England until 14th July, 1915 when they embarked at Devonport on His Majesty's Transport ship Caledonia, disembarking at Gallipoli on the 9th August.

While at Suvla Bay, on or about 12th September, 1915, Lieutenant Bate developed symptoms of dysentery and was subsequently admitted to the Cottonera Hospital in Malta. In October he was transferred to the Villa Medici in Florence, Italy for convalescence. In late December of that year he re-joined his battalion for duty and in the same month they evacuated from Gallipoli and moved to Egypt. He was soon promoted to Temporary Captain (mentioned in the London Gazette), which was relinquished the same month on ceasing to command a Company. The regiment moved to Palestine

Mr and Mrs Bate with three of their six children outside Kelsterton Hall c.1895. Left to right: Tommy, Perenna, Marjorie, Roger and Thomas Senior

and it was in the First Battle of Gaza, on 26th March, 1917, where Lieutenant Bate was killed in action.

HM Transport ship Caledonia, on which Lieutenant Bate and his regiment sailed to Gallipoli

His Colonel wrote: "He died in a noble manner, leading and encouraging his men in the attack on the Turkish Position on 26 March. All who were near him during the attack bear witness as to his gallant conduct throughout this day up to the time of his death. He was always to the fore, and showed an utter disregard to his own personal safety. He was a fine fighting soldier and a favourite with all ranks. I have put his name forward for recommendation, and I hope it will go through. You have every reason to feel intensely proud of him". His servant said: "He died a hero, if ever there was one. He was one of our best officers; his old platoon loved him. I lost my best friend when I lost Capt. BATE; I shall never forget him as long as I live. His first thought was about his men, and himself after. I never had a better master."

Lieutenant Thomas Bate is commemorated on the Jerusalem memorial on Panels 20 to 22

He has no known grave but is commemorated on the Jerusalem memorial on Panels 20 to 22 (see above). He is also remembered on the following war memorials: Connah's Quay Town, St Mark's Parish Church, Connah's Quay, and the Cottage Hospital, Flint.

He was awarded the 1914–15 Star, British War Medal and Victory Medal, and was mentioned in Despatches (London Gazette, 12th January, 1918).

Mrs J W Charlton, of Plas Bellin, near Northop, sister of Lieutenant Bate, received a telegram from the Records Office Authorities at Shrewsbury intimating that he had been killed in action recently, and the sad intelligence was received with feelings of surprise by many of the residents of the Borough of Flint.

On Sunday morning, 6th May, Canon Nicholas, the Rector of Flint, preaching in the Parish Church, alluded to the numerous letters he was receiving from soldiers serving with the Forces at the Front, and was especially pleased to read a portion of one from the son of Mr John Bowen, of Feathers Street, Flint, and who had been promoted from Corporal to Sergeant on the field of battle. Sergeant Bowen wrote as follows with regard to the death of Captain Tom Bate, of Kelsterton: "Mr Bate fell a fine soldier, game to the end. After being shot he was urging men on, giving them advice until he died, which was not long after he received the wound."

Private William Edward Metcalfe* of Carmel, near Whitford, also serving with the 1/5th Battalion

*The author's great uncle

Royal Welsh Fusiliers, was wounded and taken prisoner at the Battle of Gaza. In a letter home to his mother he stated that he was "next to Lieutenant Bate, of Kelsterton, Flint when he was killed," and added: "I was buried four times but managed to get out of it. You see I am one of the lucky ones."

In his will Lieutenant Bate left £115 14 s 11 d (£6,800 in 2014) to his mother, and his inventory kit (listed below) from the army – which was received on 13th April, 1917 – was left to his sister, Mrs J W Charlton, of Plas Bellin Hall, Northop.

1 valise containing: 1 blanket; 1 Sam Brown belt with 1 brace; 1 pyjama suit; 1 undervest; 5 pairs of socks; 1 burberry; 1 pair of shorts; 1 flask; 1 cleaning kit bag; 1 flash lamp; 3 books; correspondence; 1 trench mirror; 2 packs of playing cards; 1 whistle & lanyard; 1 revolver cleaning rod; 1 balaclava cap; 1 canvas bag; 1 sleeping bag; 1 waterproof sheet; 2 shirts; 1 pair of underpants; 6 collars; 1 khaki drill jacket; 1 camera in case; 1 canvas bucket; 1 pair of braces; 1 tube of tooth paste; 1 writing pad; 2 pipes; 1 strop; 2 handkerchiefs; 2 toothbrushes; 1 housewife; 1 tin of tobacco.

1 kit bag containing: 1 pair of gum boots; 1 canvas basin; 2 shirts; 1 pair of underpants; 1 pair of socks; 1 cardigan; 1 burberry with 4 metal stars; 1 service dress jacket; 2 body belts; 1 undervest; 1 collar; 1 canvas bag.

1 portmanteau containing: 2 pairs of socks; 1 pair of service dress trousers; 1 tie; 1 pair of khaki drill trousers; 1 pair of breeches; 1 cheque book; 2 books; 1 revolver cleaning rod; 1 comb & glass in case; 1 pair of boots; 1 towel; 1 canvas bath; 1 collar; 1 writing pad; 1 handkerchief.

1 tin box containing: 1 bag containing 1 flash, buttons, badges, stars; 1 compass in case; 1 lance; 1 bottle of shaving soap; 3 photo albums; picture postcards; 1 tin of powder; 1 trench dagger; 2 pairs of leather gloves; 1 wallet containing photos; 1 tobacco pouch; 1 cheque book; 1 pair of brown shoes; 1 pair of breeches; 1 khaki drill jacket with 4 stars and 1 collar badge, 1 flash; 1 frog sword; 13 collars; 1 ash tray; 1 packet of anti-vermin sachets; 1 bottle of castor oil; 1 fleece lining; 1 cardigan; 11 coins; negatives; 1 match box; 1 metal box; 2 cigarette holders in cases; 3 pipes; 12 books; 1 pack of playing cards; 1 wire cutter; 1 box containing shells; 1 belt; 1 lanyard; 1 diary; 1 photo mounter; 3 shirts; 1 pair of khaki drill trousers; 1 fly whisk; 1 clothes brush; 3 handkerchiefs; 1 tie; 3 towels; 1 coat carrier; 1 pair of pyjama trousers; 1 leather waistcoat

Memorial tablet in St Mark's Church, Connah's Quay with the wrong date of death for Roger

By 1918, Tommy's mother Perenna's application to the Episcopal Consistory Court (supported by the vicar and churchwardens) for a memorial tablet to be placed on the interior wall of St Mark's Church had been granted.

Tommy's elder brother, Lieutenant Roger Whitley Bate, fought in the Boer War with the 3rd Battalion Royal Welsh Fusiliers, and was killed in action by a stray bullet in a skirmish at Rostpan, near Boshof, on 5th December, 1901. He was born in October 1882 and educated at Eton, and also at Bayonne and Altenhage, Hanover. He excelled in swimming and fencing, and was a fine horseman. When war broke out, although only 17 years old, Lieutenant Bate joined the Royal Welsh Fusiliers, and early in 1901, left for South Africa with the 22nd Company Mounted Infantry. He saw considerable service and was awarded the medal with three clasps. When killed, he was in command of a section of the rearguard protecting a convoy, and was shot dead while endeavouring to prevent some Boers pressing forward, which he succeeded in doing by his skilful handling of his men. Lieutenant Bate is buried at Boshof. Had he lived it is stated that he would have been granted a commission in the regular army. He is remembered on the South African obelisk in Flint.

Their mother, Perenna, died in London 11th February, 1920, aged 62, and was buried with her husband in the family vault in St Mark's Churchyard, Connah's Quay.

Flint Cottage Hospital memorial

Since Tommy was a bachelor, the male line of the Bate family had ended. Following his mother's death his eldest sister Gwendoline and her husband stayed at the Hall for a short time but, by 1923, the birds had flown the nest and Kelsterton was alone and empty.

The great wish of Tommy's grandfather Edward Bate, expressed at the Quay House dinner of St David's Day 1871, had been for Connah's Quay to have its own volunteer corps, and that, in his words, "a worthy heir of the House of Kelsterton would take command".

It was, therefore, the saddest and bitterest of all ironies that two worthy heirs should fulfil their grandfather's dream but in doing so should also bring that very House of Kelsterton to a premature end.

The Bate family vault in St Mark's Churchyard, Connah's Quay

PRIVATE
JOSEPH BEARD

77934, 4th Battalion Royal Welsh Fusiliers

Joseph (Joe) Beard was born on 9th December, 1899 at 52, Swan Street, Flint and baptised on the 21st November, 1901 at St Mary's Parish Church, Flint. He was the second of four children to Matthew Robert Boothby Beard and Mary (Beck) and lived at 100, Swan Street, Flint.

Matthew was born at Five Ways, Staffordshire and came to live in Flint in 1897, working at the old Red Pit Colliery until it closed. He then worked as a furnace man at the Hawarden Bridge steelworks until his retirement shortly before WW2. He was an ex-serviceman and was a Lance Corporal in the Flint Company of National Reserves (Flintshire Battalion) and on the outset of WW1 he answered the call for service in response to the appeal for ex-non-commissioned officers. He served with the 10th Battalion Royal Welsh Fusiliers and was demobbed after fours years and three months' service, with the rank of Sergeant. He was also a volunteer for the Boer War, but did not go abroad. He was one of the founders of the Flint British Legion Branch and a one-time member of the local committee.

Mary was born in Swan Street, Flint and before her marriage to Matthew she had an illegitimate son named John. She had been employed as a domestic servant by a local farmer and then by the Oakenholt Papermill.

In July 1913 Matthew Beard senior was summoned to the Flint Petty Sessions in respect of the non-attendance of his boy Joseph at school. The School Attendance Officer (Mr W M Jones) said there were two boys belonging to Mr Beard, and they were truants. Neither would go to school. The Bench made an order for attendance, and directed that the costs should be paid.

At the Flint Petty Sessions in May 1916 a woman named Margaret Hough, of Swan Street, was summoned for assaulting Joseph Beard; and Edward Beck, ironworker, residing in Swan Street, was summoned for an assault upon Matthew Robert Beard, brother of the previously named complainant, on the 1st May. Hough pleaded guilty and Beck not guilty. Mr Kerfoot Roberts, solicitor, of Holywell, appeared for the Beard brothers, whose evidence was to the effect that on the evening in question they were in the house of a Mrs Jones, their aunt, enjoying gramophone selections. When they were about to leave the house they heard Hough shouting and using very abusive language in the street. When Matthew Beard was going to the assistance of his brother, Beck ran across and struck him. The Beards' father was at the Front with the Royal Welsh Fusiliers, and another brother of the youths was also serving with the Forces. Beck denied the charge made against him; and Hough said that if the occasion arose again she would do just as she had done, as she did not intend to be threatened or insulted by the Beards. The magistrates bound over Hough and Beck to keep the peace for six months in the sum of £10. They were tired of hearing such squabble. This was a family row and the whole thing was very disgraceful. The advocate would be allowed a fee of 10s 6d in each case. The other costs amounted to £1 7s 6d.

In early September 1917 Joseph Beard and two other Flint youths named William Davies, of Upper Queen Street, and Robert Haines, of 179, Chester Road, were summoned for playing football in Chester Road near a place of entertainment on the 14th August, to the annoyance of passengers. PC Parry proved the case, and said there had been several complaints. Haines said they picked up the small ball in the street, and only kicked it about three times. The Mayor said such conduct was against the law, and there were repeated complaints. Davies and Haines would be fined 6s each. Beard, who did not appear, was fined 10s, or seven days in default.

Unemployed bachelor Joe enlisted in the army at Wrexham in November 1917 and was posted to Kinmel Park Camp, Rhyl, for training. Whilst there he took ill and was sent to Kinmel Park Hospital where, on 2nd July, 1918, he died of pneumonia after contracting a severe cold. Since he never saw front-line service he was not eligible for medals.

Beard and Beck's headstone in the Northop Road Cemetery where Beck's year of death is a year out

He was buried in the Northop Road Cemetery, Flint (Line 12, South Side, Grave 10) and is remembered on the Flint Town and St Mary's Parish Church, Flint, war memorials. He is also commemorated on the North Wales Heroes' Memorial Arch, Bangor.

The impressive funeral took place on Friday, 5th July and he was accorded full military honours. A firing and bearer party under the command of Captain Armstrong (who some years since was a member of the Bank staff at Flint), was accompanied by Sergeant Instructor Phillips and Sergeant Lowe, both of Flint. The party, with the military band, arrived in the Borough about one o'clock; and shortly before five o'clock proceeded to the residence of the deceased. The coffin, which was covered with the Union Jack, and on which were wreaths and some of the deceased's accoutrements, was placed outside the house, and the Reverend Canon W Llewellyn Nicholas, VD, Lieutenant Colonel Chaplain, read the opening lines of the burial office. Afterwards, the procession, headed by the firing party, with reversed arms, moved slowly along the street, passed through the centre of the town and from thence to the Welsh Church. The band discoursed appropriate funeral marches, under bandmaster Fenwick (Connah's Quay), and the route was lined with hundreds of people. Arriving at the Church, the coffin was borne to the chancel steps, and the congregation comprised the chief mourners, relatives and friends, and only a few of the general public. Canon Nicholas read the whole of the service, and the hymns Brief Life is Here our Portion, and Peace, Perfect Peace were sung. The service at the church being concluded, the funeral procession was re-formed and wended its way to the cemetery, the military band again playing the marches. The Reverend W H Davies (curate) read the committal lines at the graveside, where the customary three volleys were fired, and the Last Post sounded. The funeral rights were of a most impressive character. The following Sunday evening a memorial service was held at the Parish Church, when Canon Nicholas preached.

At the Flint Petty Sessions in September 1919 Mary Beard, of Swan Street, summoned her husband, Matthew, for having deserted her. There was also a second charge of persistent cruelty and a separation order was applied for in consequence. Mr Kerfoot Roberts, of Holywell, appeared for the complainant, and said the parties were married on the 28th December, 1897. Their married life had been a most unhappy one. On 2nd June the defendant assaulted his wife to such an extent that she was compelled to go to a neighbour's house. The defendant left his wife on that date, and had not contributed anything towards her maintenance since. At this juncture, the Mayor appealed to the parties to make an effort to come together again. The defendant, on hearing the remark of the Mayor, shook his head in protest. The Mayor said, "Consider it for a few minutes and see if you can come together. You have been married 22 years." The defendant replied, "I don't care if it is 42 years, I won't live with her." Mr Kerfoot Roberts and Mr E H Harris (who appeared for the defendant) made an effort to bring about a reconciliation, but it was of no avail.

> ## IN MEMORIAM
>
> *Two years have passed, our hearts still sore,*
> *As time goes on we miss you more;*
> *Some may forget you, but never will I,*
> *A mother's love will never die.*
> Fondly remembered by his loving
> Mother, Brothers and Sister
> (County Herald, 9th July, 1920).
>
> *Do not ask us if we miss him,*
> *There is still a vacant place;*
> *Shall we ever forget his footsteps,*
> *Or the smile upon his face?*
> *Days of sadness still come o'er us,*
> *Hidden tears do often flow;*
> *Memory keeps our loved one near us,*
> *Though he died seven years ago.*
> Fondly remembered
> by his Mother, Father, Brother and Sister
> (County Herald, 11th December, 1925)

The complainant then gave evidence on oath and said she had a child aged 11 years. The defendant said he was 50 years of age and resided at 123, Francis Street, Chester. He was demobilised from the army in the previous February, after serving four and a half years.

The magistrates found the charge of persistent cruelty proved, but not the charge of desertion. They granted the complainant a separation order, with the custody of the child, the defendant to pay 25s weekly.

Mary and Matthew were summoned yet again on August 1920 for being drunk and disorderly. Mr F Llewelyn Jones, Mold, was for the defence, PC Lewis gave evidence for the prosecution, and PC Hughes corroborated. Thomas John Williams, a railway official, said that while collecting tickets at the railway gates, he saw both defendants, who were drunk and fighting. It was stated that defendants had that day (7th July) been on a trip to Rhyl, and were returning home when the disturbance took place. Defendants denied the offence. Mary stated that she had nothing to drink, and Matthew said he had only had three bottle of Bass. A fine of 20 shillings each was imposed.

Buried in the same grave as Joe is his half-brother John Beck who, on the 3rd September, 1924, was driving a motorcycle combination, in which were two other men, in the direction of Rhyl. When near the Tyn-y-Morfa crossing, he collided with a motorcar driven by a Prestatyn man, and received severe injuries. He was conveyed to the Holywell Cottage Hospital but, on examination, was found to be dead. His two companions were knocked out for a time, and received minor injuries. John was well known in Flint. He was an enthusiastic pigeon fancier, in which he was a successful competitor in the Flint Castle Homing Society races, having won many prizes during the season.

Joe's father died 20th July, 1952 at Lluesty Hospital, Holywell, aged 82, and is buried in the Old London Road Cemetery, Flint. His mother died on 19th August, 1948, aged 84, and is buried with her husband in an unmarked grave.

LANCE CORPORAL
HENRY BELLIS

25526, 17th (Service) Battalion Royal Welsh Fusiliers (2nd North Wales)

Henry Bellis was born in 1888 in Flint Mountain and baptised on 22nd June, 1888 at St Mary's Parish Church, Flint. He was the youngest of five children to Joseph Bellis and Mary (Thomas) and the brother of Private Samuel Bellis (page 25).

In the 1911 census he was living with his parents and brother Samuel at Bryn-y-Garreg, Flint Mountain but on enlistment in the army he was living at Cae Coch, Kelsterton, Flint and was employed as an ironworker.

He enlisted in Flint on 1st March, 1915 joining at Llandudno the following day. He went absent without a pass on 12th November that year until reporting himself at 10:00 pm on the 15th (70 hours) and was forfeited three days pay. He was promoted to acting Lance Corporal (unpaid) on the 4th December, 1915. He was severely reprimanded by the Commanding Officer 18th January, 1916 for losing government property by neglect. He was admitted to hospital suffering from scabies on 2nd March, 1916 and rejoined his battalion on the 27th March. On enlistment he was 5 ft 5 in, weighed 10st 4 lb, chest 37 in, and his physical development was good.

He was first reported missing and then declared killed in action at the Battle of the Somme between the 9th and 12th July, 1916. He was unmarried.

His service record stated he was buried in Mametz Wood, France, 4½ miles East North East of Albert, but after the war his grave could not be located. He is commemorated on the Thiepval Memorial, Somme, France (Pier and Face 4A – see above).

He is remembered on three war memorials: Flint Town (as K Bellis), St Mary's Parish Church, Flint, and the North Wales Heroes' Memorial Arch, Bangor (as K Bellis).

>
> Radcliffe House
> Greenfield Rd
> Colwyn Bay
> April 7/16
>
> Sir,
>
> Would you kindly let me know the whereabouts of the undermentioned man.
>
> Lcpl. H. Bellis 25526
> C. Company
> 17th R.W.F.
>
> I have not heard from him for a long time and recently sent a small parcel to him but it has been returned endorsed "hospital" Kindly let me know as soon as possible and oblige.
>
> I remain
> Yours faithfully
> Wm. T. Bellis

He was awarded the 1914–15 Star, British War Medal and Victory Medal.

The following is a letter sent to the War Office from Henry's concerned brother William T Bellis.

Henry's father died in February 1894 aged 50, and buried in the Northop Road Cemetery, Flint. He was born in Northop and was employed as a chemical worker. His mother, who was born in Gellifor, Denbighshire, died c. 1915, aged about 68, whilst residing at Brook House, Northop with her daughter and son-in-law.

CORPORAL
JOHN BELLIS

12583, 8th (Service) Battalion Royal Welsh Fusiliers

St David's FC, Oakenholt (1913–14)

John (Jack) Bellis was born in Flint in 1893 and baptised 10th November, 1893 at St Mary's Parish Church, Flint. He was the third of 12 children to Peter Bellis and Catherine Anne (Cooper) and was the brother of Private Thomas Bellis (page 25).

The family resided at New Western Terrace, Oakenholt for many years, however by the 1911 census they had moved to Leadbrook Cottage in the same village. Jack never married and before the war he was employed as a paper maker at the Oakenholt Paper Mill.

He enlisted in Wrexham in August 1914 and was moved to Salisbury Plain but by February 1915 was at Blackdown, Sussex. He landed at Gallipoli in about June 1915 and subsequently served in Mesopotamia (Iraq).

Private Bellis, writing to his parents under date of 21st September, 1915, stated he was with the 8th Battalion of the Royal Welsh Fusiliers at the Dardanelles. They had been out of the trenches three weeks for a rest, but instead of a rest they had been hard worked night and day, digging and unloading transports. He referred to a Jack Brockley having been badly wounded a fortnight after his brother was killed; whilst another man named 'Spikey' was also killed. Ernie Joyce, from Flint, had been down to see him and others in his battalion on the 20th September. There were two killed from Flint, and their names were Gunther and Evans. Neil Owens, who used to live in Pentre, was killed there that morning, the 21st September. He had received a copy of the County Herald.

In a further letter, dated 28th September, 1915, he wrote that the 8th Battalion had been in the thick of the fighting, just as much as had the 1/5th. He had been with others out on sniping duties and they could account for "putting a good many Turks out." Will Bennett wished to be remembered to all at home. Writing on 11th October he mentioned that the men were receiving parcels from friends in Flint, and that he was receiving his from home because they were packed securely for the long journey. It looked as though there was to be a winter campaign there, for they were preparing, making special winter dug-outs. There was a draft of reinforcements a week prior to his writing, and he was surprised to see Sammy Jones, who worked in the Co-operative Society's Stores, Flint, and who was of the 16th Battalion of the Royal Welsh Fusiliers. George Hughes, Hogan, and the Sergeant had all gone to the hospital. Hogan went with a sprained ankle. He said that he was living close to Hulley and Moulton, and both were doing all right and that Sam Williams was keeping well.

John's brother, Ben was also with the 8th Battalion at the Dardanelles and was a Dispatch Rider. In November 1915 he forwarded a letter to his parents. He said that his battalion was near that of the 1/5th Battalion, and they were visited by some of the men. They had E Joyce to tea, and Joyce was now a Lance Corporal. On another occasion they had tea with Lieutenant Alexander, of Oakenholt.

The following are more letters Private Jack Bellis wrote home.

Pte J Bellis
Mediterranean Expeditionary Force

Monday August 28th 1915

Dear Sister & Bro

Just these few lines, as I have managed to scrape an envelope & writing paper, to let you know we are both keeping quite well. We have had a stiff time of it here at it night & day and when we do get a chance of a rest in the daytime we cant get it for the flies are something terrible here its agony getting your meals with them especially when there is jam knocking about which we are very seldom without. It is a very hilly country and warm make it hard to go about but it is going very cold at night now. We get plenty of the weekly papers as there is a lot comes with every post that comes up. I had a Homing & Racing Pigeon last Saturday I don't know how they pop up here, I lot of photos of fanciers that have joined the colours. better put ours, is Joe's pigeons keeping alright. I expect you will soon be having your new teeth in soon. I shall want some if I get over this safe for they are dropping out now. I have not seen Joe Hully & Moulton for three weeks now as they are with the machine gun and are attached to another lot for a bit but we all hope to be going down to the base for a rest soon for we can do with it.

I must now conclude hoping you are all quite well. Remember me to all.

Your loving Bro
Jack

XXXXXXX
XXXXXX
To Will

Pte J. Bellis.
C. Co. R.W.F 8 Batt
Mediterranean Expeditionary Force

Tuesday Sept 21st 1915

Dear Sist & Bro

Thanks for the parcel we received here on Sunday although it had been badly damaged and got mixed up with Joe Hullys but I only think there was some cakes missing as we got soap, chocolate, licorice root, sweets and the bottle of oil which I am sure will be very handy. I shall enjoy the sweets in the trenchs into which we came last night. I have not received Lils parcel up to now. Very pleased to hear that you both enjoyed your holidays at Liverpool. I hope to have a good one if I get over this lot which I hope I shall. Things are very quiet here now, only we are preparing for a winter campaign so it looks like lasting a while yet. There is very little news to tell what there is you get from home so I now conclude hoping all are quite well as it leaves me.

Your affect Bro
Jack

XXXXXXXXX For Willie

The first part of this next letter, which was probably written in late 1915, is missing.

… days. There is very little hopes of 8th getting home for Xmas as you say the talk is it looks very like us spending it in the trenchs. Ben's knee soon got alright and he is now doing well. I expect you would feel a bit awkward having your teeth in for the first time. I wish that I could get a few of mine out as they have been plaguing me a lot.

All the boys are doing well and wishs to be remembered.

I now conclude hoping all are quite well.

Your Affect Bro
Jack

XXXXXXXXX
For Willie

12583 Lce Cpl J. Bellis
C. Co. R. W. F, 8 Batt
Mediterranean Exp Force

12/2/16

Dear Sister & Bro

Just a few lines in answer to your letter I received safe but I have not seen anything of the parcel which you say you sent along with the fiths. But all the mails were held back Christmas time owing to the evacuations of the Peninsula. I was in the both evacuations of Suvla Bay & Cape Helles as our division made a success @ Suvla we had to go to Cape Helles to do the evacuation there and we got a rough time of it too.

We are now in Egypt and out of danger at present. I don't know for how long but I believe we are out for a good spell this time. There is talk of us going to do garrison duty. I had a letter from H Forrester last week the first we had heard of him since last August he has been at hospital at Cairo with scarlet fever. He is now waiting for new teeth. It is very hot here in the day. Hulley & Co are all doing well.

I now conclude hope you are all quite well as it leaves me.

Your Affec Bro
Jack

XXXXX For Willie

112583 L/C J. Bellis
C. Co. R. W. Fus 8th Batt
Indian Exp Force 'D'

April 30th 1916

Sister

I received your very welcomed letter safe this morning April 30th also the one for Ben who you will know by now as been wounded in the hand in the second attacked we made ----- the Turks trench on the ----- when Sam Williams was also wounded. Willie Bennett from Flint was wounded in the first attack made. I have not heard from any of them yet. Surprises to hear of Uncle Tom being wounded. I expect he is right for a few weeks holiday now, they have the benefit over we out here for they are soon in Dear Old Blightie.

I think the only time as we shall get home is when the war is over although as you say we deserve a bit of leave if next at home and well deserve it the way we have been knocked about it to be hoped Joe has never to go out. Very sorry could not send you anything the short time we had in Port Said as we just had a fortnight there having a few hours notice to move and while we were there and had a chance to enjoy ourselves a little they would not pay us out. Well five shillings we got the whole second day we got there and with that we bought a bit of bread so you can see we have very little chance of buying presents to send home which I should very much like to have done. I beleave Sam Williams sent a few things home the time in was in hospital at Alesandria. I have never been to any hospital yet. I don't know how Harry got it. I was in one but I know there as been rumours about that I was wounded by some of the sick that return from home for some of them seem surprised to see me. Sorry you have not received many letters. I have had very few since we left for Port Said.

Dear Sis the sun is getting terrible hot out here much hotter than was on the Peninsular and are getting spine protectors to guard against sun strokes in spine also mosquitoes nets for these things don't have bight at night. I should be very thankful if you would send me a small parcel of a few cigs and something enjoyable that will keep.

We are all very sorry to hear of the deaths of Mr & Mrs Bushell. Hulley & Moulton are both keeping quite well and wish to be remembered. Remember me to any of the boys when they get home. I now conclude hoping you are quite well as it leaves me.

Your Loving Bro

Jack

XXXXXXXX For Willie from Uncle Jack
XXXXXXXXXXXXXXXX

And the following is a letter Jack received from his sister Gertrude.

9 Gardeners Row
Oakenholt

June 13th 16

Dear Bro

I received your welcome letter this morning of which I was very pleased & thankful of for it is so long since I had one before off you but it is better late than never as the old saying is no news good news glad to hear you are keeping well you made me feel downhearted when I read your letter where you said you would not be home until it is all over it is to be hoped that wont be long some of the Sunday papers only give it three months but I think that is to good to be true but let us hope so mother was speaking to Miss *(name crossed out)* a sister to your captain she said she had had a letter from him & he said in it as he was expecting a leave home this month or next.

Well Jack we have not heard there Ben is yet so we cannot write to him with us not hearing from him I was wondering if he could write or not if he is back with you again we have a new curate hear now & he is trying to get Dad back to Church I dont know if he is going he is very swankie & quite a young fellow to Well Jack it is Whit Tuesday to day but is nothing like it so there is no sports in Flint & all the shops open there as been no holiday throughout the Kindom this Whitsun

Willie Thomas Jones & Charlie Denton as been home from France & also gone back the time soon goes they both looked well I am sending you one of Willie's Photos he had taken in school he is quite a big boy now he is always talking about you & Ben he asks me many times a day when are you coming home for as been home for three weeks with infleu & then worked one day & then home again with blood poison foot but is much better he is remembering to you & all & Charlie Denton was also asking for you what do you think of the Naval Battle & of Lord Kitchener being drowned it is bad news but let us hope for the best

The Russians seem to be doing good work. Keep your heart up hoping to see you soon your loving sis Gert xxx

From Willie

xxxxx

I will send you something & a few cigs I will send a card to let you know they are on the road Good Luck

Private Bellis died of a fever, at No. 3, British General Hospital, Basra, Iraq on 22nd July, 1916 and was buried in Basra War Cemetery, Iraq (Plot VI, Row A, Grave 12). He is remembered on three war memorials: Flint Town, St David's Parish Church, Oakenholt, and the North Wales Heroes' Memorial Arch, Bangor. He is also remembered on his parents' headstone at Northop Road Cemetery, Flint (Line 40, South Side, Grave 2).

He was awarded the 1914–15 Star, British War Medal and Victory Medal.

It transpired by means of a telegram received by Mr and Mrs Peter Bellis that their son John was lying seriously ill with fever in one of the Eastern Military hospitals in the vicinity of the Persian Gulf and that his other son Benjamin, was reported to be wounded. The following week they received the tragic news that John had died.

On hearing this news Private John Albert Hulley (who died of wounds in 1917) and a comrade in arms (probably Albert Moulton) wrote this letter to Private Bellis's family.

> Pte J. A. Hulley
> 8th Batt. R.W.F
> 40th Brig 13th Div
> Mac. Gun. Sec, Mesopotamia Exp Force
>
> 29th July
>
> Dear Friends
>
> Just a line expressing our sympathy with you & your Mother & Father & family in the sad news in which you will have received through the loss of your brother Jack. I know it will be a sad time for you but hope you will try & bare it with the help of God. I didn't know till Albert Moulton told me & I was to busy to write then so he said he would write to your Father & I went to see him about ten days ago & he seemed to be pretty fair then, he was not in hospital then but he went the day after, I believe he left the hospital here & went into hospital down the river. I couldn't realise it myself when I heard about it I was sorry we was not nearer to him as we could pay our last respects to him As far as I can hear he died of fever you feel quite well one day & you are down the next
>
> Well I can't say any more this time their is only two of us have now out of the boy's & trusting God will watch over all & I am sure Jack served his King & Country up to the last & died for the sake of them at home, expressing our sympathy once more from his two pals X X X X
>
> Joe & Albert

On Sunday morning 20th August, at the St David's Church, Pentre, Flint, an impressive memorial service was held in connection with the deaths of Corporal John Bellis, Private Peter Evans, of 4, Bennett's Row, and Private Edward Hughes, of Gardener's Row, of the same locality. They were members of Royal Welsh Fusiliers' Battalions, having been abroad on active service for some considerable time. Bellis and Evans were first cousins, and all were respected by the residents of Oakenholt. There was a large attendance at the service, inclusive of the families, and relatives and friends of the soldiers and also representatives of the Foresters' Court County Town. The Reverend Canon Nicholas, rector of the parish, conducted the service, and in the course of his sermon made feeling allusions to the memory of the fallen soldiers. The following hymns were rendered: Art thou Weary, Art Thou Languid, I Heard the Voice of Jesus Say, and O Let Him Whose Sorrow.

The chief mourners for Bellis were:- Mr and Mrs Bellis (parents), Misses Blanche and Muriel Bellis (sisters), and Masters Eric and Edgar Bellis (brothers); Messrs. J O Jones, Liverpool and Thomas Jones (uncles); Mrs Blackwell, Mrs Hughes and Miss E Gresty (cousins); Mrs G Hooson (Bennett's Row), Mrs Jos Hooson (Boar's Head, Northop Hall), Mrs Hulley, Mrs Fred Turley and her son (Golftyn, Connah's Quay), Mr Thomas (Connah's Quay), and Mrs Williams, New Western Terrace, Oakenholt.

The chief mourners for Hughes were: Mrs Hughes (wife) and children; Mr and Mrs Hughes (parents); Mrs Small, Queensferry (sister); Mrs Richard Hughes (sister-in-law); Messrs. Thomas Hughes and Joseph Hughes (brothers); and Mrs M and E Hughes (sisters); Mr and Mrs Denton, and Mr Charles Denton.

The chief mourners for Evans were: Mr Edward Evans (father), Messrs. George Evans and E Evans (brothers), and Mrs E Joyce.

Jack's father died 19th December, 1919, aged 56, at the David Lewis' Northern Hospital, Liverpool after a long illness and was buried in the Northop Road Cemetery, Flint. He was born in Flint and had been a member of St David's Church, Oakenholt for many years, having been a prominent member of the choir and taken a leading part in the anthems and singing. He was also an esteemed member of

> IN LOVING MEMORY OF
> PETER
> BELOVED HUSBAND OF
> CATHERINE A. BELLIS
> LEADBROOK COTTAGE, OAKENHOLT
> DIED DEC. 19TH 1919, AGED 56 YEARS
>
> "THY WILL BE DONE"
>
> ALSO BELOVED SONS OF ABOVE
> CPL. JOHN BELLIS, DIED AT BASRA,
> MESOPOTAMIA, BURIED AT
> MAKINA MASUS MILITARY CEMETERY,
> JULY 21ST 1917, AGED 23 YEARS
>
> PRIVATE THOMAS BELLIS, KILLED IN
> ACTION. BURIED AT COLONIAL HILL
> MILITARY CEMETERY, GREECE.
> SEPT. 18TH 1918, AGED 21 YEARS
>
> EDGAR BELLIS,
> DIED APRIL 18TH 1921, AGED 13 YEARS
>
> "REST IN THE LORD"
>
> CATHERINE ANN BELLIS
> BURIED 17TH AUGUST 1953,
> AGED 86 YEARS

Peter and Catherine Ann's headstone (and transcription) upon which sons Jack and Thomas are also remembered. (n.b. Catherine Ann's name is not inscribed on the headstone. The information relating to Catherine, in the transcription was taken from the burial register)

the Royal Ancient Order of Buffaloes. He was employed as a paper maker.

His mother died 13th August, 1953, aged 86, at her home, 417, Chester Road, Flint, and is buried with her husband and son Edgar. She was born in Liverpool and had lived for more than 60 years in Flint and, like her husband, was a faithful member of St David's Church, and a member of the British Legion and of the Mothers' Union. In her younger days she was a fine contralto singer.

IN MEMORIAM

Day by day our thoughts do wander
To a grave not far away,
Where they laid our darling son
Just a year ago today.
From his Father, Mother,
Sisters and Brothers.
(County Herald, 27th July, 1917)

❧

'Tis hard to bear the heavy cross,
But the hardest is yet to come,
When the Pentre heroes return the roll call,
Oh, how we shall miss among the cheering crowd
Dear Jack and his comrades beloved by all.
Sadly missed by his Father, Mother,
Sisters and Brothers.
(County Herald, 26th July, 1918)

❧

"The Glorious Dead", who won for the living all
that the living have and enjoy.
Will be ever remembered
by his Father, Mother,
Sisters and Brothers.
(County Herald, 25th July, 1919)

A memorial card listing the time and place that Corporal Bellis died

PRIVATE
SAMUEL BELLIS

18360, 10th (Service) Battalion Royal Welsh Fusiliers

Samuel Bellis was born in 1885 at Bryn Morgan, Flint Mountain and baptised 31st July, 1885 at St Mary's Parish Church, Flint. He was the third of five children to Joseph Bellis (a chemical worker) and Mary (Thomas), and the brother of Lance Corporal Henry Bellis (page 13).

Samuel was a colliery labourer, probably unmarried, and still living at Bryn Morgan when he enlisted in the army at Wrexham. He landed in France on 1st June, 1915 and was killed in action there on 16th August, 1916.

He has no known grave but is commemorated on the Thiepval Memorial, Somme, France, on Pier and Face 4A (pictured above). He is remembered on two war memorials: Flint Town and St Mary's Parish Church, Flint. He is also commemorated on the North Wales Heroes' Memorial Arch, Bangor.

He was awarded the 1914–15 Star, British War Medal and Victory Medal.

PRIVATE
THOMAS BELLIS

267730, 11th (Service) Battalion Royal Welsh Fusiliers

Thomas Bellis was born 12th February, 1898 in Oakenholt and baptised 13th March, 1898 at St Mary's Parish Church, Flint. He was the third of 12 children to Peter Bellis (paper maker) and Catherine Anne (Cooper). He was the brother of Corporal John Bellis (page 15).

Thomas spent his early years in New Western Terrace, Oakenholt, but had moved to Leadbrook Cottage in the same village by 1911. Thomas never married and before the war he was employed as a silkworker.

Service record: Enlisted in Flint, 6th June, 1916, with the 4th Reserve Battalion Royal Welsh Fusiliers, No. 5607, and posted to a home base (it is not known when he transferred to the 11th (Service) Battalion RWF); admitted to the Military Hospital, Oswestry, 5th June, 1917, suffering from influenza, and transferred to Southport Convalescent Hospital and Sea Bathing Infirmary, 24th September, 1917 to 27th October, 1917; embarked Southampton, 30th January 1918; disembarked Greece, 11th February, 1918; arrived Salonica, 12th February, 1918; signed to No. 2 Base Depot, Salonica, 15th February, 1918. On enlistment he was 5 ft 5 in tall, weighed 109lb, chest 34 in and his physical development was good; he had carious teeth, stammered slightly, and had slight flat feet and forcible heart action.

He was killed in action at the Second Battle of Doiran in Salonika (now Thessaloniki), Greece 18th September, 1918 and buried in Doiran (Colonial Hill) Military Cemetery, Greece, (Plot III, Row E, Grave 20). He is remembered on two war memorials: Flint Town, St David's Parish Church, Oakenholt and also his parent's headstone at Northop Road Cemetery, Flint (Line 40, South Side, Grave 2). He is also commemorated on the North Wales Heroes' Memorial Arch, Bangor. He was awarded the British War Medal and Victory Medal.

The following is a letter Private Thomas Bellis wrote to his sister and brother.

27/2/18

Dear Sist & Bro

Just these few lines to let you know that I am quite alright hoping all at home are the same. I have not much news to tell you but as long as you get a letter from me to know how I am going on it will be all right. Tell Dad I have been speaking to George Robinson who worked at Coed-On Farm Pentre. He new me as soon as I spoke to him he was as about Joe. he wishes to be remembered to Joe & Dad. Address. Pte T. Bellis 267730. 11th Batt. R.W.Fus. B.S.E.Force. Salonica. We are out of the line and in a rest camp for a bit.

I must now conclued (sic) with best of love to all

From Your Loving Bro
Tom

XXXXXXXXX
XXXXXXX

... and a post card to his sister Gertrude and her husband, Joe Eccles.

Mrs G. Eccles
9 Gardeners Row
Pentre
Nr Flint

Dear Joe & Gerty

Just this P.C. to let you know I received your letter & tobacco quite safe and thanking you for same. Tell your mother I also got is letter & papers. Shall write to you in the week

good by for now

Uncle Tom

Private Bellis's father Peter wrote to the Infantry Records Office, Shrewsbury, enquiring about his son.

Mr P Bellis
Leadbrook Cottage
Oakenholt
Flint

1st June 1919

Dear Sir

Kindly permit me through this medium to ask you a favour if you have still heard any further news of my son 267730 Pte Thos Bellis D Coy 11th Batt RWF who was serving in Salonica. The last we heard about him that he was 'killed in action' (see envelope enclosed) yet we have nothing definite from the War Council. Could you kindly favour me with No 25621 Pte J E Williams D Coy (11th Batt RWF private address as I firmly believe he knows something respecting my son and I should like to get into communication with him.

Thank you in anticipation.

I remain your most obedient servant.

P Bellis

He received a reply just days later.

The Riding School,
Shrewsbury.

4th June 1919.

Sir,

In reply to your letter of the 2/6/19, re Private 267730 Thomas Bellis, I regret not being able to give you any definite information about your son who was reported missing 6–10–18. As soon as anything definite is received, it shall be transmitted to you at once.

As regards Private 25621 J E Williams, I beg to say the War Office regulations do not permit of the private address of soldiers being given, but, if you wish to communicate with the man, you should direct your letter to him C/O the Officer in Charge of Records No 2, The Riding School, Shrewsbury, when it will be forwarded to his last known address.

The man's Regiment and Regimental number should be stated on the envelope.

I have the honour to be,
Sir,
Your obedient Servant,

Major for Lt Colonel.
Officer i/c No 2 Infantry Records.
No 4 District.

Eight months later Mr Bellis received another letter from the Records Office.

The Riding School,
Shrewsbury.

12th February 1920.

Sir

With reference to my Notification dated the 12th November 1919, of the presumed death of your son, No 267730 Private Thomas Bellis, 11th Battalion, Royal Welsh Fusiliers, I beg to inform you a further report has been received from the War Office stating that his Grave has been located in Colonial Hill Military Cemetery, No 2 – Greece.

I am to express the regret of the army Council that it must now be definitely accepted that he was Killed in Action, and his name will shortly be published in the Official Casualty List.

I have the honour to be,
Sir,
Your obedient Servant,

B Gundle
Lieu for Lt Colonel.
Officer i/c No 2 Infantry Records.
No 4 District.

IN MEMORIAM

In loving 22nd birthday remembrance.
We have sought for him in silence,
We have sought for him in rest,
But we do still hope that he will return
To the ones that loved him best.
War's bitter cost.
Never forgotten by his dear Mother, Sisters and Brothers,
Leadbrook Cottage, Oakenholt, Flint.
(Flintshire Observer, 12th February, 1920)

PRIVATE
CHARLES BENNETT

266917, Labour Corps

Charles (Charlie) Bennett was born 19th May, 1888 in Flint and baptised 17th June, 1888 at St Mary's Catholic Church, Flint. He was the fourth of ten children to William Bennett and Margaret (McIntosh).

The family resided at 35, Church Street, Flint and before the war Charlie was employed at Messrs Summers' Ironworks, Shotton. He was unmarried.

The Bennett family home (left) at 35, Church Street

He enlisted in Flint on September 1914 with the 9th Battalion Royal Welsh Fusiliers, No. 13171. Whilst serving in France in November 1915 he was suffering from shock, owing to wounds, and afterwards transferred to the Labour Corps. In January 1916 he was invalided from France and sent to one of the Institutions in the St Helens district.

Private Bennett died of influenza at a military hospital in Limerick, Ireland on 13th July, 1918 and was buried at St Lawrence's Catholic Cemetery, Limerick, Ireland (Grave 31999).

He had recently returned to a military centre after spending a few days leave at home amongst his relatives and friends. He was seized with influenza and, eventually, information was sent per telegraph to his home that he was seriously ill. His father, Captain Bennett – who was engaged in important duties – was not at home, but Mrs Bennett journeyed, with one of her daughters, to the hospital. Private Bennett's condition gradually became worse, and the end came on the evening in question, to the grief of the relatives and friends.

A postcard Charlie sent home, which he signed at the bottom

The funeral was on Monday, 15th July, when the obsequies were of a most sympathetic and solemn nature. Thousands of soldiers participated in the last sad rites, and the military procession to the cemetery at

Private Bennett died of influenza at a military hospital in Limerick, Ireland on 13th July, 1918 and was buried at St Lawrence's Catholic Cemetery, Limerick, Ireland

Limerick was headed by the customary firing party. The funeral service was conducted in the Roman Catholic ritual by the Reverend Father Thornhill, and the remains were conveyed to their last resting place in the portion of the graveyard assigned to the Catholics. After the interment, the soldiers constituting the firing party discharged the usual number of volleys over the grave, and the Last Post was sounded. By request, the military band was not present. Mrs Bennett, mother of the deceased, was present at the funeral. The Flint soldiers extended their sympathy to Mrs Bennett, and the members of the family, in their sad bereavement.

Private Bennett is remembered on two war memorials: Flint Town and St Mary's Catholic Church, Flint and also his parents' headstone at Northop Road Cemetery, Flint (Line 41, South Side, Grave 7). He is also commemorated on the North Wales Heroes' Memorial Arch, Bangor.

He was awarded the 1914–15 Star, British War Medal and Victory Medal.

Captain Bennett died 25th September, 1924, aged 64, after an illness lasting several months and was buried in the Northop Road Cemetery, Flint. He was born at Golftyn, Northop and was a

A Bennett family wedding with Captain Bennett seated on the left and Mrs Bennett standing second from right. Charles is probably one of the boys seated on the floor

Captain Bennett's ship the 'Emma & Ester'

Master Mariner. After his school days he decided to go to sea, and eventually attained the rank of Captain. His schooner the Emma & Ester regularly sailed from Chester, stopping off at ports such as Swansea, Cardiff, Plymouth, Newry, Duddon, Belfast, Kibrush and others. During the war he performed some very useful work for the government, and in 1920 retired from active service. The last post he held was in Belgium. Captain Bennett was a most sociable but unassuming man, and gained the regard of a wide circle of friends. He was a member of an old and highly respected family, with Bennett's Row, in Oakenholt, having been built by his brother Robert.

His wife Margaret, who was born in Dublin, Ireland, died 20th May, 1920, and was buried with her husband.

In 1919 it was decided that if a man died whilst serving with the Labour Corps and had previously served in another unit (in this instance the Royal Welsh Fusiliers) his headstone would show the

The Bennett family grave at the Northop Road Cemetery, Flint (Inset, reference to Charles)

unit he was in prior to his transfer to the Labour Corps. This came about because men who had prior service, especially in the infantry, resented the idea that the burial records and headstones would record them as 'labourers'. So, generally, the headstone will not mention the Labour Corps, although the odd exception does occur.

PRIVATE
JOHN JAMES BENTHAM

240660, 1/5th (Flintshire) Battalion Royal Welsh Fusiliers

John James Bentham was born 28th October, 1893 at 28, Feather Street, Flint and baptised on 19th November, 1893 at St Mary's Parish Church, Flint. He was the eldest of six children to John Bentham and Hannah (Bellis), and resided at 39, Mount Street, Flint.

John James was employed in one of the Flint mills before the war and was unmarried.

He enlisted in Flint on 28th September, 1914 and was home based until 13th July, 1915. He embarked on HM Transport ship Caledonia (page 7) at Devonport 14th July, 1915, disembarking at Gallipoli 9th August, 1915. He was admitted to a hospital in Gallipoli 2nd December, 1915 suffering from exposure and reported for duty on 23rd December. He was subsequently posted to Palestine. On enlistment he was 5 ft 4 in, weighed 9st, chest 34½ in, and his vision and physical development were good.

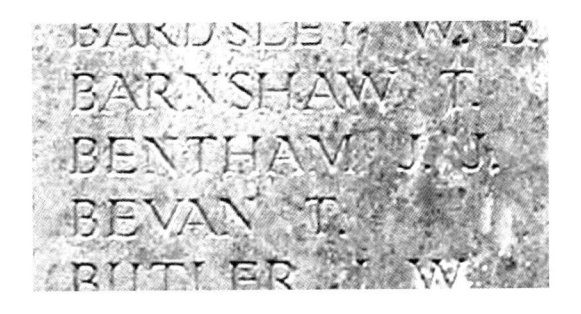

He was killed in action at the First Battle of Gaza 26th March, 1917. He has no known grave but is commemorated on the Jerusalem memorial on Panels 20 to 22 (pictured above).

He is remembered on three war memorials: Flint Town, St Mary's Parish Church, Flint, Oddfellows Hall, Flint and also his parent's headstone at Northop Road Cemetery, Flint (Line 53, South Side, Grave 8). He is also commemorated on the North Wales Heroes' Memorial Arch, Bangor.

He was awarded the 1914–15 Star, British War Medal and Victory Medal.

IN
LOVING MEMORY OF

JOHN JAMES
SON OF
JOHN & HANNAH BENTHAM
MOUNT STREET
WHO WAS KILLED IN ACTION
MARCH 26TH 1917, AND WAS BURIED AT
GAZA (HOLY LAND) AGED 23 YEARS
"HE HATH FOUGHT THE GOOD FIGHT"

ALSO THE ABOVE
HANNAH BENTHAM
WHO DIED NOV. 25TH 1924
AGED 57 YEARS
"PEACE PERFECT PEACE"

ALSO THE ABOVE
JOHN BENTHAM
WHO DIED JAN. 29TH 1938
AGED 71 YEARS

"AT REST"

The Bentham family grave and transcription

IN MEMORIAM

In loving but sad 24th Birthday remembrance.
"God's will be done," I faintly cry,
My longing heart may break;
I deemed him mine, but he is Thine,
For He who gives can take.

Some day I hope to meet him –
Some day, I know not when;
To clasp his hand in the Better Land,
Never to part again.
(One of the best, and faithful unto death).
From Father, Mother, Brothers and Sisters.
(County Herald, 26th October, 1917)

He sleeps beside his comrades,
In a hallowed grave unknown,
But his name is written in letters of love
In the hearts he left at home.

May the heavenly winds blow softly,
O'er that sweet and hallowed spot;
Though the sea divides his grave and us,
He will never be forgot.
Fondly remembered by his Uncle,
Aunt and Cousins.
Castle Hill House, Flint.
(County Herald, 29th March, 1918)

"Killed in action" says the letter,
That is all the tale they tell
Of the brave, dear boy who loved us,
Of the son we loved so well;
How his life was sped we know not,
What his last word, look, or thought,
Only that he did his duty,
Died as nobly as he fought.

Sadly missed by Father, Mother,
Brother and Sisters.
(County Herald, 28th March, 1919)

Rest on, dear one, in a soldier's grave,
Your life for your country you nobly gave,
You fought and fell for the Red, White and Blue,
Now heaven is your home, a crown you're due
Ever remembered by his loving Uncle,
Aunt and Cousins.
(County Herald, 26th March, 1920)

Deep in my heart lies a picture,
Of my good friend gone to rest,
And in memory's frame I shall keep him,
Because he was one of the best.

Upright and straight in all his ways.
Honest and just till the end of his days.
From his old Friend, Jim Ellis,
56, Feathers Street, Flint.
(County Herald, 26th March, 1920)

You did watch for my homecoming, mother,
Now I will watch for you,
And when you reach the golden gates,
I will come and lead you through.
From Father, Mother, Brother and Sisters.
(County Herald, 24th March, 1921)

I remember well my sorrow when I
stood beside him,
My deepest heartfelt anguish when
I saw that he was dead.
From his old Pal, Jim Ellis.
(County Herald, 24th March, 1922)

John senior died 29th January, 1938, aged 71, at his home, 39, Mount Street, and wife Hannah died 25th November, 1924, aged 57, at Chester Infirmary. They are buried together in the Northop Road Cemetery, Flint.

John was born in Flint and for many years he was in business on his own account as a butcher in Chester Street and was afterwards employed by Messrs E J Rogers and Sons, builders, Earl Street, retiring in 1932. He was one of the oldest members of the Flint Castle Lodge of Oddfellows. He was also a keenly enthusiastic supporter of Flint Town Amateurs Football Club and was a familiar figure at the Club's home matches on the Holywell Road ground. He was a member of St Mary's Parish Church.

Hannah was born in Flint and was a sister of Flint Councillor Thomas Bond Bellis OBE (1858–1945).

Mr and Mrs Bentham received a touching letter from Private Bentham's commanding officer which stated: "I hardly know how to word the Company's letter of condolence to you over the loss in action of your son. Your son was a brave and fearless soldier, and the Company, while mourning his death, is proud to be able to place on its honours list such an heroic man as your son. We all extend our sympathies and heartfelt regret, and hope that you may find some consolation in the thought that he died such a glorious death."

GUNNER
BENJAMIN BEVAN

673568, Royal Field Artillery 'C' Battery 275th Brigade

Benjamin Bevan was born 10th January, 1894 in Flint and was he was the seventh of eight children of Edward Bevan and Fanny (Williams) of Wesley Mount, Northop Road, Flint.

The 1911 census revealed Benjamin was a boarder at the home of a Mr and Mrs Walter Philp, of 22, Middleton Street, Moss Side, Manchester and employed as a salesman at a drapery store. He was employed elsewhere prior to joining the army but it is not known where. He was unmarried.

He enlisted in Liverpool in c. August, 1914 and was subsequently posted to France, landing at Le Havre, on 1st October, 1915.

He died from wounds received in action on 6th June, 1917 and buried at Lijssenthoek Military Cemetery, Poperinge, West-Vlaanderen, Belgium (Plot XII, Row C, Grave 39).

He is remembered on the Flint Town war memorial and was awarded the 1914–15 Star, British War Medal and Victory Medal. He is also commemorated on the North Wales Heroes' Memorial Arch, Bangor.

The information became known per telegram from the Military Authorities on Friday, 1st June that Gunner Bevan was seriously ill in one of the hospitals abroad. On Saturday morning letters were received by Mr Bevan from the Chaplain, and others connected with the Battalion, conveying the additional news that their son had met with serious shrapnel wounds, and that a portion of his right arm had been amputated at the hospital, but that he was progressing as well as could be expected under the treatment. The hopes of his relatives and friends were that Gunner Bevan would soon sufficiently recover to enable his removal to England, where he might be visited. However, the following Saturday there was received from the Chaplain the customary communication as to the hero's work in the field, and his death. Gunner Bevan was well known in the Borough and had been connected with the Peniel (Welsh Wesleyan) Church, Chester Road, where touching references were made to his death on Sunday.

Benjamin's father died 4th July, 1930 aged 73, at his home at Wesley Mount, Northop Road.

He was born in Flint, and on leaving school he was apprenticed to Mr John Lloyd Bibby, contractor, of Corporation Street, at the same time as Alderman Alfred Bibby Lloyd. He served as a brick setter and Alderman Lloyd as a joiner. When Alderman Lloyd commenced business on his own account Mr Bevan was his right-hand man, and the two were inseparable friends throughout their lives, Mr Bevan remaining with Mr Lloyd until he retired in 1927. He worked on all the big contracts carried out by the firm of Messrs A B Lloyd and Sons, acting in the capacity of foreman of the constructions. He was a member of the Flint Castle Lodge of Oddfellows and also of the Operative Bricklayers Society, in connection with which he acted as treasurer of the local branch for many years. He was a faithful member of the Peniel Welsh Wesleyan Church, where he was a Sunday School teacher for upwards of 50 years. He also held the office of Deacon for 40 years and was a 'poor steward.' In his younger days he was a singer of repute, possessing a rich baritone voice. He took an active part in the singing at Peniel Church, and he was always in great demand at concerts and socials held in connection with the church.

IN MEMORIAM

Renew our will from day to day,
Blend it with Thine, and take away
All that now makes it hard to say,
Thy will be done.
Dad, Mam and Nellie, Wesley Mount, Flint.
County Herald, 7th June, 1918)

A little card, "I am quite well,"
A letter next, "He bravely fell."
If those who caused this awful war,
Were the only ones to fight,
A brighter world this would have been
For aching hearts to-night.
From Frank and Cissi
12, Golftyn Street, Connah's Quay.
(County Herald, 7th June, 1918)

Gunner Benjamin Bevan's grave at Lijssenthoek Military Cemetery, Poperinge, West-Vlaanderen, Belgium. Plot XII, Row C, Grave 39

He was extremely well known in the town of Flint, possessing a quiet but unassuming manner; he was universally popular and highly respected. At his funeral service, addresses were given by the Reverends W H Hughes (pastor), Edward Davies and Gwynfryn Jones, all of whom paid eloquent tributes to him. The Reverend Edward Davies (Mold) commented on the fact that the late Mr Bevan, Alderman A B Lloyd and Mr Edward Hughes had been inseparable in life and now they were united in death. The Reverend Gwynfryn Jones referred to the deceased as one of 'nature's gentlemen,' and based his address on 'Blessed are the meek.' He was buried in the Northop Road Cemetery, Flint with his wife Fanny, who was also born in Flint, and died in May 1923, aged 66.

PRIVATE
ROBERT BEVAN

10807, 9th (Queen's Royal) Lancers

Robert Bevan was born 8th October, 1894 in Flint and was the third of five children of William Smedley Bevan and Margaret (Williams) and resided at Penypalment, Coleshill, Bagillt Road, Flint.

Robert was employed as a brick setter by Alderman Alfred Bibby Lloyd, JP, builder, Flint and was a well-known and respected member of the Welsh Wesleyan denomination. He was unmarried.

He enlisted in Flint in January 1916 with the 13th East Surrey Regiment, No 25795, then transferred to the 2/1st Troop Welsh Horse 'C' Squadron, No 743, and then again to the 9th Lancers, No GS/17240 and, finally, the Corps of Lancers, No L/10807.

He was killed in action at the Battle of Pozieres, France on 27th March, 1918. He has no known grave but is commemorated on the Pozieres Memorial, Somme, France, on Panel 4.

He is remembered on three war memorials: Flint Town, Bagillt Village and St Mary's Parish

A greetings card Private Bevan sent home

Pictured here with the 1st Troop Welsh Horse 'C' Squadron, Private Bevan is seated in the second row, third from the right

Church, Bagillt. He is also remembered on his parents' headstone in the Northop Road Cemetery, Flint (Line 10, North Side, Grave 8). He is also commemorated on the North Wales Heroes' Memorial Arch, Bangor. He was awarded the British War Medal and Victory Medal.

Robert's father died 9th June, 1925, aged 67, at Stanley Hospital, Liverpool, and was buried in the Northop Road Cemetery, Flint. He was born in Flint and he and his wife emigrated to New York, possibly in the late 1880s, but returned within a few years. He was employed by Alderman Alfred Bibby Lloyd for many years as a brick setter, but for some time had been assisting his son, who carried on business in Church Street. He was well known and highly respected and a faithful member of the Peniel Welsh Methodist Church.

William's wife Margaret died 2nd April, 1935, aged 75, at The Glyn, Coleshill, Flint and is buried with her husband. Like her husband she was also well known and highly esteemed in the town, and a member of the Peniel Welsh Methodist Church.

The Bevan family grave in the Northop Road Cemetery

PRIVATE
HAROLD BITHELL

13452, 9th (Service) Battalion Royal Welsh Fusiliers

Harold Bithell was born in Flint in 1890 and baptised 22nd January, 1890 at St Mary's Parish Church, Flint. He was the sixth of nine children to William Edwards Bithell and Margaret (Jackson).

Harold grew up living at the Blue Bell Inn, Castle Street, moved to 12, Earl Street before settling with the family at 60, Earl Street.

He was one of the best-known footballer players in Flintshire and North Wales, having been a member of the Flint Club's team some seasons. A single man, he was employed as a beamer at the local silk works and was a member of the Loyal Flint Castle Lodge of Oddfellows.

Harold enlisted in Flint sometime in 1914 and at one time was a Lance Corporal, so for some unknown reason had been demoted. He landed at Boulogne, France 27th July, 1915.

Private Bithell was killed by a shell in France on 20th November, 1916. He has no known grave but is commemorated on the Thiepval Memorial, Somme, France, on Pier and Face 4A. He is remembered on three war memorials: Flint Town, St Mary's Parish Church, Flint and Oddfellows Hall, Flint. He is also commemorated on the North Wales Heroes' Memorial Arch, Bangor.

He was awarded the 1914–15 Star, British War Medal, Victory Medal and the Military Medal for bravery in the Field (without citation), which was published in the London Gazette on Wednesday, 23rd August, 1916.

The Captain of the Company in which Private Bithell was a member conveyed to his parents the sympathy of the officers and men at the death of their "splendid son", who was killed by a shell. "The remains were laid to rest where he fell, with two comrades who shared the same fate. His loss to the Company and to me personally is immense. He was a splendid soldier and a noble man who had a great and good influence with the men. His heroism was prominent at the time; and it is very satisfactory to know that it has not gone by unheeded, for he was the proud wearer of the Military Medal. Such noble fellows as these cannot be dead. They and their influence and their works live after them."

Private E B Morris, whose home was in Park Avenue, Flint, and who was one of the comrades of Private Bithell, wrote to Mr and Mrs Bithell, and furnished them with particulars of the death of their son, and stated his remains were respectfully interred. The funeral service was read at the grave. A cross had been erected to mark the spot, so that the parents would now know how highly respected was Harold by all his comrades. Harold was always cheerful and always the same, and his death – along with that of many other poor fellows – had made them sad and more thoughtful men.

On the same day the intelligence reached his parents and friends that Private William Carr, the son of

Mr Thomas Carr, florist, of Chester Road, Flint, and brother of Company Sergeant Major George Carr (page 61), had been seriously wounded. Private Bithell and he were in the trenches, and a portion of the shell which killed Bithell came into contact with his arm. He was removed to the dressing station, and then to the hospital.

The following extracts were taken from the personal diary of H Lloyd Williams (A/Lt-Col: T/Major) 9th (Service) Battalion Royal Welsh Fusiliers recounting his experiences during the years of the Great War concerning the action in which Private Bithell was killed:

"On the morning of the 19th November 1916, the 56th and 57th Brigades had made the oft-postponed attack on Grandcourt. A thick mist prevailed, and the attack, which was supposed to have about four turning movements, and which the brigades made their several attacks in directions which were at right angles to each other, resulted in hopeless

Private Harold Bithell

confusion although some points were seized and some progress made. The 58th Brigade was ordered to continue the progress and to make good the already captured positions and to consolidate them. The instructions were not one whit more definite than that. No-one knew the situation in front, and when we of the two front companies (B. and C.) called at the 57th Brigade H.Q. in Stuff Redoubt for information on our way up, neither the General (Jeffreys) nor any of his staff had the remotest idea of what had happened or of the position of the troops in front. It was thereupon arranged between us that B. Company should occupy Blue Trench – a position they held on their previous visit – and that C. Company should make good a certain trench to the left front of that position. It was not known in whose possession this latter was, and I was advised to proceed carefully and warily, because it was certain that there were many of our wounded lying about and there was a likelihood of its being held by the enemy. Our orders generally were to construct and consolidate a line from Fergusson Communication Trench to Lucky Way. There were no guides provided, and the two Companies struggled along behind Matt Davies who was directing himself by means of a compass. We ultimately arrived at Blue Trench, and leaving the Company lying behind that Trench, Lt. E. O. Roberts and I reconnoitred forward and fixed on positions in which to place the Company, and around which we could establish strong points.

There certainly were numbers of our wounded lying about, and in the dug-out which we made our H.Q., was a wounded sergeant of the Gloucesters, who had gone insane. After raving for several hours, the poor fellow died there before we could arrange to have him sent down. Our time was feverishly employed in rescuing and sending down the wounded and in consolidating our position, for we had not the remotest idea of how far or how near the enemy was. During the next day our position was rendered uncomfortable by accurate sniping and artillery fire. The very door of our dug-out was accurately ranged, and when a group of men dashed for the dug-out in the middle of a bombardment, the destruction was awful. The entrance was blocked, and the steps inside also, with our dead, who included the C.S.M's Staff – Bithell, Brennan, and Kingsbury. It was a brutal state of affairs, and when an order came through from Battalion H.Q., who had never once been down to see the situation for themselves, to carry out another difficult operation, I felt very mutinous indeed. It was so obviously an operation conceived by the drawing of lines on the map by someone who had not the remotest idea of the conditions in front. Before proceeding to carry out this order, I made enquiries of Battalion H.Q., and was informed that it emanated from a certain junior captain who had spent his whole time bluffing at H.Q., an outsider and sycophant, who had so influenced the C.O. while we were enduring as we were in front, that the latter, on proceeding to take over the command of the 12th Brigade, left his junior in command. From that moment I dropped the reigns, and so did Matt Davies. We brought our Companies back to the comfort of Battalion H.Q. in Bainbridge trench and later went even further back to Bulgar trench. It was a bold proceeding, but we were desperately 'fed up' with this treatment.

On Saturday, 28th April Lieutenant Colonel Chaplain the Reverend Canon Nicholas, of the Rectory, Flint, received from the Authorities the Military Medal, which had been awarded to the late Private for bravery in the field. It is known that the act of bravery was very conspicuous, and it was most unfortunate that in a later action he received a fatal shrapnel wound, and therefore was deprived of the opportunity of being presented with the honour at Buckingham Palace. The Canon delivered the medal to the mother of the deceased soldier who had already received the prayer book and other small articles belonging to her son, and which were in his possession at the time of his death.

Harold's brother, Albert Francis, served in the war as a Quarter Master Sergeant with the 2/5th Battalion Royal Welsh Fusiliers from 1915–19. He and his wife Mary Ann were both killed in WW2 by enemy bombing over their home at 22, Well Lane, Rock Ferry on 12th March, 1941.

Their father, William, died on 15th October, 1920, aged 65, at his home, 60, Earl Street, and buried in the Northop Road Cemetery, Flint. He was born in Flint and was at one time Licensed Victualler at the Blue Bell Inn, Castle Street, Flint, and for many years he was in the employ of Mr Henry Taylor, Clerk to the Borough Justices, and subsequently he held the position of School Attendance Officer, and also that of Coal Controller. He was a solicitor's clerk, managing clerk (law), accountant and Inspector of Nuisances. He was a gentleman who was held in high esteem and greatly respected by the residents of Flint. He was a member of the local Conservative Club, and out of respect to him after his death the Club's flag was flown at half-mast. He was also a Freemason.

His wife Margaret, also born in Flint, died 2nd November, 1940, aged 84, at 54, Earl Street, Flint and is buried with her husband. She was very well known and highly esteemed in the town, of which she was one of its oldest residents. She was a daughter of Mr and Mrs Robert Jackson, of the Castle Inn, Flint and a faithful member of St Mary's Parish Church.

IN MEMORIAM

A loving hero, true and kind,
A beautiful memory left behind.
Sincerely mourned by his Parents,
Brothers and Sisters.
(County Herald, 23rd November, 1917)

SERGEANT
FREDERICK WILLIAM BOWEN

9452, 2nd Battalion Royal Welsh Fusiliers

The 2nd Battalion Royal Welsh Fusiliers (RWF) in India. The International Order of Good Templars Red Dragon Lodge. Sergeant Bowen is in the middle row 3rd from right

Frederick (Fred) William Bowen was born in Flint in 1886 and baptised 15th June, 1886 at St Mary's Parish Church, Flint. He was the second of four children to John Taylor Bowen and Mary Elizabeth (Williams).

In Fred's early years the family lived in Halkyn Street then moved to 25 Chester Street before settling at 54, Feathers Street. He was employed as a baker and was unmarried.

It was reported in the County Herald that on Tuesday the 24th July, 1906 Fred – who was one of the employees at the Holywell Company's Works, in Holywell Road, and was then living at Chester Street – met with a severe accident. "It appears that in the course of his employment the unfortunate young man tried to turn on a tap, but finding it too tight for his hand, he used his foot, when the whole thing collapsed, and young Bowen fell into a hot vat and was severely scalded."

He enlisted in the army at Flint, 17th May, 1907, as a Private, with the Army Service Corps, and his service record is as follows: joined at Wrexham, 18th May, 1907, then transferred to the Royal Welsh Fusiliers; posted to India, 8th January, 1908; arrived at Northbrook, 31st January. 1908; Shwebo, 25th February, 1908; Bhamo, 24th February, 1908; hospital suffering from diarrhoea, 17th September, 1908 to

25th September, 1908; awarded 3rd Class Certificate of Education, 14th November, 1908; Shwebo, 25th February, 1909; granted Proficiency Pay, 7th May, 1909; passed classes of Instruction in Nursing Duties, 17th May, 1909; appointed to unpaid Lance Corporal, 6th July, 1909; awarded 2nd Class Certificate of Education, 18th February, 1910; appointed to paid Lance Corporal, 3rd February, 1911; Quetta, 31st March, 1911; hospital, 28th August, 1911 to 15th September, 1911, suffering from the effects of parasites; hospital, 27th May, 1912 to 3rd June, 1912, suffering from tapeworm; promoted to Corporal, 1st December, 1912.

In the same month he forwarded a military Christmas greetings card to the Rector of Flint. The card was exhibited in the clothiers' establishment of Messrs Thomas and Son, Chester Street, and presented a view of a military parade with the 'Silver Drums' of the regiments.

His service record continues: permitted to extend his period of army service to complete 12 years with the colours, 29th November, 1913; home based, 10th March, 1914; appointed unpaid Lance Sergeant, 1st May, 1914; landed in France, 11th August, 1914; promoted to Sergeant, 28th October, 1914, for special conduct in the field. On enlistment he was 5 ft 5¾ in tall, weighed 114lb, chest 32 in, his physical development was fair and had loss and decay of eight teeth, a fresh complexion, brown eyes, brown hair and an irregular scar on front of left leg.

In the first week of November 1914 several letters and postcards were received by relatives of the local soldiers who were at the Front in Ypres. Sergeant Bowen stated that he received the parcels of gifts, which had been forwarded from his home and friends in Flint, and that he had distributed portions of the gift to his comrades, who were, along with himself, extremely grateful for the kindness.

Sergeant Bowen was killed in action in France 14th November, 1914 and buried at Pont-Du-Hem Military Cemetery, La Gorgue, Nord, France (Plot XI, Row C, Grave 3). He is remembered on two war memorials: Flint Town and St Mary's Parish Church, Flint. He is also commemorated on the North Wales Heroes' Memorial Arch, Bangor.

He was awarded the 1914 Star, Clasp, British War Medal and Victory Medal.

By the first postal delivery on Friday morning 20th November the sad intelligence of the death of Sergeant Bowen reached Flint and this is how it was reported in the local newspaper:

The deceased was 28 years of age and displayed an especial aptitude for military duties, making excellent progress in the ranks with his promotions. When the Regiment returned to England, and became quartered at Portland, he received a further promotion, and held the non-commissioned rank of Sergeant.

At the time he was expecting a furlough, but by some means it was never accomplished; and then the war broke out. The Regiment and others which were near were constituted as one of the first drafts of the British Expeditionary Force; and the 2nd Battalion of the Royal Welsh Fusiliers arriving in France were with the 1st Battalion engaged in several marches. The positions they held were not definitely known to the general public on this side of the Channel, but letters which occasionally reached friends in Flint were sufficient indications that they were on the line of communication, and that afterwards they had been engaged in some desperate skirmishes. Time proceeded, and eventually it became known that the 1st Battalion of the Royal Welsh had been heavily engaged in the firing line, with serious losses, of which the public had been anxiously awaiting the publication of a casualty list. Then it was also intimated privately by means of other letters that the men of the 2nd Battalion had also been in the thick of the battles in villages and districts not far from Lille. It is believed that it was near this town where Sergeant Bowen was shot, and his remains interred on the 14th instant.

Additional information respecting the death will be found hereunder in a letter received from Colour-Sergeant Thomas Davies, of Flint, who was a close friend of the deceased. As soon as the intimation of the death of Sergeant Bowen was spread in the Borough general expressions of regret were heard, and the heartfelt sympathies of numerous residents were conveyed to Mr and Mrs Bowen in their sad bereavement. The news created a painful sensation inasmuch as Sergeant Bowen was well known in the town; and there was no doubt that the intelligence was also received with much sorrow amongst the men of the Flint Company of the 5th Battalion at Northampton, and of which Company the deceased's elder brother is a member. At the latter end of last week Mr and Mrs Bowen received a postcard from the Sergeant stating that he was quite well, and asking that he should be forwarded gloves because of the cold weather. The articles were obtained, and were to have been dispatched on Friday morning, when the news of his death was gently broken to the parents. This is a circumstance which tends to make the grief more poignant. Those parents who visited the bereaved parents on Friday saw the splendid gloves on a table. Bowen has died in the cause of his country. When his father wrote to him soon after the hostilities commenced, and when he was reminded of his military work, he wrote a reply, which was received at home, containing the pointed and brief sentence, "I will do my best." No one can gainsay that he did his best for his King and Country; his name will be revered as one of the country's heroes; and when the proper time arrives his name should be enrolled on the golden monument of fame. The proprietors of the "County Herald" desire to tender their sympathies to Mr and Mrs Bowen.

We learn that on the day previous to his death Sergeant Bowen had been promoted to the position of Colour-Sergeant.

In the previous two issues of the County Herald the statements had been furnished to provide the friends and relatives of the RWF with the vague information that the battalions of the RWF were in the fighting line, and taking a prominent and gallant part in driving the Germans back. It was stated at the same time that it was understood that the 1st Battalion of the Royal Welsh had suffered many casualties, and that the 2nd Battalion had also been "thinned". These statements have received verification in several details, and as far as we are permitted to mention them.

Colour-Sergeant Thomas Davies, of the 2nd Battalion RWF, of Sydney Street, Flint, and who is a brother of Sergeant D E Davies, of the E Company, 5th Battalion RWF, at Northampton, in a letter home under date of 15th November, stated that the men of the Battalion had had a terrible time of it, as would be seen from the casualty list; and he was surprised he was alive to be able to write home. They went into the trenches, where they had been until that day. The weather had been very cold and wet, and in addition the Germans had been pouring shells towards their trenches. The continual bursting of the shell and rifle fire had made it a very trying time. The 2nd Battalion had lost, it was said, about 300 men;

and one Company had lost many men and their officers. To "cap the lot," Sergeant Fred Bowen, of Flint, was shot in the head and killed on the spot. The letter continues: "I had him buried last, poor Fred: he was only made full Sergeant the day before, and we were arranging to have such a good time when we got home." He also says that he himself had some narrow escapes with shrapnel. One of his ammunition pouches was blown away and a piece of shell went through his haversack. His overcoat had been torn to pieces by a shell dropping on it on the bank of the trench, at the same time wounding one officer and a man who were next to him. So they could guess he had been in a 'hot shop,' and he thought himself lucky to have come out safe. They were afterwards placed into billets for a few days, and did not know when or where they would be going next. He believed that the 1st Battalion had had a worse time, for it is said they had lost officers and about 700 men. The 2nd Battalion was only a few miles from [censored] and were giving the Germans "socks." The Germans were trying to break through the lines of the British, but had found the British too stubborn for them. He had killed several of the enemy in the daytime, and very likely accounted for a good many more at night-time when they had been charging the trenches of the British. It was a sight to see the amount of dead Germans in front of our trenches; they were even hanging dead on our wire fencing like clothes on a line.

Sergeant Bowen's parents John Taylor and Mary Elizabeth Bowen

Private Morris stated in a letter home that on the 12th November he was speaking with Colour-Sergeant Fred Bowen, when he had taken water to the men in the trenches in the evening; and on the following morning he was sorry to hear he had been killed.

On his return from the Front in early December Sergeant-Major T Davies said, "On the morning of the 14th November he left Sergeant Fred Bowen in order to join the Headquarters, which were at the rear, and about ten o'clock the same morning he was informed that Bowen had been killed with a bullet which entered the right side of the forehead. During the night the stretcher-bearers brought several bodies to the burial ground near the rear of the supports of the Battalion, and amongst the bodies he recognized that of Bowen. In the presence of four members of the Battalion a clergyman read a brief service and the remains of Bowen were interred. Sergeant-Major Davies states that he was the only Flint man present at the time of the interment, as the others were some distance away."

Fred's father was born in Llangollen and had resided in Flint since he was 10 years of age and until his retirement carried on a confectionery business in Chester Street. He was a founder member of the Flint Borough Working Man's Club. He died in Manchester 4th December, 1948, aged 86, and was buried in the Northop Road Cemetery, Flint.

Fred's mother was also born in Flint and was a faithful member of St Mary's Parish Church, where as a young woman she was a Sunday school teacher. She died 18th September, 1938, aged 76, at her residence, 54, Feathers Street, Flint, and buried with her husband. Mr and Mrs Bowen had been married 55 years and celebrated their Golden Wedding in 1933.

DRIVER
PATRICK JOSEPH BRADLEY

172730, 'B' Battery, 281st Brigade, Royal Field Artillery

Patrick Joseph Bradley was born 28th January, 1899 in Sydney Street, Flint. He was the sixth of seven children to Arthur Bradley and Mary (Murphy) and resided at 43, Sydney Street, Flint. Patrick was unmarried and his occupation is unknown.

He enlisted in Wrexham in July 1916. A driver's job in the Royal Field Artillery was to care for and maintain the horses needed to move the artillery pieces around the battlefield.

He was killed in action 6th September, 1918 at St Leger, France, along with seven others and 63 wounded, caused by 5.9 HV (high velocity) shelling of wagon lines.

He was buried at Mory Street Military Cemetery, St Leger, Pas de Calais, France (Plot A, Grave 9). He is remembered on two war memorials: Flint Town and St Mary's Catholic Church, Flint. He is also commemorated on the North Wales Heroes' Memorial Arch, Bangor.

He was awarded the British War Medal and Victory Medal.

Patrick's father, who was born in County Down, Ireland, died in late March 1909, aged 46, and buried in the Northop Road Cemetery, Flint. He was employed as an ironworker.

His mother, who was also born in County Down, Ireland, died 24th March, 1926, aged 64, at her residence in Sydney Street, Flint, and buried in the Northop Road Cemetery with her son Peter, but not her husband.

PRIVATE
JOHN JAMES BRAMFIELD

25937, 17th (Service) Battalion Royal Welsh Fusiliers (2nd North Wales)

John James Bramfield was born 1st April, 1883 at the Hawarden Union Workhouse, Broughton Hall, near Chester, and the second illegitimate son of Mary Alice Bramfield who was born at Knotty Ash, West Derby, Liverpool and was employed for a time as a domestic servant.

John James, with his mother and half-brother Samuel, lived for a number of years at 8, Chemistry Cottages, Saltney.

He married Charlotte Ann Martin at the Register Office, Holywell, 28th September, 1912, and they had two children: John James junior, who was born in 1913, and died 13th March, 1916 of "convulsions and bronchitis," and Edward James (1916–97). They resided at 21, Evans Street, Flint and John James was a labourer at the Shotton Paint Works.

On 2nd April, 1913 John's mother died of cardiac disease, aged about 65, at the Hawarden Union Workhouse, Broughton, near Chester, and was buried in St Mary's Churchyard, Broughton. She remained a spinster all her life.

Before the war John had served three years with the Volunteer Battalion Royal Welsh Fusiliers. He enlisted in Flint, 26th April, 1915, signing with an X, and joined at Llandudno the following day. He moved to Winchester in August 1915 and landed in France in December 1915. On enlistment he was 5 ft 4½ in tall, weighed 10st, chest 34 in, and his physical development was good.

He died on 25th March, 1916 from wounds received in action in France, and was buried in the Guards' Cemetery, Windy Corner, Cuinchy, Pas de Calais, France (Plot III, Row O, Grave 3). He is remembered on two war memorials: Flint Town and St Mary's Parish Church, Flint.

He was awarded the 1914–15 Star, British War Medal and Victory Medal.

Private Bramfield's wife Charlotte who, it was reported, was in a delicate state of health, received the following letter on Friday 31st March, 1916: "DEAR MADAM, – It is with regret that I write to inform you of the death of your husband, 25937, Pte J J Bramfield, of the Royal Welsh Fusiliers. He died under my care and without any suffering, from wounds received in action. – With deepest sympathy, yours, H J BARKER, Supt, RAMC."

On Saturday morning Mrs Bramfield was awaiting the official intimation of the death from the War Office; but there was no reason to doubt the authenticity of the letter written by the medical Superintendent of the Field Hospital Ambulance.

Charlotte Ann wrote the following letter enquiring about her husband's death plaque:

Mrs C A Bramfield
21 Evans Street, Flint,
North Wales

23/5/21

Sir,

Could you kindly inform me above where I can get a memoriam plate relating to my husband Pte J J Bramfield No 25937 17th Batt Royal Welsh Fus. He was killed in France March 1916. Hoping you will favour me with an early reply.

... and received this reply:

> Infantry Record Office
> (RWF Section)
> Shrewsbury
>
> 28/5/21
>
> I am in receipt of your letter of recent date, in respect of the Memorial Plaque relative to the late No 25937, Private J J Bramfield, Royal Welsh Fusiliers, and in reply thereto have to inform you that the Plaque will be forwarded to you direct from the Plaque Factory.
>
> As there are many thousands of the Mementoes to be issued, some time may elapse before you receive same, but you may rest assured that your case will be dealt with with all possible speed.
>
> In the meantime further correspondence on the subject is unnecessary.
>
> Major,
> For Lieut-Colonel,
> O i/c Infantry Record Office.

Charlotte Ann died in July 1936, aged 54, and is buried in the Northop Road Cemetery, Flint.

PRIVATE
PATRICK BRETT

901, 1/5th (Flintshire) Battalion Royal Welsh Fusiliers

Patrick Joseph Brett was born 1st March, 1871 at Carra Na Gepple, Sligo, Ireland and was the third of seven children to Thomas Brett and Catherine (Gallagher).

Thomas and Catherine were both born in Sligo, Ireland and brought the family to England in the 1880s.

In the 1891 census the Brett family were living at 26, Ireton Street, Horton, Bradford, Yorkshire, where Mr Brett was listed as an unemployed confectioner and Patrick as a woollen mill hand.

Mr and Mrs Brett both died in Bradford, Yorkshire; Thomas in 1892, aged about 46, and Catherine in 1899, aged about 44.

It is not known exactly when Patrick moved to Flint but in the late 19th and early 20th centuries Messrs Summers' Ironworks, Shotton were employing in large numbers, including migrants from various English counties, so it is almost certain he came over for that reason, and he was employed as a dyer.

He married Harriet Stacey née Bithell at St Paul's Parish Church, Seacombe, Wirral on 26th November, 1906. She was born in Flint in 1879 and the daughter of Edward Bithell (1852–1944), a fisherman, and his wife Alice (1860–1928), of Sea Villa, Flint. Patrick and Harriet lived at 7, Chester Street, Flint and had three children – Norah (1907–33); Delia (1912–?); Patrick Joseph (1915–74).

Harriet was first married at St Mary's Parish Church, Flint, 24th December, 1900, to Isaac Stacey, a merchant seaman, who served as a mate on board the merchant ships Winifred and John. He was serving as a master on the latter when, on 6th October, 1903, it foundered on the River Mersey and he drowned aged 24. They had two children named Isaac and Alice Gertrude.

Prior to WW1 Patrick served for twelve years with the Royal Irish Fusiliers, No. 347, then with the 2nd Volunteer Battalion of the Royal Welsh Fusiliers from 17th January, 1907 to 23rd April, 1909. On 29th August, 1908 he passed a most successful examination qualifying as a first-class signaller. Captain E J H Williams, Flint, was regimental instructor, and his brother Sergeant H O Williams (who is written about elsewhere), Flint Company, was assistant instructor, to whom the credits of the excellent results were due. On 23rd May, 1911 he signed for four years' service with the 5th Battalion of the Royal Welsh Fusiliers Territorial Division based at Flint Castle with the rank of Private. His Medical Inspection Report described him as 5 ft 5½ in tall, chest 37 in, dark brown hair, brown eyes, a dark complexion, with good vision and physical development. Mr George Clews, hairdresser, of 5, Chester Street, Flint, who provided a character reference for Private Brett, stated he had known him for 10 years and described him as sober and honest. He completed his preliminary training at Flint on 30th July, 1911 and was posted to Pembroke where he remained until the 13th August of the same year. There is a blank in his service record for the next three years until he enlisted at Flint with the Regular Army on the 5th August, 1914. He was discharged as medically unfit at Northampton 6th October, 1914.

He died on 22nd October, 1914 at his home, 7, Chester Street, Flint, of bronchopneumonia, and was buried in the Northop Road Cemetery, Flint (Line 28, South Side, Grave 4). He is remembered on the Oddfellows Hall memorial in Flint but was not eligible for any military awards.

The following report of his death appeared in the County Herald:
"About ten o'clock on Thursday morning the death occurred at his residence in Chester Street, Flint, of Mr Patrick J Brett, who had been for some years a well-known resident. The Deceased, who was 38 years of age, had been employed in local works and for a long period had been a member of the local Company of the Royal Welsh Fusiliers. He volunteered with others of the Regiment and was with the Regiment during the South African War. At the time of the mobilization of the 5th Battalion of the Royal Welsh Fusiliers, three months ago, he was numbered with the "E" Company of Flint, and left with the Battalion for Northampton. Three weeks since he was discharged from the Regiment as medically unfit, and returned home, when he sought medical advice. Eventually, he was seized with a serious illness, and strength gradually failing he expired as stated. He had identified himself with the Conservative Party and was one of its staunchest workers during elections, and it is said he was able to

wield some influence amongst a certain class of the voters. He was a member of the "Loyal Flint Castle Lodge" of Oddfellows, and his death is lamented by many in the ranks of the Territorials, as well as others who are living in Flint. He leaves a widow and three children to mourn his loss. – The funeral took place on Monday afternoon and was of a military character. Under the control of Company Sergeant-Major Williams, of the Headquarters' Staff, 5th Batt. RWF, Flint Castle, the whole of the men at present stationed there, to the number of about 156, paraded, and proceeded to the residence, and the main thoroughfares leading to the cemetery were lined with spectators. The coffin was placed upon a hand-bier covered with the "Union Jack," and on which were placed a number of pretty wreaths. The cortege was headed by the representatives of the "Loyal Flint Castle Lodge" of Oddfellows, who were followed by the Fusiliers' Firing Party, with arms reversed. Then came the remains, which were borne by several of the Fusiliers. The members of the family, relatives, and general mourners were next in the mournful procession, the rear of which was composed of the remainder of the Fusiliers. At the Cemetery gate the remains were met by the Very Rev Canon Jennings, of the St Mary's Catholic Church; and the interment was conducted with the ritual of that church. Immediately the prayers were concluded, the detachment of the Fusiliers fired three volleys over the grave, and the "Last Post" was sounded by Private J Owens, of Queensferry, who is connected with the National Reserves. An immense crowd of people were in the cemetery grounds. The Fusiliers were marched to the castle where they were dismissed."

The Brett family grave at the Northop Road Cemetery, Flint

Harriet married a third time in 1921 to Charles Dutton (c.1872–1955). She died on 7th February, 1928 and was buried with second husband Patrick. For many years she conducted a toy and confectionery shop in Chester Street, and was well known and highly respected in the town. She was a keen member of the Women's Guild and Mothers' Union.

PRIVATE
AMOS BROADSTOCK

10558, 2nd Battalion South Staffordshire Regiment

Amos Broadstock was born 26th February, 1877 at Bull Lane, West Bromwich, Staffordshire and the second of three children to John Broadstock and Mary (Bamford).

In the 1891 census, when Amos was 14 years old, he was employed as a tube maker, and the family had left

16, Bull Lane and were now living at 59, Foredraft Street, Greet's Green, West Bromwich before moving again by 1901 to 12, Tasker Street in the same town. Mrs Broadstock, who was a native of Wednesbury, Staffordshire, had died in 1897 aged 53. Mr Broadstock, a native of West Bromwich, died in 1911 aged 80. He was previously married to lady named Sarah who died in 1871 aged about 40. He was employed as a collier but in his later years he was an invalid.

Amos married Ada Price, of Wednesbury, Staffordshire, at the All Saints Parish Church, Moxley, Staffordshire on 23rd November 1902, and the 1911 census found them living at 63, Mount Place, Chester Road, Flint. Amos had gained employment at the Hawarden Bridge Ironworks, Shotton. They had five children – Walter (1905–93), Ernest Amos (1908–87), Jack (1911–54), Doris (1912–?) and Vera May (1914–84).

He enlisted in Wrexham in 1914 and landed in France 28th November, 1914.

He died on 26th March, 1917, of bronchopneumonia at the No. 1 Canadian General Hospital, Etaples, France and was buried at the Etaples Military Cemetery, Pas de Calais, France (Plot XXII, Row C, Grave 3A). He is remembered on two war memorials: St David's Parish Church, Oakenholt and St Gabriel's Parish Church, Walsall.

He was awarded the 1914–15 Star, British War Medal and Victory Medal.

Two greetings cards Amos sent home to his wife

PRIVATE
JOSEPH BRODERICK

15114, 5th (Service) Battalion Connaught Rangers.

Joseph Broderick was born 13th December, 1883 at 2, Moore Street, Cork, Ireland and the son of James Broderick, a farm labourer, and Jane (Healy).

In the Irish Census of 1911 Jane was a widow, aged 50, living with a daughter Jane, aged 11, at Cork Hill, Cork. It was stated that neither could read.

Meanwhile, back in the UK, the 1911 census revealed Joseph to be lodging at the home of a Mr Albert Edward Rogers of 70, Swan Street, Flint, and employed as a pitch worker at a Pitch and Tar Works. He was later employed as a chemical labourer.

He married Edith Parry at the Register Office, Chester on 6th July, 1912 and they lived at 4, Upper Queen Street, Flint. They had two children – James (1913–88) and Joseph (1915–99).

Joseph enlisted at Tralee, County Kerry, Ireland in August 1914, with the 6th Battalion Leinster Regiment, No. 6689 having previously served with the Territorial Army. It is not known when he transferred to the Connaught Rangers.

The County Herald of 6th August 1915 reported the following:

"A man named George Jones, residing in Upper Queen Street, Flint, appeared before the Magistrates in answer to two charges of threats made by a Mrs Edith Broderick, of 4, Upper Queen Street. Mrs Broderick said that some dispute had arisen between her mother and the defendant on Monday evening last. There was a quarrel and Mr Jones threatened he would take her life if she went from her house to the water tap. He also threatened to "pull her liver out.". He had also struck her and threatened her upon another occasion. Mr Jones responded: "It is all through her mother telling fortunes and cutting the cards for the little girl in the house." Mrs Janet Williams gave corroborative evidence of the defendant's threats; and Police Inspector Jones said he had been called to the neighbourhood several times in consequence of the defendant's conduct, the defendant being under the influence of drink each time. The complainant's husband was a soldier at the Front. The Mayor said it was the duty of all men at the present time to protect women whose husbands were serving their country and fighting at the Front. Defendant would be bound over in the sum of £10 to keep the peace for six months in each of the two cases, and to pay 4 s as costs in each case."

What became of Joseph's mother after this incident is not known. It is quite possible she returned to Ireland.

In September 1915 it was reported that Private Broderick was wounded in the arm in France. He recovered from the wound sufficiently to enable him to be granted a period of leave, whereupon he returned to Flint, and to his friends in Swan Street, receiving a hearty welcome.

He died in a hospital at Rouen, France on 25th November, 1918 from wounds received in action, and is buried in St Sever Cemetery Extension, Seine-Maritime, Rouen, France (Block S, Plot II, Row C, Grave 4).

He is remembered on two war memorials: Flint Town and St Mary's Parish Church, Flint. He is also commemorated on the North Wales Heroes' Memorial Arch, Bangor. There is a John Broderick remembered on the St Mary's Catholic Church war memorial too. This could be him also, and someone simply got the name wrong, as no-one of that name could be traced.

Private Broderick was awarded the 1914–15 Star, British War Medal and Victory Medal.

Edith re-married, as Edith Louisa Brodrick, at St Mary's Parish Church, Flint, on 6th July, 1919, to widower John Thomas Paynter (c.1868–1957). She died in Nantwich in 1953 aged 72.

PRIVATE
FRANK BROWN

240643, 1/5th (Flintshire) Battalion Royal Welsh Fusiliers

Frank Brown was born on 12th August, 1897 at 191, Moorside Road, Swinton, Lancashire and was the eldest of five children to William Brown and Emma (Chapman).

The 1901 census revealed they had moved a short distance away to 27, Ellesmere Street, Swinton. From there they moved to 68, Mount Street, Flint before settling at 19, Mount Street, by which time Frank was employed as a stamper at the Oakenholt Paper Mill. He was later employed at the Mercerisers Silk Factory, Holywell Road. He was unmarried.

> **IN MEMORIAM**
>
> *Loving memory of him brings many a silent tear*
> Our dear Frank, the dearly loved eldest son of
> William and Emma Brown
> (County Herald, 5th November, 1920)

Frank enlisted in Flint on 23rd September, 1914 and his service record is as follows: embarked on HM Troopship Caledonia (see Lieutenant T Bate for photo) 14th July, 1915 for Gallipoli; sick in hospital in Gallipoli, 30th November, 1915; in a Cairo hospital suffering from frostbite, 3rd December, 1915; re-joined battalion for duty, 8th January, 1916; deprived of 10 days pay for not complying with an order in Egypt, 22nd May, 1916; granted Class 2 Proficiency Pay, 27th September, 1916; in a field hospital suffering from scabies, 5th May, 1917; re-joined battalion for duty, 21st May, 1917. On enlistment he was 5 ft 7 in tall, 10st, 2lb, chest 33 in, had a fresh complexion, grey eyes and light hair.

Private Brown wrote a welcome letter home, dated 17th August, 1915, where he explained that after the landing of the battalion on the Gallipoli shores it was marched to the firing line; and in the battle that ensued he stated that Colonel Basil E Philips, Major B Head and other officers were killed, and others had been wounded. He believed that the total casualties of those killed and wounded amongst the Battalion had been rather heavy. He mentioned that the Turkish snipers had been very busy amongst the men of the Battalion, who had since become entrenched. The men had been in the trenches several days, had afterwards been resting, and were returning to relieve others in the trenches at the time of writing.

In October 1915, amongst the letters that were received from the soldiers at the Dardanelles was one from Frank. His friends were glad to hear that he was quite well, it was reported. The men of the Battalion at the time he wrote were practically resting, but were engaged in fatigue duty; which meant they were away from the firing line and given domestic duties around the camp to keep them occupied. The men had had payments made to them.

Private Brown died from wounds received in action in Egypt on 7th November, 1917 and was buried in the Beersheba War Cemetery, Israel (Plot A, Grave 52).

He is remembered on two war memorials: Flint Town and St Mary's Parish Church, Flint. He is also commemorated on the North Wales Heroes' Memorial Arch, Bangor. He was awarded the 1914–15 Star, British War Medal and Victory Medal.

In March 1918 his parents were sent his identity disc from the Infantry Records Office, Shrewsbury, and in June 1919 they received from the following: 1 devotional book, 1 diary, a letter and 4 buttons.

Frank's father, William, was born in Swinton, Lancashire in c.1875 and was employed as a long chain beamer in a cotton mill. His mother, Emma, was born in Patricroft, Lancashire in c.1875 and was also employed in a cotton mill as a coner. They were both still alive in 1919 but it is not known for certain what became of them after that.

PRIVATE
FRANK BROWN

W/496, 13th (Service) Battalion Cheshire Regiment

Francis (Frank) Brown was born in Flint in 1882 and the sixth of nine children to Thomas Brown and Margaret (Bradshaw). Thomas and Margaret were both born in Ireland, with Thomas employed as a chemical yard labourer in Flint. They resided at 4, Commercial Road, Flint.

It was reported in the County Herald that at the Flint Petty Sessions, in March 1889, Thomas Brown of Commercial Road was summoned by Police Constable Ward to recover the sum of 16s, being the amount due in respect of the maintenance of the defendant's boy, now confined to the Birkdale Industrial School. An order was made for payment forthwith or 14 days in gaol. It is not known which son it was referring to. The Birkdale Industrial School was the Birkdale Farm Reformatory School for Roman Catholic Boys at Ainsdale, near Southport.

Frank's mother Margaret died in 1901, aged about 47. His father collapsed and died suddenly on the evening of 22nd November, 1910 of a heart attack whilst out walking on Corporation Street. An inquest took place the following evening at the Town Hall where the Jury returned a verdict of death from 'natural causes.' He was 56.

The 1911 census revealed Frank to be a boarder at 2, Commercial Road, the home of a Mr and Mrs George Foulkes. Later that month, on 17th April, 1911, he married Liverpool born Ellen (Nellie) Whitty at St Anne's Roman Catholic Church, Rock Ferry, Birkenhead.

They lived at 54, Meadow Lane, Rock Ferry, Wirral and Frank was now employed at the nearby Port Sunlight Soap Works. Nellie was also employed there working as a soap packer. Frank was at one time a member of the Loyal Flint Castle Lodge of Oddfellows. They had two children: Thomas Francis (1911–1969) and Dennis (1914–1985).

Frank enlisted at Port Sunlight, Wirral and landed in France on 25th September, 1915.

The Port Sunlight war memorial on which Private Brown is remembered

He died on 8th July, 1916 as a result of a bullet wound to the neck received in action in France on the same day and was buried in the Warloy-Baillon Communal Cemetery and Extension, Somme, France (Plot III, Row C, Grave 16).

He is remembered on two war memorials: St Mary's Catholic Church, Flint and Port Sunlight Village, Wirral, Cheshire.

He was awarded the 1914–15 Star, British War Medal and Victory Medal.

Ellen remarried at Birkenhead in 1919 to Thomas Vincent Murphy and they had three children. Thomas was killed in an accident at Cammell Laird's Shipyard on 11th April, 1929 aged 50. Ellen died in Holywell on 13th November, 1963, aged 80, and was buried with Thomas in Bebington Cemetery.

PRIVATE
PETER BURKE

256, 1/5th (Flintshire) Battalion Royal Welsh Fusiliers

Peter (Jumbo) Burke was born on 11th January, 1902 at 3, Wilmott Terrace, Wilmott Street, Everton, Liverpool, and was the fourth of eight children to Peter Burke and Caroline Mary (Edwards).

Peter senior and wife Caroline were both born in Flint, and at the turn of the century they had moved to Liverpool where Mr Burke was employed as a sugar warehouse porter. By 1904 they had returned to Flint, residing at 8, Rose Cottages, Chapel Street, and Peter was now working as a bricksetter's labourer.

Peter junior, a single man, was employed at Courtaulds Castle Works, Flint, and when the call was made for the Defence Corps, he joined and was stationed at Kinmel Park. On Thursday 23rd June, 1921, along with 170 comrades, he was taking part in a bathing parade at Pensarn, about the time the Royal train conveying their Majesties from Ireland was passing, and he was drowned. On Saturday the body was brought home to his parent's house.

On Sunday night the body was removed to St Mary's Roman Catholic Church, where it lay until interment. A requiem Mass was celebrated by Father McGrath.

On Monday afternoon, at the Northop Road Cemetery, the funeral took place with military honours and by permission of the Lieutenant-Colonel Freer Ash, commanding officer of the regiment, a firing party of 14 men in charge of Sergeant Hough, of Flint, and a number of comrades of the deceased, and the buglers of the regiment, in charge of Drum-Major Homer, attended the funeral. The cortege was preceded by the Flint Town Band, of which both the deceased and his father were members. There were also present a large number of members of the Catholic Young Men's Society, of which the deceased was a member. The funeral service was conducted by Father McGrath, in the presence of a very large gathering. The firing party then fired three volleys over the open grave, and the buglers sounded the Last Post. A large number of beautiful wreaths were sent, including one from Lieutenant-Colonel Freer Ash and officers of the regiment, and a bunch of flowers from his comrades.

Peter is remembered on two war memorials: Flint Town and St Mary's Catholic Church, Flint. He is also commemorated on the North Wales Heroes' Memorial Arch, Bangor.

Peter senior died, aged 81, in November 1956, at his home, 3, Rose Terrace, Chapel Street. He ended his working career at Messrs Courtaulds Castle Works at the age of 75. He was associated with Flint Carnival in which he helped to raise considerable sums of money with his 'mule,' which he made himself and was a feature of the annual procession. He was also a member of the old Flint Town Silver Prize Band in which he played the euphonium. Mr Burke was a member of St Mary's Catholic Church and was one of the founders of the Catholic Parochial Hall.

Mrs Burke was also born in Flint and died just 10 days after her husband. As a young woman she worked in the British Glanzstoff Company at Aber Works. She was a member of the Catholic Church. Mr and Mrs Burke had been married more than 60 years. They were buried with son Peter (Grave 12, Line 43, South Side).

PRIVATE
JOHN CAMPBELL

16238, 10th (Service) Battalion Royal Welsh Fusiliers

John (Jack) Campbell was born in Chester in 1880 and brought up in the Great Boughton area. He was the second of five children to Duncan Alexander Campbell and Jane Gwyneth (Ledsham).

Duncan Alexander and Jane Gwyneth were both born in Chester and after their marriage in 1876 resided in Great Boughton, Chester.

Jack married Emily Williscroft at St Oswald's Parish Church, Bidston, Cheshire on 27th November, 1907. She was born in Colton, Lichfield, Staffordshire, and a daughter of John Williscroft, a gardener, and his wife Hannah, of Park Road West, Birkenhead.

In the 1911 census Jack and Emily were found to be living at 136, Harrowby Road, Tranmere, with Jack employed as a domestic gardener. By 1914 they were living at Mount Cottage, Waen-y-Balls, Flint Mountain, where Jack was still working as a gardener but was soon to start work at the British Glanzstoff Works, Flint.

They had three children – John Duncan (1913–2002), Jean Mary (1914–?) and Elsie Gwyneth (1915–2013).

Jack enlisted in Flint circa. October 1914 and landed at Boulogne, France on 27th September, 1915.

He was killed in action in France, 17th February, 1916, as a result of the enemy heavily bombarding the Battalion trenches for over half an hour, from 5:30 am, leaving 24 dead and seven wounded.

He has no known grave but is commemorated on the Ypres (Menin Gate) Memorial, Ieper, West-Vlaanderen, Belgium, on Panel 22. He is remembered on two war memorials: Flint Town and St Mary's Parish Church, Flint. He is also commemorated on the North Wales Heroes' Memorial Arch, Bangor.

136, Harrowby Road, Tranmere, today

He was awarded the 1914–15 Star, British War Medal and Victory Medal.

Private Campbell's widow received the following sympathetic communication:

> 22, Feb, 1916. B.E.F.
>
> DEAR MRS CAMPBELL – It is with great sorrow and deep sympathy that I write to you, for I am afraid that this letter is the bearer of very bad news for you. It is about your husband, John Campbell, of the 10th Royal Welsh Fusiliers. He was up in the trenches last Thursday, February 17th, when the Germans opened a very heavy shell fire, and I am deeply grieved to say that he was killed instantly with several others of his company. I know what a heavy blow this will be, and that it will take all your courage to bear it bravely; but try to give him up as bravely as he gave himself. He will be sadly missed by all his comrades, for he was a good soldier, and very highly spoken of by his officers. He was always so keen and ready to do his duty, and now he is gone from us. He has made the great sacrifice – the greatest man can make. He has given his life for what is dearer than life itself – the honour of his Fatherland and the safety of his Home. He has indeed followed in the footsteps of His Master, and passed with Him from the storm of war through the valley of the shadow of death to the glorious mansions of the blest beyond. We must not grudge him his well earned rest or his new found joy; he is gone forever, but has made the great journey a little ahead of us. But one day we shall all catch him up again and be re-united never again to be separated. Think of the Great Day, and try to find comfort in the thought of seeing him again under perfect conditions, where sorrow and sighing are unknown and everything radiates with the everlasting love of the Father. May your husband rest in peace and may the God of all mercies comfort you with his own consolation. We all Officers and men alike, offer you our deep and true sympathy in your great bereavement.
>
> In all true sympathy,
> Believe me,
> Yours very sincerely,
> M. P. G. LEONARD, Chaplain
> 10th R. W. Fusiliers

Private Campbell, having been home on several days' leave of absence from the trenches, left Flint on Saturday, 12th February, returning to the Battalion. He had, therefore, only been again in the trenches two or three days when he was killed.

Emily re-married on 4th March, 1919, at St Mary's Parish Church, Flint, to widower John Roberts, a farmer of Waen Farm, Flint Mountain.

Jack's father, of 165, Christleton Road, Boughton, died in Chester, after an illness of 18 months, on 27th December, 1934, and was buried in an unmarked grave in the Overleigh Cemetery, Chester. He was aged 79 and had served on the London, Midland and Scottish (LMS) Railway company for 58 years. He commenced his railway career as a cleaner when only 11 years of age, and he was promoted step by step until he became an express driver. On several occasions Mr Campbell had driven royalty, and tokens of appreciation are proud possessions of the family. One reads: "The King and Queen wish their appreciation of the arrangements made in connection with their Majesties' recent tour over the London and North Western system conveyed to all concerned, and I have pleasure in communicating their Majesties' gracious message to you. – Mr. D. Campbell. June 8th, 1917."

He retired in 1924 as a No. 1 driver at Chester LMS sheds.

Emily Campbell, John's wife

Jack's mother, Jane Gwyneth, died on 11th September, 1938, at the age of 82, at the Royal Infirmary, Chester, as a result of an accident. An inquest was held at the Royal Infirmary the following day. It was revealed that Mrs Campbell lived with her adopted daughter, Miss Angela Ledsham, and on

Duncan Alexander and Jane Campbell with their grandchildren. The tallest boy and the two girls to his left are John and Emily's children John Duncan, Jean Mary and Elsie Gwyneth. In front of Mr Campbell is Lilian, Emily's daughter from her second marriage

2nd September she was sitting in a chair in the kitchen, and Miss Ledsham left her for a moment to go into the next room. She had only been gone a second or two, when she heard Mrs Campbell calling. She went to her, and found her sitting on the floor, having apparently fallen when attempting to get up from her chair. Dr Woodruffe was called and ordered her removal to the Royal Infirmary, where she died nine days later. Miss Ledsham said Mrs Campbell had been able to walk about without assistance but was not very steady. She slept downstairs because of her infirmity. Dr Fallon, house surgeon, said Mrs Campbell was suffering from a fracture of the neck of the left femur. Her heart condition, which was not good on admission, became worse on Saturday, and she died on Sunday from heart trouble. The Deputy Coroner recorded a verdict of accidental death, and expressed sympathy with the relatives. "At this age it is distressing to go out of life through an accident," he said.

165, Christleton Road, Boughton, pictured on the right hand side, as it is today. This was the last home of Mr and Mrs Duncan Alexander Campbell

The funeral took place on 14th September and Mrs Campbell was buried with her husband.

Emily and John had a daughter Lilian who, on the 3rd November, 1936, aged 15, while riding her bicycle down past the Coach and Horses Inn, collided with two pedestrians and died instantly. At the inquest, held the following evening at the Village Hall, Flint Mountain, the Coroner said: "In all probability had there been proper footpaths along this road this bright life would not have been lost. It is a terrible tragedy, and the tragedy is largely due to the neglect of public authorities in not carrying out their duties as they should do."

Lilian's half-sister, Elsie, recalled that she was in the back of the car when they took her from the scene, with Lilian lying on her lap. Lilian was buried in Northop Churchyard.

John Roberts died 11th April, 1952, aged 90, and Emily 14th November, 1963, aged 84.

The resting place of Emily, John and Lilian

Both were buried with their daughter Lilian.

COMPANY SERGEANT MAJOR
GEORGE CARR

19408, 16th (Service) Battalion Royal Welsh Fusiliers

Thomas George Carr was born in Flint and baptised on 17th June, 1877 at St Mary's Parish Church, Flint. He was the third of 11 children of Thomas Carr and Emily (Jones) of 'Seafield,' Chester Road.

George lived in Swan Street throughout his childhood before the family moved to Seafield. His first job was as an office boy before joining the army, seeing active service in the South African Campaign (Boer War 1899–1902), and his name is commemorated on the South African War obelisk in Flint.

Upon returning home he gained employment at the United Alkali Company's Works, Flint, as an engine fitter, and was a member of the Flint Company of the Territorials some years but resigned.

On 7th February, 1904 he married Eliza Gertrude Jones Bishop at St Mary's Parish Church, Flint. They resided at Vryburg, 127, Chester Road and had three children – Gertrude May (b.1904), Thomas Charles Bishop (1906–1973), George (1908–1978) and Vera Mary Emily (1909–2001).

Company Sergeant Major George Carr is buried at St Sever Cemetery Extension, Seine-Maritime, Rouen, France (Plot A, Row 27, Grave 21)

Some time after the commencement of the war, circa January 1915, and when the Pals' Battalions were being recruited and trained at Llandudno, he enlisted in Flint, and his previous experience was of benefit to him. He began his training in Llandudno and then moved to Winchester where the troops were reviewed in early December by the Queen. About the same time he was promoted to Quartermaster Sergeant from Warrant Officer Class 2. It is not known when he was promoted to Company Sergeant Major. He landed in France in December 1915.

In April 1916, George's father, Thomas, who ran a successful business as a market gardener and florist on Chester Road, claimed absolute exemption from the armed services for his married son, Herbert Walter, 26 years of age, and who was in his employ. He stated in his claim that he had two sons at the Front who, when at home, used to assist him a little in the business. The young salesman he had had also enlisted and was away at the Front. He had two large gardens of several acres, and a large quantity of fruit in cultivation under glass, and if there was not anyone regularly watching the plants it would entail considerable loss. Much of the fruit, etc., might be spoilt in half an hour. His son had been in the business since he left school, and thoroughly understood the work, as well as conducting the retail trade in the town. He was granted three months' exemption.

There were statements circulating the town that Company Sergeant Major Carr had been wounded, and that further information was awaited on the evening of Tuesday, 25th July, 1916. On the following morning a postcard was received intimating that he had been wounded but in the evening a telegram conveyed the sad tidings of his death. The message was an exceedingly painful one, and the news created a mild sensation. There then followed the usual document from the Territorials' Records Office, Shrewsbury, with the confirmatory evidence that the Company Sergeant Major had, on the 18th July, died in one of the general hospitals in France of wounds received in action. The wounds were the results of gunshots in the body.

He was buried at St Sever Cemetery Extension, Seine-Maritime, Rouen, France (Plot A, Row 27, Grave 21) and is remembered on three war memorials: Flint Town, St David's Parish Church, Oakenholt and Oddfellows Hall, Flint. He is also commemorated on the North Wales Heroes' Memorial Arch, Bangor.

No. – General Hospital, ----, France

July 18th, 1916.

Dear Mrs Carr,

It is with the deepest regret that I have to write to tell you that your dear husband has passed away. We had hoped he would have recovered. I was with him yesterday and had a nice talk with him. You have my deepest sympathy. I am burying him tomorrow in the St. Sever Cemetery, where so many of our brave heroes are lying.

Yours truly,

T. J. James,
Chaplain (C. of E).

On Friday, 28th July, his widow, Eliza received the following letter:

> 16th R.W.F.
> B.E.F.,
> July 22, 1916.
>
> DEAR MRS CARR,
>
> It was with very great sorrow that I heard yesterday that your husband had died of wounds in hospital. He was wounded when the Battalion went into action; but I was given to understand at the time that his wound was not serious, and I hoped that he would soon have been in England, and would recover in course of time. It was therefore a great shock to me yesterday to hear that he had died. I had a great admiration for Sergeant Major Carr. He had been with the Company the whole time we were in the trenches, and I had grown to depend on him absolutely for getting things done. I regarded him as the best Company Sergeant Major in the Battalion. I remember him joining the Company as a Private when we were at Llandudno, and I was struck then by his steadiness. And when he came back to the Company as its Sergeant Major I soon learned that he carried that steadiness and trustworthiness into everything he did. He was greatly respected by all the men, and so made the working of the Company very easy and smooth. I hope it will be a comfort to you to know in what respect we held him, and what a good man we all thought him to be. Please accept this small tribute to the memory of a good soldier.
>
> Sincerely yours,
>
> H. H. PAINE, Captain.

Mrs Carr received a touching tribute to the memory of her husband and the letter reads as follows:

Mrs Carr received several other letters of condolence from the Front, and elsewhere.

George's brother, William Albert, served in the war for five years and six months with the 9th Battalion Royal Welsh Fusiliers and was seriously wounded on the 20th November, 1916 by a portion of the shell that killed Private Harold Bithell who has been written about elsewhere.

Eliza Gertrude re-married in 1917 to Edward Walker, a butcher, who carried on business at Flint Mountain, and lived at Chester Road, Flint. He committed suicide on 19th September, 1922, by shooting himself in the head at his mother-in-law Mrs Bishop's residence at Wern Cottage, Flint

Mountain. He was 39 years of age. They had three children – Edward (Teddy) (1918–1919), Pearl (1920–2002), and William Arthur (1923–2003).

George's father was born in St Helen's, Lancashire and died 18th January, 1936, aged 81, and was buried in the Northop Road Cemetery, Flint. He was well known and highly esteemed and in his younger days was a very keen sportsman, his favourite pastimes being cycling, shooting and skating. He was an enthusiastic member and secretary of the old Flint Cycling Club in the days of the Penny Farthings and later, when the safety machines became popular. He was one of the first people in the town to ride a bicycle. At the early age of nine, he was employed at the old chemical works of Messrs Muspratt Brothers and Huntley, which stood on the site later occupied by Messrs Courtaulds Castle Works. He became a foreman in the crystal house and retained that position until the works were taken over by the United Alkali Company. At the turn of the century he retired from the chemical industry and commenced a successful business as a market gardener and florist at Seafield, Chester Road. Mr Carr, who enjoyed good health until about three weeks before he died, had an excellent memory and used to delight in recalling events which happened in the town and district many years ago. He would relate an incident told to him by his mother that he was taken to the banks of the River Dee in his mother's arms to see the famous ship Royal Charter passing down the river following her launch at Sandycroft. He was a member of St Mary's Parish Church, and one of the oldest members of the Flint Castle Lodge of Oddfellows.

George's mother was born in Flint and died on 20th November, 1933, aged 78, after an illness of two years, and was buried with her husband.

> **IN MEMORIAM**
>
> *In France he rests in peace,*
> *A soldier true and brave;*
> *And there with honour now he sleeps*
> *In a British soldier's grave.*
> *He gave his life, his all,*
> *That those he loved might live.*
> His Wife and Children.
> (County Herald, 20th July, 1917)
>
> *To memory ever dear.*
> *And with the morn those angel faces smile,*
> *Which I have loved long since, and lost awhile.*
> From Father and Mother, Brothers and Sisters.
> (County Herald, 20th July, 1917)

Eliza Gertrude is buried in the Old London Road Cemetery, Flint with her son Thomas Charles

Eliza Gertrude was born in Wrexham and died on 30th April, 1969, aged 87, at 115, Chester Road, Flint. She is buried in the Old London Road Cemetery, Flint with her son Thomas Charles. In her younger days she was a well-known violinist and pianist, and was a member of the Flint String Orchestra.

PRIVATE
JAMES CARROLL

46599, 17th (Service) Battalion Welsh Regiment (1st Glamorgan)

James Carroll was born on 2nd March, 1896 near the Block, Coleshill Fawr, Flint, and baptised on 8th March, 1896 at St Mary's Catholic Church, Flint. He was the illegitimate son of Dora Carroll née Kennedy and a half-brother to Private John Carroll (see below).

Dora died in 1900 and James was raised by his half-brother John and half-sister Catherine at 19, Redfern Row, Chester Road. Catherine married Edward Bartley in 1906 and lived at 59, Chester Road, and took James with them.

James was first employed as a cutter boy at the Oakenholt Paper Mill before moving to the Hawarden Bridge Ironworks, Shotton. He was unmarried.

He enlisted in Flint circa September 1914, with the Royal Welsh Fusiliers, No. 14928. He landed in France 28th September, 1915. It is not known when he was transferred to the Welsh regiment.

He was killed in action in France, 5th May, 1917, and buried at the Fins New British Cemetery, Sorel-le-Grand, Somme, France (Plot VI, Row G, Grave 7).

He was awarded the 1914–15 Star, British War Medal and Victory Medal and is remembered on two war memorials: Flint Town and St Mary's Catholic Church, Flint. He is also commemorated on the North Wales Heroes' Memorial Arch, Bangor.

PRIVATE
JOHN CARROLL

292997, 15th (Service) Battalion Cheshire Regiment (1st Birkenhead)

John Carroll was born in Flint on 3rd March, 1883 and was the third of five children to John Carroll and Dora (Kennedy). He was a half-brother to Private James Carroll (see above).

John senior was born in Ireland and died in early 1894 aged 58. He was a general labourer but in the 1891 census he was described as a disabled army pensioner suffering from tuberculosis.

Dora was also born in Ireland and in the early 1870s she had a relationship with a Mr Porteus, by whom she had a daughter named Alicia, who was born in Aldershot, Hampshire in 1874. However, no record of a marriage could be found.

John junior was raised at 23, Mount Street, Flint, but after his mother died in 1900, aged just 47, he went to live with his sister Catherine and half-brother James at 19, Redfern Row, Chester Road, Flint. His occupation was a collier.

John married Mary Catherine Bartley at the Register Office, Chester on 22nd December, 1906, and resided at 35, Chapel Street, Flint, with John was now employed as an ironworker. They were to have five children: John Bartley (February 1907–March 1907), William John (1909–1937), Thomas (1911–1978), Dora (1913–1991) and Edward James (1916–1989). By the time the war started they had moved to 69, Mumforth Street, Flint.

John enlisted in Flint in 1914 with the 1/5th Royal Welsh Fusiliers, No. 86. He landed at Gallipoli on 8th August, 1915. It was after this date he transferred to the Cheshire Regiment and moved to France.

He was killed in action in France, 24th March, 1918, and buried at the Grand-Seraucourt British Cemetery, Aisne, France (Plot VII, Row E, Grave 8).

He was awarded the 1914–15 Star, British War Medal and Victory Medal, and is remembered on two war memorials: Flint Town and St Mary's Catholic Church, Flint. He is also commemorated on the North Wales Heroes' Memorial Arch, Bangor.

John's wife, Mary Catherine, was born in Flint and died in September 1957, aged 73. She was buried in the Northop Road Cemetery, Flint, with her son William John and his wife Sophia Mary.

Private Carroll's headstone with "BELIEVED TO BE" engraved at the top

The resting place of Mary Catherine Carroll

PRIVATE
ROBERT CARTWRIGHT

63459, 141st Infantry Battalion Machine Gun Corps

Robert Henry Cartwright was born in Flint in 1893 and was the youngest of five children to Henry Cartwright and Emma (Beck).

Robert grew up in 51, Swan Street, Flint before the family settled at No. 87. He was a bricklayer's labourer, employed by a local firm of building contractors and was unmarried.

He enlisted in Flint in 1915 with the Royal Welsh Fusiliers, No. 3699, before transferring to the Machine Gun Corps.

He was killed in action in Belgium on 29th May, 1917, and buried at Bedford House Cemetery, Ieper West-Vlaanderen, Belgium (Enclosure No. 4, Special Memorials, Grave 38).

He is remembered on two war memorials: Flint Town and St Mary's Parish Church, Flint. He is also remembered on his parents' headstone at the Northop Road Cemetery, Flint (Grave 5, Line 8, West Side). He is also commemorated on the North Wales Heroes' Memorial Arch, Bangor.

He was awarded the British War Medal and Victory Medal.

Robert's father died at his home, 87, Swan Street, on 28th May, 1931, aged 82. He was a native of Little Ness, Neston, came to Flint in about 1879, and was employed as a horseman at Cornist Hall, later with Mr Read at Northop Hall, and for 28 years with Mr Matthew Rogers (builder), Flint. He was also employed by the United Alkali Company for a time. He was a member of the Church of England, and was highly respected.

His mother was born in Flint and died at her home, after a long illness, on 13th July, 1936, aged 77. She is buried with her husband. She was a member of St Mary's Parish Church and was well known and esteemed.

Private Robert Cartwright is remembered on his parents' headstone at the Northop Road Cemetery, Flint (Grave 5, Line 8, West Side)

IN MEMORIAM

We have lost you, we who loved you,
But like others must be brave,
For we know you are lying
In a British soldiers' grave.

If we could have raised his dying head,
Or heard his last farewell,
The grief would not have been so hard,
To those who loved him well.
Deeply mourned by Father, Mother and Sisters.
(County Herald, 17th May, 1918)
In loving memory of Robert Cartwright and
William Hughes, his chum.

ঞ

Their duty called them, they were there,
To do their bit and take their share;
Their hearts were good, their spirits brave,
They are resting in a hero's grave.

If those who caused this awful war
Were the only ones to fight,
A brighter world this would have been,
For all our aching hearts to-night.
Their memory will always remain
in the hearts of their mates.
Sergt W G Davies, 13, Feathers Street, Flint.
(County Herald, 16th August, 1918)

ঞ

Never a day but his name is spoken,
Never an hour but he is in our thoughts,
A link in our family chain is broken,
Gone from our home, but not from our hearts.

This day brings back to memory
A loved one gone to rest,
And those who think of him to-day
Are those who loved him best.
Sadly missed by Father and Mother.
(County Herald, 30th May, 1919)

ঞ

Sleep on, dear brother in a foreign grave,
A grave we may never see,
But as long as life and memory last
We will remember thee.
From his sisters
Emma and Maria and Lizzie.
(County Herald, 30th May, 1919)

ঞ

Days of sadness still come o'er us,
Hidden tears do often flow,
But memory keeps our dear one near us,
Although he died three years ago.
Never will be forgotten by his
Father, Mother,
and Sisters,
Lizzie, Emma, and Maria.
(County Herald, 28th May, 1920)

ঞ

Mourn not for him whom God hath blest,
And taken to His heavenly rest;
Freed from all sorrow, grief and pain,
Our loss is his eternal gain.
Gone, but not forgotten
by his loving
Father and Mother
and Sisters
Emma, Maria and Cissie.
(County Herald, 27th May, 1921)

ঞ

His memory is as fresh today
As in the hour he passed away.
What would we not give to grasp his hand,
His dear kind face to see,
To hear his voice and see his smile,
That meant so much to me.
Sadly missed by
his loving
Father and Mother and Sisters.
(County Herald, 25th May, 1923

ঞ

COMPANY SERGEANT MAJOR
JOHN CLARK

**15522, 10th (Service) Battalion
Royal Welsh Fusiliers**

John (Jack) Clark was born on 2nd June, 1876 at Platt Bridge, Wigan, Lancashire. He was the only son of John Clark and Jane (Jones).

It is not known where John senior was born but Jane was born on 16th April, 1856 in Tunstall, Staffordshire.

They married 16th May, 1875 at St Mary's Parish Church, Flint. John was the son of John Clark, miner, and Jane the daughter of William Jones, miner.

John senior was accidentally killed on 17th May, 1876, aged 23, whilst working at the Bamfurlong Colliery, Ashton-in-Makerfield, Lancashire, belonging to Messrs Cross, Tetley, and Co., Limited, by a roof falling upon him. An inquest was held at Abram, Lancashire and a verdict of accidental death was returned. He was buried in the All Saints Churchyard, Hindley, Lancashire.

Mrs Clark re-married at St Mary's Parish Church, Flint on 20th October, 1878, to bachelor John Hughes, of Chapel Street, Flint, who was employed by the United Alkali Company's works, Flint.

By 1896 Mr and Mrs Hughes had had eight children together and were living at 8 and 10 Chapel Street. Jack was now employed as a chemical labourer in the town, and Mrs Hughes was a grocer and shopkeeper in Chapel Street.

Sometime in the 1890s Jack joined the army and served with the Royal Welsh Fusiliers in China during the Boxer Rising of 1900. He was awarded the China Medal.

On the 10th October, 1903, at the Wesleyan Chapel, Barton, Lancashire, Jack married Jane Chapman of Patricroft, Lancashire, and was now employed as a tool grinder with an engineering company.

In 1905 they had a daughter named Bessie, then in 1906

CSM John Clark, out of uniform and with his wife Jennie and children Bessie and Edith

Edith was born but sadly, in 1911, Bessie died. They were now living at 36, Reginald Street, Patricroft, Lancashire, but were soon to move to Flint, where they lived at 12, Chapel Street, and Jack was working as a commission agent.

Jack re-enlisted with the 10th Battalion Royal Welsh Fusiliers (RWF) on 14th September, 1914, at Ferndale, Glamorganshire. He was one of the 'pensioned soldiers' who proceeded to Wrexham for the purpose of training recruits. He remained at the Wrexham Depot some time, and when the Battalion with which he was concerned left for France on the 27th September, 1915 he journeyed with it. His service record stated that on enlistment he was 5 ft 5½ ins tall, fresh complexion, blue eyes and fair hair.

On 24th September, 1915 he drew up a will in the presence of Corporal Mitchell, of St Domingo Vale, Liverpool, and Sergeant George Bowen, of Rhos-Robin, Wrexham, both of the 10th RWF, and sent the documents with the following moving letter to his half-brother Mr William Henry Hughes, of 34, Hardy Street, Peel Green, Patricroft, Manchester:

> Barrona Bks
> Aldershot
>
> 26/9/15
>
> Dear Will
>
> I am writing hoping these lines will find you in the enjoyment of perfect health as they leave me at present.
>
> Well old fellow the day has come & tomorrow (Monday) at 4.30 pm we leave here for France. If you care to follow our movements in the papers you can do so by the number of the division & the Brigade. Our Divisional number is 25 & we are the 76th brigade so by watching those numbers you will know when we have been in action. Now I have made out my will & I have made you executor of it & should anything happen to me I want you to see that Jennie gets everything. I want you to keep the will yourself. I shall have to get it signed by the doctor before I send it. I am very busy as you will understand so you will please excuse this short letter. Good bye old chap it may be we may never meet again. These are strenuous times, these are times of sacrifice, the weeding of the gold from the dross. If this bit of dross goes under, the world I dare say will be all the better for it, but before that happens I shall have done my little bit for the salvation of the country I love. Gallant little Wales, keep your eye on the old home see to it that the grand old people, (whom we have the honour to call Father & Mother never want for anything & if I die tell them from me that to me there is no man I know nobler & grander than my Father & no woman so loving so tender & self sacrificing as my mother & I loved them dearly always. God bless you all, my brothers, my sister, & may your lives be pure, full of love & full of real true life

follow after righteousness, shun evil, & your reward will be true happiness here & now. I would like to say a lot but have not the time. Give a helping hand to dear old Jennie & little Edith her burden is a very heavy one be kind & gentle with her & do all you can to turn her mind from me. What a fine pal she's been to me. What a gem for a man to possess. How I have missed her love & tenderness. See to it Will lad that her & her child never want for anything. & now I will close knowing that the sacred burden I have laid upon you will be faithfully borne & I shall go overseas knowing that whatever happens you my brother will do your duty by my loved ones. God be with you always is the prayer of your loving

Bro John

Four months later he wrote a very touching letter to his daughter Edith:

Dedicated to my darling daughter Edith

Jan 25) 16

My darling Edith I am writing just a line to let you know I received your pretty post card, and appreciate it so and the lovely lines upon it, brought the tears to Daddys eyes as I pictured you my darling, with the lovelight in your eyes with my photo standing near you were trying to let me know how you wish me safely home again because you love me so. And how each day you miss me, and how each night you pray God bless my Daddy at the war and bring him home someday. Your Dad will keep that post card darling always very near his heart and not for all the riches in the world with it would part. So I want you to be brave and good, always kind and true and help your mother all you can and nothing will you rue for her heart is often sad dear lass, for she misses daddy too. So for Daddys sake just do for mum, the best in you to do. Be obedient, helpful, cheerful, then God will hear you pray and bless your Daddy at the war, and bring him home someday. I know you don't quite understand, just why I came away but someday you will know it was, to break a tyrants sway just for a scrap of paper for we had given our word and Britains word is sacred and trusted o'er the world. So Daddy wouldn't stay at home to fight I had to go to save old England's honour, as Britons ought to do. The task is heavy darling but grows lighter when you pray God bless my Daddy at the war and bring him home someday. But I want you to remember, that your Daddy went to war not because he was ambitious, or loved the cannon's roar, for he loathes the cruel monster, which has caused such grief and woe. But honour called and duty so your Daddy had to go to fight for home and beauty, dear old England great and free. And for you my little darling and your mother so you see

> I couldn't help it could I. So just tell God when you pray to bless your Daddy at the war and bring him home someday. And now my darling Edith this letter I must close with fondest love and heaps of kisses for my little rose. And every night ere I lay down I will to God commend my little lass and mother and the cause which I defend so we'll live in hope my darling that the day will not be long when victory crown's our efforts and we sing the victors' song and Dad comes marching home again no more from you to stray. Our reunion blessed and hallowed, by our little darling's prayer.

In early March 1916 Mrs Clark received a letter from her husband which passed through the Field Post Office in France on 29th February, and stated that he was in the best of health and spirits. He was hoping to obtain leave of absence in the course of a short time in order to visit his family and relatives in Flint. He wrote:

> The famous choir of the 10th Battalion gave another concert on Saturday night, but these concerts make one sad because every time there is someone missing. Dear young Corporal Jack Roberts was missing this time. He has gone to his eternal home. He was hit by a piece of shrapnel and died in my arms. Ben Davies, of Flint Mountain, was also killed. I was hit, but it only tore the sleeve of my coat. God has indeed been good to me, and I am thankful.

Continuing, he exhorts his wife and relatives not to worry about him, for he believed he was performing the greatest work of his life. It was hard, it was cruel, but it was necessary, for life would be intolerable for the world if Germany won. The Germans must be beaten at all costs, and would be beaten; but the price must be paid. But, he prayed to God the end was not far off, for the sacrifice of young life was terrible.

A greeting card Jack sent home from the Front

As a throb of affectionate remembrance of Corporal Roberts* he attached to his letter the following verses which he composed:

---

*Corporal John Edward Roberts, of the 10th Battalion Royal Welsh Fusiliers, was killed in action in Flanders on 17th February, 1916. aged 23. He was the son of John and Susannah Roberts, of 3, The Grove, Holywell. He is remembered on the Ypres (Menin Gate) Memorial, Belgium

> He fell and died,
> Jacky, with his cheery and winsome smile,
> In my arms he died.
> Yes, he's dead, died doing his duty
> For King and Home and beauty,
> For Justice, Hope and Liberty,
> Jacky died.
> Yet, Jacky lives,
> In the eternal arms of Jesus, resting awhile,
> Jacky lives,
> And we'll meet again in the morning,
> When we hear reveille sounding,
> His martyr's crown he's wearing,
> Jacky lives.

Company Sergeant Major Clark received recognition for distinguished service in the field on the 2nd and 3rd March, 1916, and when he was on short leave of absence to his home he placed into the procession of his step-father and mother a letter written by the Major of the Battalion, which was as follows:

To CSM John Clark

It had been my intention to present this Card to you on Battalion parade. I appreciate your feeling in the matter, and I wish to congratulate you most heartily on your Distinguished Conduct on the Field and to congratulate you on its recognition by the "Divisional General."

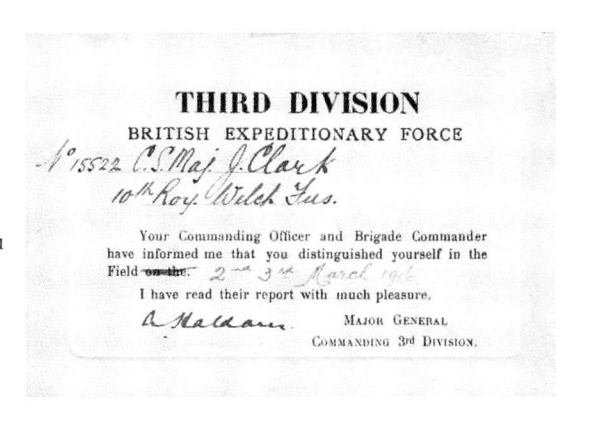

THIRD DIVISION
BRITISH EXPEDITIONARY FORCE

N° 15522 C.S. Maj. J. Clark
10th Roy. Welsh Fus.

Your Commanding Officer and Brigade Commander have informed me that you distinguished yourself in the Field on the 2nd–3rd March 1916.
I have read their report with much pleasure.

A. Haldane.
Major General
Commanding 3rd Division.

Company Sergeant Major John Clark was killed in action in France on 16th August, 1916. He has no known grave but is commemorated on the Thiepval Memorial, Somme, France (Pier and Face 4A). He is also remembered on the Flint Town memorial and on a stone pot on his wife's grave at Peel Green Cemetery, Eccles, Manchester (Plot 6562, Section C2).

He was awarded the 1914–15 Star, British War Medal and Victory Medal.

When news reached Flint that he had been killed the following letters were received by his mother:

Wesleyan Methodist Church,
Central Buildings,
Westminster,
London, S.W.

7th October 1916.

Dear Mrs. Hughes,

I have just heard, from the Rev. A. Shipman, of the great loss you have sustained in the death of your son, Coy. Sergt.-Major John Clark. I deeply sympathise with you. May the Comforts of the Loving Spirit of God abound to your heart.

Yours is indeed a heavy loss, and I am afraid that your heart will be well-nigh broken, but it is when the heart is breaking, and our need of Christ is greatest, that He Himself come near to us blessing. He Who bore our sins also carries our sorrows, and I am sure that His Presence and Voice will bring comfort to you.

I am trying to secure some particulars from the Front as to the manner in which your son was killed.

In deepest sympathy,

Yours sincerely,
J. H. Bateson (Rev.)

Secretary, Wesleyan Army and Navy Board.

27th October 1916

Dear Mr. Shipman,

You wrote to me some little time ago concerning Co. Sergt. Major John Clark of the R.W.F.

I have now heard from the chaplain concerning him. He writes as follows:-

"His company made an attack on the way to Guillemont on 17th August. Shortly after going over the parapet Sergt. Major Clark was wounded in the leg. His Captain (Capt. Hale) told him to return. But he preferred to go on towards the German trench. Before he got there he was hit by a bullet in the head and died. He was buried later by our Pioneers. This would be where he had fallen and so, I fear, this makes it somewhat difficult for his dear ones to get a photograph of the grave in the usual way . . . . I was very fond of Sergt. Major Clark and so were all that knew him. He showed much sympathy with me in an effort to arrange a service, and was present whenever his duties would allow him. I have every confidence that sudden death meant sudden glory to him."

Will you kindly pass on the information to his mother?

Please express to her my deep sympathy with her in her sorrow; but how proud she must feel of such a son.

With kindest regards,
Yours sincerely,
J. H. Bateson.

Grosvenor Manse,
Mold,
28th October, 1916.

Dear Mrs. Hughes,

The enclosed letter, which you may keep for your own, reached me this afternoon. With Mr. Bateson, I am very sorry that the report of your son Sergt. Major John Clark's death is confirmed; but it is some relief to be no longer in doubtful suspense. You now rank with many thousands of mothers who have lost their sons in defence of their country and for the sake of GOD's righteousness. If they had not fought for us, our dear land would have been overrun by a barbarously cruel enemy, our women would have been outraged, our children and old folk tortured and massacred. From all these horrors, by the grace of GOD, we have been delivered through their bravery and courageous endurance. The cost is tremendously sorrowful; yet it was worth while. We who benefit by their sacrifice cannot be too grateful, not only to the men who fight and fall, but also to the wives &

mothers who gave them up on our behalf.

Just now your heart will be too sore to think quietly or reason calmly, but in time to come you will acknowledge that it was better for them to have gone and not return, than never to have gone at all. The world has never known anything equal to this Great War; may GOD grant that the like of it may never be known again!

Any persons who have declined to take any part in the conflict, whether by serving in the Army & Navy or by letting their dear ones serve, will live to be ashamed of themselves and to be objects of public reprobation. You are not among these; you gave your son for GOD, King, & country; for righteousness, truth, & mercy. Be thankful to have had such a son and to have made such a sacrifice.

Be sure also that the precious life, though cut short, has not been wasted. All who lay down their lives in the faith of Jesus Christ, for love of GOD and neighbour, will continue their lives in a better world, where sin & sorrow, suffering & death, have no place. Let us, by patiently running the appointed race and by looking into Jesus, win that world for ourselves. The card enclosed exactly expresses my conviction in this matter. Be comforted, & live as Jack would have you live.

I write as a father who has lost his eldest and his youngest son, each aged 25, one of whom was killed by accident on the railway. I know & I sympathize.

Will you kindly allow Mrs. Clark to read this?

I am,
Yours sincerely,
Arthur Shipman.

John's mother Jane died on 12th June, 1920 aged 64, and her husband on 22nd May, 1941, aged 90.

Company Sergeant Major Clark's widow, Jane, did not marry again and died on 13th December, 1956 at 31, Sydney Street, Flint. She was buried in Peel Green Cemetery, Eccles, Manchester, with daughter Bessie (pictured right and inset).

PRIVATE
THOMAS PIERCE CLARK

41517, 5th Battalion South Wales Borderers

Thomas (Tom) Pierce Clark was born in Flint in March or April of 1899 and was the youngest of three children to James Clark and Elizabeth (Pierce) of 15, Halkyn Street, Flint.

Tom was educated at Holywell County School, never married and his occupation is unknown.

He enlisted at Wrexham in January 1917 and had previously served with the Territorial Reserve Battalion, No. 40483.

He was killed in action in Belgium on 16th April, 1918.

Early in May 1918 much anxiety was experienced concerning the absence of information as to the whereabouts of Private Clark. He was home on leave about Easter, and left shortly afterwards for the Front. A letter written on 19th April by a personal friend was received by Mr and Mrs Clark enquiring whether they had any official information as to their son, as the last he saw of him was lying on the ground, having been wounded. The writer stated that he was unable to render his comrade any assistance, but informed the stretcher-bearers of the locality where Clark was left. He had since made several enquiries but had failed to ascertain anything as to his whereabouts. Mr Clark paid a visit to the Records' Office at Shrewsbury but nothing could be gained; and since then a communication had been forwarded to the Commanding Officer of the Battalion, and consequently a reply was being awaited. Nearly one month had then elapsed since Private Clark had written home; and the hope was expressed that he had been removed for medical treatment, probably as a prisoner of war in the hands of the Germans. Information was subsequently received from a comrade that he had died after only two days in the line. In his last letter home, dated 31st March, 1918, he wrote:

> Do not worry, mother dear, remember I go out for a good cause, and you can rest assured your son will not fail in his duty to his King and Country and the dear folk at home. I have put all my trust in God, and I feel quite safe. Au revoir.

He has no known grave but is commemorated on the Tyne Cot, Zonnebeke, West-Vlaanderen, Belgium, on Panels 65 to 66.

He is remembered on three war memorials: Flint Town, St. Mary's Parish Church, Flint and Holywell County School (now in Holywell High School). He is also remembered on his parents' headstone in the Northop Road Cemetery, Flint (Grave 9, Line 6, West Side). He is also commemorated on the North Wales Heroes' Memorial Arch, Bangor.

He was awarded the British War Medal and Victory Medal.

Tom's father died 28th April 1929, aged 63, at his home, Mohrcroft, Halkyn Road, Flint, after a long illness, and was buried in the Northop Road Cemetery, Flint. He was born at Gateshead-on-Tyne, but had lived at Flint practically all his life and was well known and highly respected. He had been employed by the United Alkali Company for 44 years as bookkeeper but in his later years was in the service of the Chester, Wrexham and District Savings Bank at their Flint Branch in Holywell Road. He was a faithful member of the English Wesleyan Church, Holywell Road, of which he was a trustee. He was also a member of the Tower of Refuge Tent of the IOR, and was one of the pioneer workers in connection with the Juvenile Tent at Flint. He acted as their auditor and at one time held the office of Chief Ruler of the Chester District. For a short period he was a member of the Flint Town Council, being elected unopposed at a by-election, but when his term of office expired he did not seek re-election.

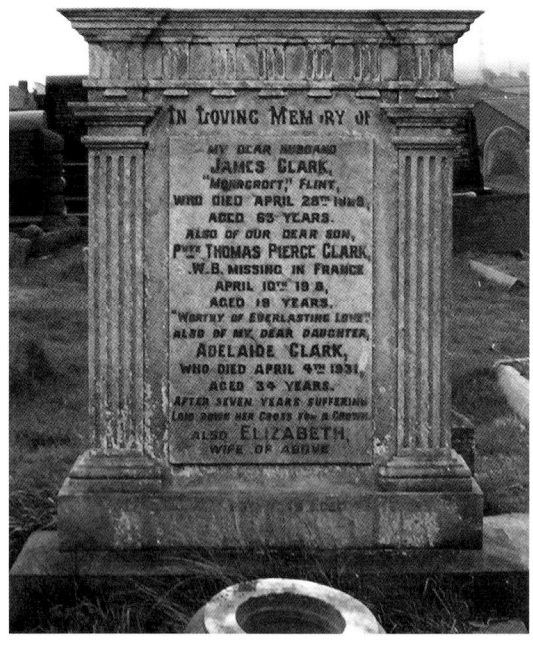

Private Thomas Pierce Clark is remembered on his parents' headstone in the Northop Road Cemetery, Flint (Grave 9, Line 6, West Side).

His mother was born in Flint and died on 29th November, 1956, aged 88. She was buried with her husband and their daughter, Adelaide.

IN MEMORIAM

In sad but loving Birthday remembrance of our dear boy.
I sigh all times to see thy face,
But since this cannot be,
I'll leave thee to the care of Him
Who cares for thee and me;
"I'll keep you both beneath my wings,"
This comforts, dear,
One wing's o'er thee, and one o'er me,
So are we near,

He holds thy hand, he claspeth mine,
And keeps us near.

'Tis a weary wait, but have never given up hope.
His grieved Parents, Brother and Sister.
15, Halkyn Street, Flint.
(County Herald, 4th April, 1919)

❧

Rest well dear son, for at the great awakening,
When Christ shall call His soldiers to His side,
His promise stands, there shall be no forsaking,
Of those who fought for Him, and fighting died.
Sadly missed by all at home.
15, Halkyn Street, Flint.
(County Herald, 19th December, 1919)

❧

In sad but ever loving 21st birthday remembrance of our dear nephew.
Gone to rest through pathway of duty,
Venturing his life that others may live,
One of the best that God ever lent,
A beautiful life so nobly spent.

His voice still sounds in memory's ear,
Like distant music once so clear,
In fond remembrance yet he smiles,
Though from our sight he is lost awhile.

He loved not war, but at his country's call
He made the great surrender, leaving all;
Friends, plans, ambitions, all the hope of years,
He laid upon the altar – with our tears.
Sadly missed by his loving Uncle and Aunt, Leslie and Margery.
Bodoryn Road, Abergele.
(County Herald, 2nd April, 1920)

❧

In very sad but ever loving 21st birthday remembrance of our dear son.
He willingly gave his life that others may live,
Lying wounded, my boy, how your thoughts must have flown,
To your father and mother, and the loved ones at home,
What would I give to have only been there,
To soothe your last moments with mother's care.

Days of darkness still come o'er me,
Sorrow's path I often tread,
But the Saviour still is with me,
By His hand I am safely led;
He will keep me till the river
Rolls the waters at my feet,
Then He'll bear me safely over
Where my dear boy I shall meet.

Two years have passed, how long it seems,
In all our thoughts his face still beams,
And so we sadly yearn
For the old time step and the dear old smile,
We cannot say, and do not say
That he is dead, he's just away.
Mother's lifelong sorrow.
Sadly missed by Father, Mother, Brother, Sister, Mamie and Annie.
15, Halkyn Street, Flint.
(County Herald, 9th April, 1920)

❧

In very sad but ever loving 22nd Birthday remembrance of our dear son.
What would I give his hand to clasp,
His dear sweet face to see,
His loving smile and cheery words,
Which meant so much to me.
We doubt not that for one so true
God will have other nobler work to do.
Surely for him, whose earth's last fight is fought,
God did not give that martial soul to end at last at naught ,
That steadfast soldier's heart was not for this brief life alone,
'Tis as a soldier he will stand before the Great White Throne.
Mother's lifelong sorrow.
So sadly missed by Father, Mother, Brother, Sister, Grandmother and Aunt.
15, Halkyn Street, Flint.
(County Herald, 1st April, 1921)

❧

In very sad but ever loving 22nd Birthday remembrance of our dear nephew.
He loved not war, but at his country's call
He made the great surrender, leaving all;
Friends, plans, ambitions, all the hope of years,
He laid upon the altar – with our tears.

Sadly missed by Uncle, Aunt, Leslie and Madge.
Bodoryn Bach, Abergele.
(County Herald, 1st April, 1921)

In sad but ever lasting remembrance of my loved ones.
My dear Addie; my dear son; also my dear husband, James Clark (our dad).
Oft are the days of sadness,
When my eyes are dim with tears,
I can hear their sweet voices calling
Hush Mum, we'll meet again on the Golden Shore.
Your lonely and sorrowing mother, Caroola, Prestatyn, and Frank (Widnes).
(County Herald, 3rd April, 1936)

PRIVATE
JOSEPH CLEWS

882, 1/5th (Flintshire) Battalion Royal Welsh Fusiliers

Joseph Clews was born 7th August, 1882, at Chester Street, Flint and baptised on 17th December, 1882 at St Mary's Parish Church, Flint. He was the third of six children to George Clews and Rosa (Seal).

As a boy Joseph and his family were living at 7, Chester Street before moving next door to No. 5.

George was born in Kidsgrove, Staffordshire and was a master barber by trade with a business in Earl Street. He died 7th June, 1895, aged 41, at his home in Chester Street and was buried in the Northop Road Cemetery.

Rosa was born in Audley, Staffordshire and died 14th May, 1909, aged 49, and was buried with her husband. The funeral was of a public character and it took place at the Welsh Church where the first portion of the burial service was read by the Reverend W Llewelhyn Nicholas (Rector), and the Reverend R Owens read the committal service at the graveside. She was highly esteemed and there was a large attendance of sorrowing relatives at the cemetery, and many beautiful floral tributes were placed upon the coffin.

The 1911 census revealed Joseph was still residing at 5, Chester Street with his sister Stephanie and her husband Herbert Bellis, and his occupation was a galvanised sheet worker at the Hawarden Bridge Ironworks, Shotton. He never married.

He enlisted in Flint and for some years previous to the war he was in the Royal Anglesey Engineers (Militia), and subsequently in the Volunteers and Territorials.

He was killed in action on 10th August, 1915 at Suvla Bay, Gallipoli and buried in the Green Hill Cemetery, Turkey (Plot II, Row B, Grave 8).

He is remembered on two war memorials: Flint Town and St Mary's Parish Church, Flint. He is also remembered on his parents' headstone at Northop Road Cemetery (Grave 9, Line 21, North Side). He is also commemorated on the North Wales Heroes' Memorial Arch, Bangor.

He was awarded the 1914–15 Star, British War Medal and Victory Medal.

A letter was received in Flint on the morning of Wednesday, 1st September, 1915 through the message of Quarter Master Leo Schwartz, of Holywell, conveying the sad intelligence that Private Clews had been killed in action. Clews was well known in the Borough, and was a very popular comrade with his fellow men in the Battalion.

Private Albert Frimstone, of the 1/5th Battalion, wrote to Mrs Frimstone, of 27, Mumforth Street, Flint, under date of 16th August, stating that Thomas, Robert, John and himself had: "… a devil of a do the other day. Poor Private Tom Hewitt, of Trelawny Square, and Private Joseph Clews, were shot dead. There were several of the men of the Battalion slightly wounded. The boys of the Flint Company were in the pink."

He concluded: "Cheer up, all at Flint; we will do our duty; the Turks are a bad lot."

Private Joseph Clews' parents' headstone at Northop Road Cemetery (Grave 9, Line 21, North Side)

CIVILIAN
SAMUEL JOHN COCKS

Samuel (Sam) John Cocks was born in 1870 in Wandsworth, Surrey, and was the third of nine children to Samuel Cocks and Ellen (Grace).

In Sam's early years the family were living at 2, Ann's Cottages, Wandsworth and Mr Cox was employed as a beater at a paper mill. Then, by 1881, they had migrated to Oakenholt to live at

Crystal Terrace. Mr Cox was employed by the North Wales Paper Mill in Oakenholt doing the same job he did before. Sam was still a boy and attended the Flint Church of England School. They were to move again to 4, Marine Terrace, Oakenholt before eventually settling at 100, Marine Terrace.

Sam's first occupation was as a railway goods clerk, and on 5th August, 1896 at the Holy Trinity Church, Chester, he married 26-year-old Alice Jones. Their address was given as Watergate Street, and Sam was an office clerk with the London and North Western Railway Company, Chester. Their first child, a daughter named Edith Marjory, was born in Chester in 1899.

Samuel (Sam) John Cocks

That same year, on 27th August, Sam's Putney-born mother died of heart failure at the residence of her daughter, 494, Glossop Road, Sheffield, aged just 51.

When Ronald, their second child, was born, c.1902, they were living in Dublin, Ireland where their next two children, daughters Lily and Maud, were also born. The Irish census of 1911 found them living at 8, Faughart Terrace, Dundalk; Sam had gone up in the world and had become General Manager of the Dundalk and Newry Steam Packet Company, Dundalk.

Life must have seemed rosy for Sam but tragedy was just around the corner, as his wife Alice died. The exact date of her death is not known but on the 28th December, 1915, at the Register Office, Liverpool, Sam married 46-year-old widow Jane (Jennie) Davies of 9, Groes Road, Cressington, Liverpool. She was the daughter of the late William Williams, a hotel proprietor.

Sam's younger brother, William Gladstone Cocks, who was on the clerical staff at the head office of the London and North Western Railway Company, Dublin, commenced his railway career at Flint, and various local stations on the North Wales Coast, in about 1899. He was transferred to North Wall, Dublin in 1905 and died at his residence in Dublin on 6th October, 1918 of acute pneumonia aged 33.

The funeral took place at the Welsh Church, Flint on Wednesday afternoon, 9th October, the remains having been brought over from Dublin the previous day. A memorial service was held the following Sunday morning at the Presbyterian Church. The Pastor (Reverend D James, MA) took as his text Psalm 49, verse 15, and in his discourse referred to the life of the deceased as full of cheer and brightness wherever he went, and his kindness of disposition, with his generous heart, made him beloved by all. There was a large congregation, who listened with rapt attention to the able discourse. At the close, the Dead March in Saul was rendered on the organ by Mrs Robert Jones, of Park Avenue.

Both Sam and Jennie attended the funeral and on Saturday, 12th October Sam set out without Jennie to return to Ireland, and left Liverpool on the SS Dundalk on the evening of Monday, 14th October. She was a victim of German U-boats (UB) and sunk five miles north-north-west of the Skerries, off

Anglesey, by UB123 and UB90. Nineteen of her crew, including the captain, who left a widow and five children, were killed on the way across. The Daily Telegraph gave the following account of the tragic occurrence: "Five members of the crew of the steamer Dundalk, of Dundalk, all Irishmen, were landed at Douglas (Isle of Man) last Tuesday evening, having been picked up in a half-clothed condition from a boat in which they had spent sixteen hours in a heavy sea. They stated that their vessel was torpedoed at twenty past eleven on the previous night without warning, and sank in four minutes. The ship's company numbered thirty two. There were two raft boats on deck, which floated off when the vessel foundered, but most of the crew were left struggling in the water. A collier steamer appeared on the scene, but the men are uncertain whether she rescued any of their comrades. The submarine, which was described as a large and powerful one, came to the surface while the men were struggling in the water, and, without offering assistance, headed south and west out of sight. The five men in the boat had to be continually baling out water to keep her afloat. They were starved with hunger, suffered greatly from exposure, and were exhausted when rescued. They were provided with food and clothing, and a collection was made for them on board the rescuing vessel. Another message states that twelve of the crew have been saved, and eighteen are missing. The missing include the general manager of the company (Mr S J Cocks), Captain O'Neill (master of the Dundalk), and the chief engineer."

The Irish Telegraph, Belfast, stated: "The affair has created a general wave of indignation. One public official remarked to a representative that it was up to the young men of the town to have revenge for this cruel outrage, and he observed that this did away with the myth of Germany's love for Ireland. Five members of the crew have arrived in Dundalk, showing signs of hardships they have undergone."

Sam's body was not recovered but he is commemorated on a memorial plaque in St Patrick's Church, Dundalk (above), and is remembered on his brother William and sister Fanny's headstone in the Northop Road Cemetery, Flint (Grave 8, Line 36, South Side).

Sam's father was born in Wandsworth, Surry and died on 16th October, 1928, aged 83, and buried with his wife in the Northop Road Cemetery. He had been a member of the Presbyterian Church, Chester Road, for 45 years and a memorial service was held there on the Sunday following his death and was conducted by the Pastor, the Reverend J Martin Davies. He referred to the great loss which the church had sustained, to the deceased's great faithfulness and the keen interest which he took in the work of the management committee of the church, of which he was a life member. References to Mr Cock's death were also made at the Sunday School, in which he had been deeply interested.

Sam is remembered on his brother William and sister Fanny's headstone in the Northop Road Cemetery, Flint (Grave 8, Line 36, South Side).

> PRAY FOR THE SOULS OF THE FOLLOWING
> WHO WERE LOST ON THE S.S. DUNDALK
> TORPEDOED DURING THE GREAT WAR.
> EDWARD BENNETT   PATRICK HUGHES   VINCENT MORGAN
> SAMUEL COCKS   EDWARD JOHNSTON   JOHN MUCKIAN
> MARGARET CREEGAN   FRANCIS KEIRAN   HUGH O'NEILL (CAPTAIN)
> JOSEPH FOX   WILLIAM McKEOWN   PETER SLOANE
> JOSEPH HALPENNY   PETER MATTHEWS   JOHN STACKS
> JAMES HERNON   PATRICK MELIA   DANIEL STOWELL
>   THOMAS TUITE
> THIS WINDOW WAS ERECTED TO THEIR MEMORY
> BY THE DUNDALK STEAM Cº
> AND S.S. DUNDALK DISASTER COMMITTEE.

Sam's body was not recovered but he is commemorated on a memorial plaque in St Patrick's Church, Dundalk

The SS Dundalk was torpedoed and sunk on the evening of Monday, 14th October, 1918, off Anglesey, by UB123 and UB90.

In the summer of 2004 divers Steve Cowley and Dave Copley, assisted by Adrian Corkill, dived the wreck of the steamship Dundalk 17 nautical miles south off Port St Mary. The wreck lies in approximately 60 metres of water so the divers were using trimix to safely dive this sort of range. The shot landed about midships and despite the dark and low visibility condition, the two divers made a complete inspection of the wreck. She was so shattered by the torpedo attack that she sank instantly. The wreck is largely upright and intact but aft of the boiler the hull is split, caused by the massive torpedo explosion and the stern section is angled at 45 degrees. The ship's gun was seen to one side, lying on the seabed. The boiler was large – more than 6 metres in diameter. The cargo holds are empty and the bow section is quite flat. Large lobsters and congers were noted; but the most notable feature was the abundance of marine animals attached to the wreck, which appears white out of the gloom.

LANCE CORPORAL
HENRY FRANCIS CONWAY

240692, 1/5th (Flintshire) Battalion
Royal Welsh Fusiliers

Henry Francis Conway was born in Flint 25th April, 1891 and baptised on 14th June, 1891 at St Mary's Catholic Church, Flint. He was the seventh of 10 children to Thomas Conway and Sarah Ann (Hayes) of 1, Castle Terrace, Flint, where they lived for many years, and the brother of Private James Conway (page 87).

Henry's father, Thomas, was born in Widnes, Lancashire in c.1854 and died in March 1907, aged about 50, and buried in the Northop Road Cemetery, Flint. He was employed as a chemical labourer.

Henry's first job was as a labourer at a cotton factory before gaining employment at the Hawarden Bridge Ironworks, Shotton.

He married Sarah Emily Cartwright in 1914. She was born in Gardeners Row, Oakenholt on 6th September, 1894, and a daughter of George Francis Cartwright, painter, and his wife Mary Elizabeth, of West View, Oakenholt.

Henry and Sarah Emily began their married life at 299, West View, Oakenholt and had a son they named Wilfred (1915–1982) who was known as Bud.

He enlisted in Flint on 5th October, 1914 as a Private with the 1/5th Battalion Royal Welsh Fusiliers, and his service record is as follows: forfeited 6 days pay being absent from 10:00 pm 29th January, 1915 to 10am, 3rd February, 1915; embarked on His Majesty's (HM) Troopship Caledonia at Devonport, for Gallipoli, on 14th July, 1915; admitted to hospital in Gallipoli suffering from exposure, 28th November, 1915; admitted to hospital in Nanders suffering from frost bite, 22nd December, 1915 and invalided to England on the Aquitania, 26th December, 1915; admitted to Netley Hospital on 3rd January, 1916 to 21st January, 1916 suffering from frost bite in both feet and recommended for ten days furlough; embarked on HM Troopship Tunisian at Devonport for Egypt, 30th April 1916; disembarked at Alexandria, Egypt, 9th May, 1916 and joined the Battalion on 18th May, 1916; he was granted Class 2 Proficiency Pay on 5th October, 1916; appointed paid Lance Corporal in the field, 1st November, 1916; admitted to hospital in the field, suffering from abrasions on his feet, 25th February, 1917; re-joined Battalion for duty in the field, 6th March, 1917. On enlistment he was 5 ft 5 in tall, chest 37 in and his vision and physical development were good. His wife was awarded a widow's pension of 26s 3d per week.

Lance Corporal Conway was killed in action in the first battle of Gaza, Palestine on 26th March, 1917.

He has no known grave but is commemorated on the Jerusalem Memorial on Panels 20 to 22. He is remembered on two war memorials: Flint Town and St Mary's Catholic Church, Flint and was awarded the 1914–15 Star, British War Medal and Victory Medal. He is also commemorated on the North Wales Heroes' Memorial Arch, Bangor.

Sarah Emily Conway

Sarah Emily died 23rd November, 1953, aged 58, and was buried in the Old London Road Cemetery, Flint

Sarah Emily re-married in 1919 to Patrick Burke (1894–1948); they had nine children and lived at 35, Woodfield Avenue.

Henry's mother was born in Flint and died on 19th August, 1946, aged 84, at 59, Sydney Street, Flint, the residence of her daughter and son-in-law, and was buried with her husband.

Sarah Emily died 23rd November, 1953, aged 58, and was buried in the Old London Road Cemetery, Flint with her second husband Patrick and their son Kenneth Patrick, who died in mysterious circumstances in 1993.

PRIVATE
JAMES CONWAY

713, 1/5th (Flintshire) Battalion
Royal Welsh Fusiliers

James (Jim) Conway was born in Flint on 17th April, 1888 and baptised on 17th June, 1888 at St Mary's Catholic Church, Flint. He was the fifth of 10 children to Thomas Conway and Sarah Ann (Hayes) of 1, Castle Terrace, Flint and the brother of Lance Corporal Henry Conway (page 85).

Like his brother Henry he was employed at the Hawarden Bridge Ironworks, Shotton but subsequently moved to the United Alkali Works, Flint.

James married Margaret Burke in 1912. She was born in Flint and a daughter of Thomas Burke, bricklayer, and his wife Mary, of Roskell Square. James and Margaret resided at 16, Roskell Square and had no children.

Previous to the war he had been a member of the Territorial Army for seven years.

He enlisted in Flint but it is not known exactly when. Since he had served with the Territorials for a number of years it is most likely he joined in August 1914. He landed at Gallipoli on 8th August, 1915.

He was killed in action at Suvla Bay, Gallipoli on 22nd August, 1915 and buried in the Green Hill Cemetery, Turkey (Plot II, Row B, Grave 7).

He is remembered on two war memorials: Flint Town and St Mary's Catholic Church, Flint and was awarded the 1914–15 Star, British War Medal and Victory Medal. He is also commemorated on the North Wales Heroes' Memorial Arch, Bangor.

Since the departure of the 1/5th Battalion of the Royal Welsh Fusiliers for the Dardanelles, Turkey, several relatives of the members of the Battalion had been without news of soldiers, and Mrs Conway made enquiries per letters to the Territorials' Records Office, Shrewsbury, respecting her husband. After the landing of the Battalion on the 10th August, 1915 at Suvla and the subsequent battle charge Private Conway was missed from the ranks by his fellow comrades. The information at that time was that he had been removed to one of the hospitals; but there was a remarkable and mysterious absence of news regarding him at the base and at home. On the 18th September there was information that he was believed to be suffering from wounds at one of the Alexandria Hospitals; but there were still no letters from him, or any intimation from anyone as to his condition, or whereabouts. One afternoon, in mid-October, however, Mrs Conway was shocked to receive direct from the War Office an official intimation, dated the 14th, in reply to her letter of the 27th September that he had been "killed in action," but no date was given. Private Conway was very popular amongst his friends in Flint.

Private Benjamin George Bellis, of Leadbrook Cottage, Oakenholt, was a Dispatch Rider with the 8th Battalion of the Royal Welsh Fusiliers at Gallipoli, and in a letter to his parents he said that his Battalion was near that of the 1/5th Battalion, and they were visited by some of the men. They had Ernie Joyce to tea, and Joyce was now a Lance Corporal. On another occasion they had tea with Lieutenant Alexander, of Oakenholt. They were located at Suvla and while walking round a field a few days previous to the date of his letter, their sniper Sergeant came across the grave of a Private J Conway of the 1/5th Battalion of the Royal Welsh Fusiliers. He thought the number of Conway was 713. The name and regiment were written on an old envelope. He believed the man belonged to Flint. The earth was only just thrown over him; but the comrade had "tidied it up" and put a nice little wooden cross over it.

Private Conway's wife, Margaret, never re-married and she died on 19th May, 1958, aged 70, at the Cottage Hospital, Flint, and buried in Pantasaph Cemetery.

PRIVATE
PETER PATRICK COSTELLO

14917, 10th (Service) Battalion Royal Welsh Fusiliers

Peter Patrick (Patsie) Costello was born in Flint on 14th November, 1896 in Flint and baptised on 29th November, 1896 at St Mary's Catholic Church, Flint. He was the sixth of nine children to Patrick Costello and Ellen (McManus) and the brother of Private William Costello (page 90).

In Patsie's early years the family were living at 35, Mumforth Street, before moving to No. 59.

His father, Patrick, was born in Salford, Lancashire and died on 16th March, 1910, aged 50, at his residence, 45, Mumforth Street, Flint, after an illness of only a few days, and buried in Pantasaph Cemetery. He was employed as an ironworker and had previously worked as a caustic maker, probably at the British Glanzstoff Chemical Works, Flint.

The following year Mrs Costello married John Mears Logan (1862–1946)

At Flint Borough Sessions, on Wednesday 6th December, 1911, George Jones, ironworker, 57, Mumforth Street, was summoned for using threats to Ellen Logan, a married woman, on 3rd November. Mr T W Hughes appeared for Mrs Logan and said the parties lived next door to one another and Mr Jones was continually annoying her. Mrs Logan said she was in bed on the night in question when she heard Mr Jones shouting to her from the street. He threatened to kill her, called her Mrs Maybrick, and used a great deal of abusive language, charging her with all sorts of immorality. On the following day he repeated his conduct, saying she had poisoned her husband and had her children heavily insured for the same purpose.

Ellen Costello with four of her children

Mr Jones said Mrs Logan drew all the bother on herself; she was the aggressor. Police Constable Hughes spoke to being called to the house and being insulted by Mr Jones. Mr Jones's wife said Mrs Logan was always carrying on with her ever since Mrs Logan's son was locked up. Mr Jones and his wife both said he was at work all the night of 3rd November. He went next morning and told her what he thought of her. The Mayor described the proceedings as discreditable, and said both would be bound over for six months. Mrs Logan strongly objected at first, but was ultimately persuaded to abide by the decision of the Bench.

Patsie was employed at the Hawarden Bridge Ironworks, Shotton and was unmarried.

He enlisted in Flint on 7th September, 1914 and landed at Boulogne, France on 27th September, 1915.

Private Costello was killed in action in France 16th August, 1916. He has no known grave but is commemorated on the Thiepval Memorial, Somme, France, on Pier and Face 4A. He is remembered on two war memorials: Flint Town and St Mary's Catholic Church, Flint, and was awarded the 1914–15 Star, British War Medal and Victory Medal. He is also commemorated on the North Wales Heroes' Memorial Arch, Bangor.

His mother, who was born in St Asaph, died 8th January, 1922, aged 57, and was buried with her first husband Patrick.

Patsie's parents' grave in Pantasaph Cemetery

PRIVATE
WILLIAM COSTELLO

11682, 8th (Service) Battalion Royal Welsh Fusiliers

William Costello was born in Flint on 24th July, 1886 and baptised on 8th August, 1886 at St Mary's Catholic Church, Flint. He was the eldest of nine children to Patrick Costello and Ellen (McManus) and the brother of Private Peter Patrick Costello (page 88).

William was raised in 17, Princes Street then the family moved to 35, Mumforth Street until settling at No. 59.

He could not be located in the 1911 census; however, in 1901 his occupation was listed as ostler (groom) at an hotel. He was unmarried.

He enlisted in Flint on 14th August, 1914 and joined at Wrexham the same day. He landed at Gallipoli circa June 1915 and subsequently posted to Mesopotamia, where he was killed in action on 3rd February, 1917. On enlistment he was 5 ft 7½ in tall.

He has no known grave but is commemorated on the Basra Memorial, Iraq, on Panel 15. He is remembered on two war memorials: Flint Town and St Mary's Catholic Church, Flint. He is also commemorated on the North Wales Heroes' Memorial Arch, Bangor.

He was awarded the 1914–15 Star, British War Medal and Victory Medal.

PRIVATE
EVELYN NAPIER CRAVEN

51728, 16th Battalion Cheshire Regiment

Evelyn Napier Craven was born in Flint on May 1885 and baptised on 26th June, 1885 at St Mary's Parish Church, Flint. He was the third of about 13 children to John Craven and Theresa (Mooney). He was a half-brother to Private Richard Craven (page 93).

The Craven family lived in Oakenholt Cottages, which were also known as the Villas, and Evelyn served an apprenticeship in the offices of the North Wales Paper Mill, Oakenholt.

The 1911 census revealed Evelyn to be a boarder in the

A newspaper photo of Evelyn Napier Craven

household of a Mr William Darrock, a station master of 16, Birley Street, Newton le Willows, Lancashire, and his occupation was clerk in a printing works. It was here he met his future wife Minnie who was Mr Darrock's daughter.

In March of 1912 Minnie gave birth to Evelyn's daughter Annie and they had her baptised at St Mary's Parish Church, Flint on 19th April that year.

Evelyn and Minnie married at St Peter's Parish Church, Newton le Makerfield, Warrington, Lancashire on 27th May, 1912 and, shortly after, Evelyn was offered a post as a commercial traveller with paper merchants T W Leigh & Company of Thomas Street, Liverpool, and they set up home at 28, Ingram Road.

They were to have two more children – William John (1913–1995) and Clifford (1915–?).

On 12th April, 1913 Evelyn's father died of pneumonia at his residence in Oakenholt, and was buried in the Northop Road Cemetery. The following is his obituary, which appeared in the County Herald: "Mr Craven was a gentleman who had earned for himself an indisputable and esteemed reputation in the papermaking world and had enjoyed a somewhat interesting career. He was a native of Radcliffe, Lancashire and he came, when he was a comparatively young man, to the North Wales Paper Mills at Oakenholt, and had been employed at the Mill for a period of forty years. His duties were always characterized by a quiet persistence and indomitable perseverance and diligence. Years ago, his work in the Mills was recognized by the Company when he received the appointment of foreman paper-maker, and which duties he continued to discharge with entire satisfaction for his employers. Throughout these duties he displayed exceptional energy and activity, combined with a most marked ability; and he was keenly interested in the welfare of the Mills in regard to any improvements in the art of papermaking. He was a member of the Loyal Flint Castle Lodge of Oddfellows for over thirty years, being one of the oldest members, and he was also an active member of the Flint Horticultural Society; a Conservative in politics, and a devoted Churchman."

He was previously married to Winifred Mooney (mother of Private Richard Craven – page 93), who was an older sister to John's second wife Theresa.

Evelyn enlisted in Liverpool on 11th December, 1915 with the 3rd South Lancashire Regiment, No. 40902, and his service record is as follows: joined at Warrington;

Private Craven was buried in the Minty Farm Cemetery, Langemark-Poelkapelle, West-Vlaanderen, Belgium

formerly with the 2nd Volunteer Battalion Royal Welsh Fusiliers; on enlistment he was 5 ft 7¾ in, weight 134lb, chest 35 in and his physical development was good; he had a varicocele in the left side of the scrotum and had to wear a suspender bandage; home base until 15th October, 1917; embarked Southampton, 17th October, 1917; disembarked Le Havre, France, on 21st October, 1917; transferred to Cheshire Regiment, 27th October, 1917; his personal effects sent home to his wife were: identity disc, letters, pipe, mirror, pouch, nail clippers in case, and one coin; Mrs Craven was awarded a widow's pension of 29s 7d per week for herself and three children, with effect from 10th June, 1918.

He died 26th November, 1917, at the Main Dressing Station, France, as a result of a gunshot wound in the right thigh, and was buried in the Minty Farm Cemetery, Langemark-Poelkapelle, West-Vlaanderen, Belgium, (Plot II, Row D, Grave 7).

Private Craven is remembered on his parents' headstone in the Northop Road Cemetery, Flint (Grave 8, Line 24, South Side)

He is remembered on two war memorials: St David's Parish Church, Oakenholt (now in St Mary's Parish Church, Flint) and Oddfellows Hall, Flint. He is also remembered on his parents' headstone in the Northop Road Cemetery, Flint (Grave 8, Line 24, South Side).

He was awarded the British War Medal and Victory Medal.

It was early in December of 1917 when the sad information was received in a letter by Mrs Craven that her husband was wounded and had died. A letter from the Chaplain stated that the remains were interred in a cemetery on the following day. Private Craven was respected by his comrades amongst whom he served. He was well known in his home town of Oakenholt and also by many people in Flint, by whom he was esteemed for his bonhomie and exceedingly entertaining character, being a most versatile musician with an excellent knowledge of operatic and other musical works.

His mother, Theresa, was born in Sheffield, Yorkshire, and died 1st January, 1919, aged about 56, at 4, Halkyn Street, Flint and buried with her husband and her step-daughter Jane.

By March 1918 Minnie was living at 1, Mount Tabor, Newton-le-Willows, Lowton, Lancashire. She re-married in 1920 at St Luke's Parish Church, Lowton, Lancashire to Brook Ellwood (1876–1954), and they resided at 25, Sobley Buildings, Carlinghow, Batley, Yorkshire. She died at Dewsbury, West Yorkshire in 1958, aged 69.

PRIVATE
RICHARD CRAVEN

36389, 14th Battalion Cheshire Regiment

Richard Craven was born in Oakenholt in 1875, and the third of five children to John Craven and Winifred (Mooney). He was a half-brother to Private Evelyn Napier Craven (page 90).

John and Winifred's fourth child was born in 1879 but, sadly, Birkenhead-born Winifred died in October the following year aged just 27, and was buried in St Mark's Churchyard, Connah's Quay.

The 1881 census found widower John living in Flint Lane, Oakenholt with his four daughters, Mary Esther, Martha C, Margaret and Jane, whilst Richard was staying with his uncle and aunt, William and Mary Craven, at 21, Seymour Street, Radcliffe, Lancashire.

On 31st December, 1881 John married Winifred's sister Theresa Mooney at St Mary's Parish Church, Chester (see Private Evelyn Napier Craven, page 91).

Richard was to return to Oakenholt where he attended the Pentre School, and the school log book entry for 10th April, 1888 revealed the following: "Re Richard Craven – Richard Craven, a boy of 11 years, has been a source of great trouble and anxiety to the teachers. His intellect is very weak and he is much given to pilfering & stealing. Last week he purloined some of his mother's jewellery and destroyed them. In fact he has become so unmanageable that his parents have procured his admission into a reformatory school, where he will be more strictly guarded; & I hope, cured of his evil habits. An attempt was made last year to get him on to the training ship "Clio" but it was unsuccessful."

The Clio was an industrial training ship that served North Wales, Chester and the Border Counties during the period 1877–1920. During this time it was moored in the Menai Straits, near Bangor. The ship had a dual purpose – namely, to take care of, and train, boys under the age of 14 who were regarded as being in need of special educational or custodial care; and also, to provide a regular supply of seamen for the Royal Navy and Mercantile Service. Although boys who had been convicted of crimes were not permitted to enter industrial training ships, the Clio was regarded by many people as a 'reformatory' ship.

The industrial training ship Clio in the Menai Straits

Richard was sent to Bradwall Reformatory School for Boys (sometimes referred to as Bradwall Training School) in Sandbach, Cheshire where, at the time of the 1891 census, he was, listed as a "boy under detention," but it is not known for how long he was there.

The 1911 census revealed him to be residing at Oakenholt Hall, in the employ of Mr John Lee Bohannan, as a gardener (domestic). However, prior to his army service he was a farm labourer living at Cotton Farm, Lache, Chester. He never married.

He enlisted in Chester on 11th December, 1915 but never saw front line service; on enlistment he was 5 ft 5in, 124lb, chest 36 in, and his physical development was good.

He died at 3:20pm on 26th April, 1916, of pneumonia and exhaustion, at the Military Hospital, Prees Heath, Whitchurch, Shropshire, where he was a patient for 24 days. He was buried in Whitchurch Cemetery, (Grave 153) [see right].

He is remembered on St David's Parish Church war memorial, Oakenholt, and was awarded the British War Medal and Victory Medal.

PRIVATE
ALFRED DAVIES

240634, 1/5th (Flintshire) Battalion Royal Welsh Fusiliers

Alfred Davies was born on 1st May, 1891 at Mount Pleasant, Flint and baptised on 17th June, 1891 at St Mary's Parish Church, Flint. He was the eldest of 12 children to William Davies and Elizabeth (Jones).

It is not known where William and Elizabeth were in the 1901 census but Alfred and his five-year-old brother Richard were staying with their grandparents Robert and Margaret Davies at 1, Mill Brow, by Bryn Houses, Flint.

In the 1911 census the Davies family were living at 23, Swan Street and Alfred's occupation was a Corporation labourer.

Alfred's father William, who was born in Flint, died on 22nd February, 1912, aged 53, and was buried in the Northop Road Cemetery. He had been employed as a collier and chemical labourer.

Alfred married Edith Eccles at the Register Office, Holywell on 26th December, 1912. She was born in Flint and was a daughter of William Eccles, farm labourer, and his wife Mary, of 1, Gardeners Row, Oakenholt, and sister to Private John William Eccles (page 116).

The lived at 265, Brook Place, Chester Road, Oakenholt, and had two children – William (1913–?) and Florence (1915–?). Alfred was now employed as a carter in the chemical works.

He enlisted in Flint on 21st September, 1914, and his service record is as follows: forfeited 10 days' pay for absence from 6:00 pm 30th January, 1915 to 9:30 am 8th February, 1915; embarked His Majesty's (HM) Troopship Caledonia at Devonport for Gallipoli on 14th July, 1915; hospitalised at Gallipoli with a bayonet wound in the left leg on 5th September, 1915; hospitalised in Malta on 10th September, 1915 and in the Wesleyan General Hospital, Cardiff, on 17th October, 1915; embarked HM Troopship Ivvenie at Devonport, on 23rd April, 1916; disembarked at Alexandria, Egypt, on 3rd May, 1916; joined Battalion at Wadi Natrun on 13th May, 1916; attached to CRE (Divisional Commander Royal Engineers) Australian Division as Railway Man at Ismailia, on 28th May, 1916; rejoined Battalion ex-attachment at Egypt, on 3rd August, 1916; embarked for El Arish, Port Said, 25th December, 1916; rejoined Battalion ex-El Arish in field, on 29th December, 1916; granted Class 2 Proficiency Pay, on 27th September, 1916; wounded in action at Gaza, on 26th March, 1917; on enlistment, he was 5 ft 9 in, chest 36 in, fresh complexion, grey eyes and black hair. His wife Edith was granted a widow's pension of 44s 2d per week for herself and two children with effect from 2nd February, 1920.

A concerned Edith wrote a letter to the Record Office, Shrewsbury, dated 21st July, 1917, stating that her husband had been a prisoner of war in Turkey and she had not heard from him for two years, and would they look into the case for her.

A report was received by the War Office from No. 241227 Private R Johnson, 1/5th Royal Welsh Fusiliers to the effect that No. 240634 Private A Davies of the same regiment died at Bor, Turkey whilst a prisoner of war since he was wounded in action at the First Battle of Gaza, Palestine on 26th March, 1917. The relatives were informed that this report had been accepted for official purposes, and that the date of death taken as, "on or since 1st August, 1917." The cause of his death was not stated.

He was buried in the Baghdad (North Gate) War Cemetery, Iraq (Plot XXI, Row U, Grave 32), and is remembered on the Flint Town war memorial. He is also commemorated on the North Wales Heroes' Memorial Arch, Bangor. He was awarded the 1914–15 Star, British War Medal and Victory Medal.

Edith re-married in 1920 to Albert Leighton Hughes (1896–1968), residing at 21, Woodfield Avenue, Flint. She died on 18th July, 1959, aged 65, and is buried with her second husband in the Old London Road Cemetery, Flint (see right).

Alfred's mother, Elizabeth, was born in Flint and died on 16th March, 1930, aged about 65, and was buried with her husband.

LANCE CORPORAL
BENJAMIN DAVIES

15183, 10th (Service) Battalion Royal Welsh Fusiliers

Benjamin (Ben) Davies was born on 31st October, 1892 at 1:20 am at Bryn-y-Garreg, Flint Mountain (his twin sister Sarah Elizabeth was born at 1:45 am). He was the eighth of nine children to John Davies and Ellen (Jellicoe).

On 12th October, 1912 Ben's father, John, died of pneumonia at his home, aged 60, and was buried in the Northop Road Cemetery, Flint.

Halkyn-born Mr Davies was an exceedingly popular resident of the Mountain district, where he was a faithful member of the Welsh Wesleyan cause, and he took a keen and active interest in the work of the church, being always prominent in whatever was a movement for the benefit of the denomination. He was the custodian of all the literature circulated amongst the members of the church, as well as the adherents and exhibited an absorbing concern. He was well read and well versed in all matters pertaining to Methodism, and was also the Treasurer to the Flint Mountain Eisteddfod. He had been employed by Messrs Summers' Ironworks, Shotton, and previously a check-weighman at the old Flint Colliery.

Another tragedy was soon to befall the Davies family when Mrs Davies, who was born in Neston, Cheshire, died under horrific circumstances on Sunday 4th October, 1914, at Dee View Cottage, Bryn-y-Garreg.

She died as a result of extensive burns from the ankle to the neck when she fell and knocked over an oil-lamp at her home.

The following evening, at Dee View Cottage, the Flintshire Coroner (Mr F Llewellyn Jones) held an inquiry into the death of Mrs Ellen Davies, a widow, aged 60 years of age, who resided at the address named. Mr William Davies, Post Office, was elected as the foreman of the jury. John Davies deposed that he was a son of the deceased and resided at Dee View. He identified the body, which the jury had viewed as that of his mother.

The County Herald of 9th October gave a full report of the inquiry: "Mary Catherine Bellis, living at Bryn-y-Garreg, stated that about five minutes past nine o'clock she was returning home from Flint along the Cwlta Road, which is about 200 yards from here and just at the bottom of the hill I saw Mrs Davies open the door of her house and run out. She was enveloped in flames. She was screaming at the time. She ran up Bryn-y-Garreg Terrace; and then I ran to Richard Hughes's house. I opened the door and said that the old lady was on fire. He is her son-in-law, and he ran and tried to do what he could for her.

Richard Hughes went out and called for Thomas Williams, of Inglenook, to come to assist him and they both went up the road to look for the deceased, and found her in Mrs Hogg's house. The house was full of smoke and in darkness and the door partly open. She was sitting on the sofa and appeared to be in pain. Her clothes were partly on fire and he took her to the door; got her outside; asked for some water from Mrs Hogg, and poured it on her clothes to put the fire out. He removed other portions of the fire with his hands.

Then Mrs Annie Owens came up the entry and asked Mrs Hogg for a rig or a cloak. Mrs Hogg handed me a cloak, which I put round the deceased, and then we carried her home and put her to bed.

Charlotte Dennis, who lived next door to the deceased, gave evidence and said that on Saturday night about ten minutes past nine o'clock she heard someone screaming and went out to see what was the matter. I noticed a smell coming from her cottage into mine, and the smell resembled that of a candle having been extinguished. I tried to find what was the cause of the smoke, and I came and put my nose to the door of the deceased's cottage. Then I said that it was something next door, and they must have been burning something. I went out to the back, and I could not see a light; but I could hear a low screaming. When I got into the garden the screams seemed to be at the top of the garden; and I thought there was some drunken brawl. I went to the gate and said, "Oh, is that Mrs Hogg; there must have been some dreadful screaming." Afterwards I heard the voices of two men, and a voice "We will throw water over her." My first thought was, as the deceased had been on fire, for the safety of the cottage, and I rushed back into it to see if it was on fire, because my house is next door. I saw that the kitchen table had been overturned, a chair had been overturned, and the lamp was lying in pieces on the floor. There was paraffin on the floor. There was only a very small fire in the grate. I afterwards saw the men carrying the deceased up the lane to her house. I was with her until 1.30 on the following morning.

I asked her how it happened and she said it was a pure accident and she fell. I said "Why didn't you run into my cottage?" and she said "I did not like." She conversed with me, and she said, "I have been breaking my heart about my children." I understood she referred to her three sons who had enlisted to go to the Front.

Dr J H Williams, of Flint, said he was summoned per telephone about ten o'clock on Saturday night, and he was at the house of the deceased about a quarter past that hour. Deceased was in bed and suffering from extensive burns – the most extensive burns he had ever seen – practically all over her, with the exception of the head. The burns extended from the ankles to the neck. She died on Sunday morning as a direct result of the burns.

The jury returned a verdict that the deceased died from burns accidentally caused.

The funeral took place the following Wednesday afternoon. At the residence the service was opened by the Rev D R Thomas (Welsh Wesleyan), of Flint, and the Reverend Gwynfryn Jones (Welsh Wesleyan), Flint Mountain, engaged in prayer. The remains were then conveyed to the cemetery where the ministers again officiated at the graveside; and the beautiful hymn, "Bydd myrdd o'ryfeddodau" was sung."

Ellen is buried with her husband and their son Peter, of 60, Maes-y-Dre Avenue, Flint, who died in 1947, aged 69.

After the death of his parents, Ben moved in with his sister, Mary Ellen, and her husband,

Richard Hughes, at Rock Cottage, Flint Mountain. He never married and his occupation is not known. He enlisted in Shotton in August 1914 and landed at Boulogne, France on 27th September, 1915.

He was killed in action in France on 19th February, 1916.

He has no known grave but is commemorated on the Ypres (Menin Gate) Memorial, Ieper, West-Vlaanderen, Belgium on Panel 22. He is remembered on the Flint Town war memorial and was awarded the 1914–15 Star, British War Medal and Victory Medal. He is also commemorated on the North Wales Heroes' Memorial Arch, Bangor

Ben's sister, Mary Ellen, received the following letter dated 20th February, 1916:

> DEAR MADAM,– I'm not sure whether you've heard that your brother Private Benjamin Davies, was killed yesterday, as a result of shell fire. His death was instantaneous. I've felt the news very much, for as Chaplain in the Battalion, I was very fond of your brother. He was such a nice lad, and a good lad. You need no doubt but that he is safe for evermore. I saw your other brother today, and while he naturally feels it he is holding up as well as you could expect. Please allow the consolations of religion to have their influence, and I believe them to be substantial, and particularly so when they have to do with us so gentle, so Christian-like a character as your brother, Benjamin. Please accept my expression of very deep sympathy with you.
>
> Believe me to be,
>
> Sincerely yours,
>
> D. C. WILLIAMS (Chaplain),
> Attd. 10th R. W. F.

Private Joseph Hamlet Davies, of the same Battalion, and the brother of Private Ben Davies, writing to his sister, Mrs Richard Hughes, under field post office, dated the 22nd February, said he hardly knew how to let her know of Ben having been killed on the 19th. He had only been talking to his brother a few minutes before, and he was not further than 10 yards away from him when he was killed by a shell. Another young man who was near his brother was also killed and four others were wounded. He asked his sister to try and bear up, as he must do so. Ben was killed instantly. He didn't see Ben after he was killed, but their Sergeant Major informed him that he was buried very shortly after he was killed, and that he was buried quite respectably. He had received her letter and he noticed she stated that she saw Private Campbell when he was home. He told her that he had been killed also. Private Davies made further reference to the terrible fighting which was proceeding at the time he was writing.

IN MEMORIAM

A light from our household gone,
The voice we loved is still'd,
A place is vacant in our home
Which never can be filled.
Sadly missed by Brothers and Sisters. Rock Cottage, Flint Mountain.
(County Herald, 23rd February, 1917)

Days of sadness still come o'er us,
Tears of sorrow often flow,
But memory keeps our loved one near us,
Although he fell two years ago.
Rock Cottage, Flint Mountain.
(County Herald, 22nd February, 1918)

'Tis sweet to think we'll meet again,
Where partings are no more,
And that the one we loved so well
Is only gone before.
Aunt, Uncle and Cousins. Runcorn View, Halkyn.
(County Herald, 22nd February, 1918)

PRIVATE
DANIEL DAVIES

13484, 9th (Service) Battalion
Royal Welsh Fusiliers

Daniel Davies was born on 28th December, 1890 at Bryn Llwyni, Llandrillo yn Rhos, Colwyn Bay, Denbighshire, and the seventh of 11 children to Daniel Davies and Catherine (Davies).

Daniel junior lived at Bryn Llwyni throughout his bachelor life and was employed in one of the outfitting establishments in Flint.

Daniel Davies senior died on 12th April, 1913, aged 66, and buried in Bron-y-Nant Cemetery, Colwyn Bay.

On Wednesday, 9th April Mr Davies was about as usual and attended the music festival at Engedi. He was taken ill on the Thursday, and passed away on Saturday, after only two days' illness. He was a native of Mochdre, and had resided in Upper Colwyn Bay for many years. He was a faithful member of the Seion Welsh Calvanistic Methodist Chapel, where he acted as a deacon since the inception of the cause 14 years previously. For many years before coming to reside at Bryn Llwyni he was in business as a butcher, but in the latter part of his life he had taken to market gardening. His funeral was well attended and there was an unusually large attendance of ministers and the general public. In the evening, at Seion, a memorial service was held, at which the Reverend W R Owen, the pastor of the church, preached a special sermon. References were made to the sterling qualities of the deceased, and the faithful manner in which he carried out the duties in connection with the cause at Seion Church.

Private Davies's brother, Hugh Goronwy, also served in the war as a Private with the 10th Battalion Royal Welsh Fusiliers, No. 40571, and was killed in action in France on 16th August, 1916, when he was hit by shellfire, and is remembered on the Thiepval Memorial, France and Colwyn Bay Town memorial. He was employed by Brookes Brothers the Drapers in Llandudno.

Private Daniel Davies

Daniel Jnr married Jane (Jennie) Horrobin in the Register Office, Conway on 9th June, 1913, and they set up home at 24, Sydney Street, Flint. Jennie was born in Greenfield and a daughter of Walter Horrobin, storekeeper, and his wife Eliza Abigail, of 55, Holywell Road, Flint.

They had two children – Herbert Gordon (1913–1983), and May (1914–1999). Herbert was a tax inspector who served in WW2 with the RAOC. He married Hilda Culley (1919–?) and they lived in Cardiff. May was a spinster and employed at London House, Flint.

Jennie Davies

Mr Daniel Davies Senior

Mrs Catherine Davies

Daniel Davies Jnr enlisted in Shotton in September 1914 and landed at Boulogne, France on 19th July, 1915, and was wounded in action in September of that year.

In an undated postcard from the Front addressed to his son, Master G H Davies, c/o Mrs Horrobin. 55 Holywell Road. Flint, he wrote:

To Dear little Gordon

Hoping you are all well see you all soon drop me a line love to all yours Daniel

To little Gordon
From Dada
xxxxxxx
xxxx

In September 1917 Private Davies, who was a Stretcher Bearer, forwarded to his wife a Military Card, signed by the Brigade General, intimating that the General Officer had brought to his notice his gallant conduct in the field at the time of a certain engagement. And on the morning of Saturday 22nd September she received from her husband a letter, in which he said: "You will be pleased to hear that I have won the D.C.M." and that every one of his friends in the Company were pleased to learn the news, and that he had been congratulated by the officers of the Company.

The citation for his DCM (Distinguished Conduct Medal), which appeared in the London Gazette on 22nd October, 1917 & Edinburgh Gazette on 28th January, 1918, read as follows: "for conspicuous gallantry and devotion to duty as stretcher bearer during an attack. He continually attended to the wounded under rifle and shellfire, and on one occasion he left the trench under heavy fire and rescued a badly wounded comrade in the open. He set a splendid example of courage and devotion to duty."

Private Davies was killed in action during the battle of Arras, France on 22nd March, 1918.

He has no known grave but is commemorated on the Arras Memorial, Pas de Calais, France on Bay 6.

He is remembered on four war memorials: Flint Town, St Mary's Parish Church, Flint, Caersalem Chapel, Flint and Colwyn Bay Town.

He is also remembered on his wife's headstone in the Old London Road Cemetery, Flint, on

A tribute to Private Davies

Grave C914, Section D, and his parent's headstone in Bron y Nant Cemetery, Colwyn Bay, on Grave D350, as well as being commemorated on the North Wales Heroes' Memorial Arch, Bangor.

Along with the DCM he was awarded the 1914–15 Star, British War Medal, Victory Medal.

> **IN MEMORIAM**
>
> *Dearer to memory than words can tell,*
> *Are the thoughts of one we loved so well.*
>
> He nobly responded to his country's call, and did his best.
> Sadly missed by his Wife and Two Children.
> (County Herald, 19th March, 1920)

In the family bible, presented to Daniel and Jane, on the occasion of their marriage, by Mrs Davies, Jennie wrote the following:- "In loving memory of my dear husband killed in France March 22nd 1918 aged 26 years. He stood a soldier until the last sad end. A perfect patriot and a noble friend."

In June 1919 the Mayor of Flint made an official presentation of gallantry medals to the Flint soldiers but in the case of Private Daniel Davies the DCM was pinned on the breast of his son Herbert Gordon.

Daniel's mother Catherine was born in Colwyn Bay, Denbighshire and died 17th February, 1932, aged 75, and is buried with her husband and children William Griffith, Catherine Rachel and Deborah.

Jennie, who didn't remarry, was residing at 73, Sydney Street, Flint when she became seriously ill and died in hospital a fortnight later on 22nd December, 1962, aged 73. She was the superintendent of Muspratt's Sunday School for many years and a devoted member of St Mary's Parish Church. She was buried in the Old London Road Cemetery, Flint, with her sisters Edith and Elizabeth Mary.

Private Daniel Davies is remembered on his wife's headstone in the Old London Road Cemetery, Flint, on Grave C914, Section D, (above) and on his parent's headstone in Bron y Nant Cemetery, Colwyn Bay, on Grave D350 (right)

SERGEANT
WILLIAM DAVIES

349, 1/5th (Flintshire) Battalion
Royal Welsh Fusiliers

William (Will) Davies was born on 21st May, 1874 near Eyton's Colliery Office, Flint, and the third of seven children to William Davies and Sarah (Williams).

By 1891 the Davies family were living in Swan Street and Will was employed as a blacksmith's labourer.

In February 1899 Will's mother Sarah, who was born in Flint, died at the age of 56, and was buried in the Northop Road Cemetery with her daughter Ann, who died in 1895, aged 23.

On 10th September, 1898 Will married Mary Jones in the Register Office, Holywell, and they set up home at 10, Salisbury Street. Will was now employed as a labourer at the chemical works in Flint.

He was for some years a member of the Territorial Army, for which he was awarded the Territorial Force Efficiency Medal on 1st October, 1909.

By 1911 Will and Mary had moved home to live at Tyddyn Mesham, Bagillt, and Will had changed his job yet again; at this time, he was a labourer at the Shotton Iron Works.

Mary Davies (above) and (right) seated with her children (left to right): Bertie, Poll, Jen (front), Gladys (back), Mrs Davies, Margaret, William and Bob

Will and Mary had at least eight children and would move home once again to live at 1, Commercial Road, Flint.

He enlisted in Flint (probably as soon as the war began), and landed at Gallipoli on 8th August, 1915. He died on 14th September, 1915 from dysentery, at St Patrick's Hospital, Malta, and was buried at the Pieta Military Cemetery, Malta (Plot B, Row XI, Grave 5).

The gravestone inscription of Sergeant William Davies

Will is remembered on two war memorials: Flint Town and St Mary's Parish Church, Flint. He is also remembered on his wife's headstone in the Northop Road Cemetery, Flint (Grave 8, Line 8, South Side). He is also commemorated on the North Wales Heroes' Memorial Arch, Bangor.

He was awarded the 1914–15 Star, British War Medal and Victory Medal.

Will's father, William, who was born in Flint, died at the Workhouse Infirmary, Holywell on 3rd September, 1916, aged 72, and was buried with his wife. He was a chemical labourer.

Will's wife, Mary, was born in Flint and died on 23rd January, 1942, aged 63, at 9, Salisbury Street, Flint. She is buried in the Northop Road Cemetery with two of her children, William and Agnes (see below). Mary was a member of St Mary's Parish Church, and well known and highly esteemed.

IN MEMORIAM

Could I have raised his dying head,
Or heard his last farewell.
The grief would not have been so hard
For one who loved him well.

Sleep on, my dear husband, in a soldier's grave,
A grave I may never see;
But as long as my life and memory last
I will always think of thee.
Sadly missed by his sorrowing
Wife and Children.
1, Commercial Road, Flint.
(County Herald, 15th September, 1916)

IN MEMORIAM

Sleep, my dear brother, in a soldier's grave,
Your life for your country you nobly gave;
No one stood near you to say goodbye,
But safe in God's keeping now you lie.
Still in thought by his sister-in-law, Maggie.
Cicely House, Ansdell.
(County Herald, 15th September, 1916)

❧

To an unseen grave far away,
A sad wife's thoughts wander to-day,
Unseen by the world he stands by my side,
And whispers, dear wife, don't fret,
death cannot divide.
Sadly missed by his loving Wife and Children.
1, Commercial Road, Flint.
(County Herald, 14th September, 1917)

❧

Could I, his wife, have clasped his hand,
The husband I loved so well,
To kiss his brow when death was nigh,
And whisper, "Will, farewell."

We have lost a loving father,
We have lost a loving friend,
But we will cherish him in memory
And love him to the end.
Sadly missed by his loving Wife and Children
1, Commercial Road, Flint.
(County Herald, 13th September, 1918)

SAPPER
JOHN JOSEPH DEAN

WR/253215, Royal Engineers (Railway Operating Division)

John (Jack) Joseph Dean was born on 19th March, 1897 at 23, Charles Street, Chester, and the eldest of three children to John Dean and Mary Philhelmina (Davies). He was a nephew to Private Samuel Dean (page 108).

In 1901 the Dean family were living at 18, Romily Street, Manchester, and 10 years later they were living at 12, Brampton Street, Newton Heath, Manchester; Jack's occupation was given as "learning in cotton factory." He eventually became a silk spinner and remained unmarried.

John and Mary Dean

Jack's mother took ill and was admitted to the Winwick County Asylum in Warrington, where she died of "general paralysis of the insane" on 11th January, 1915, aged 40. She was buried in All Saints churchyard, Newton Heath, Manchester.

By September 1916, Jack and his two brothers, George and Thomas, had been taken in by their aunt, Mrs Katie Jones, of 74, Duke Street, Flint, who became their next of kin. On 25th May, 1917, at the Royal Infirmary in Chorlton-upon-Medlock, their father, John, died aged 42, of "cirrhosis of the liver and heart failure." He was buried with his wife.

Aunt Katie and her husband Robert with their daughter and Thomas

The Dean brothers – Thomas, John Joseph and George

Jack's army service record revealed he enlisted in Flint on 1st November, 1915 with the 3/5th Royal Welsh Fusiliers Territorial Force, No. 3461, and he was discharged for re-enlistment on 19th March, 1916 with the Regular Army of Royal Engineers, No. 130561, at 6d per day. Sometime in 1917, he was tested in the Railway Operating Workshops in the field, and proved he proficient at locomotive cleaning; raised to skilled rate of pay, 3rd July, 1918.

On enlistment he was 5 ft 2 in, chest 32¾ in, his physical development was good and his vision was adequate; his personal effects sent to his next of kin were: gold ring, waist belt, watch & chain, £6 in English money and about 160 Francs.

He died on 9th January, 1919 after he was admitted to No. 12 Stationary Hospital, France, on 3rd January, suffering from influenza and bronchopneumonia. Military service was considered to have aggravated the condition from which he died.

He was buried in the St Pol British Cemetery, St Pol-Sur-Ternoise, Pas de Calais, France (Plot II, Row E, Grave 2) and is remembered on three war memorials: Flint Town, St Mary's Parish Church, Flint and Oddfellows Hall, Flint. He is also commemorated on the North Wales Heroes' Memorial Arch, Bangor.

Sapper J J Dean was buried was buried in the St Pol British Cemetery, St Pol-Sur-Ternoise, Pas de Calais, France

Jack was awarded the British War Medal and Victory Medal.

The following is a letter his aunt wrote to the Royal Engineers Record Office at Tavistock Square, London dated 24th January, 1919:

> Sir
>
> Will you kindly let me know who Sapper J J Dean WR253215 let 130561 has made his will for as I note by the form you have sent notifying us of his death that it is addressed to his brother G Dean whom is now serving with His Majesty's Forces in Russia & if he has made his will for him it will make it very inconvenient to get different documents signed by him. I have seen his Pay Book when he was home on leave & he drew my attention that he had made everything for me. An early reply will be appreciated by
>
> Yours Truly
>
> K Jones

Jack's brother Thomas was born in Newton Heath, Manchester, in 1912 and in World War 2 served as a Gunner, No. 1457646, with the 85th Anti-Tank Regiment, Royal Artillery and died on 1st October, 1943 whilst a Japanese prisoner of war, working on the infamous Burma–Siam railway. He was buried in the Chungkai War Cemetery, Kanchanaburi, Thailand.

Katie died of a stroke in 1924, aged 58; her husband, Robert, died in 1942 aged 78. Both were buried in the Northop Road Cemetery.

Gunner Thomas Dean

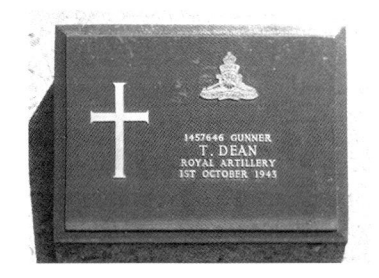

The resting place of Katie and Robert Jones

PRIVATE
SAMUEL DEAN

17607, 6th (Service) Battalion King's Own Scottish Borderers

Samuel (Sammy) Dean was born on 30th June, 1870 at West View, Little Lever, Bolton, Lancashire, and was the third of five children to Thomas Dean and Jane (Jones). He was an uncle to Sapper John Joseph Dean (page 105).

Sammy's father, Thomas, was a bricklayer, born in Flint and his trade took him to Bolton for a few years. However, the 1881 census shows that he had returned to Flint with his growing family, where they lived at Haywood's Court.

Thomas's Liverpool-born wife, Jane, died on 11th June, 1900, at Castle Street, Flint, aged 63, and was buried in the Northop Road Cemetery.

The 1901 census shows Sammy was employed as a bricklayer's labourer and lodging at the home of a Mr George Downie and his wife Ann, of 18, Mill Street, Ashton-in-Makerfield, Lancashire.

On 14th November, 1906, Sammy's father died at Sydney Street, Flint, aged 66, and was buried with his wife.

By 1911, Sammy was lodging at the home of a Mr and Mrs John Love at 251a, Florence Terrace, Wigan Road, Bryn, Ashton-in-Makerfield, Lancashire. He was a bricklayer's labour at a colliery. He was a single man and remained that way.

He enlisted in Ashton-in-Makerfield, Lancashire in January 1915 and joined at Berwick-on-Tweed. He landed at Boulogne, France on 12th May, 1915.

Private Dean was killed in action in France on 10th February, 1916 and buried in the Tancrez Farm Cemetery, Comines-Warneton, Hainout, Belgium (Plot I, Row B, Grave 10).

He is remembered on two war memorials: Flint Town and St Mary's Parish Church, Flint, and was awarded the 1914–15 Star, British War Medal and Victory Medal. He is also commemorated on the North Wales Heroes' Memorial Arch, Bangor.

Private Dean is buried in the Tancrez Farm Cemetery, Comines-Warneton, Hainout, Belgium

Thousands of patrons of football in Flint, Flintshire, several towns in North Wales, Cheshire and in Lancashire, learned, with regret, of the reported death of Private Samuel Dean, of Flint. There was, however, a conflicting condition. Mrs Robert Jones, residing at 74, Duke Street, Flint, sister of Private Dean, said that on the previous Monday afternoon she received a letter from him from France, dated the 11th February, whereas he was stated to have been killed on the 10th February. On the 9th February he received a letter from his brother, who resides in Widnes and, as circumstances have proved, he wrote a reply that day, but which was evidently not posted to leave the field post office. The letter was, however, forwarded to the brother at Widnes, with a covering letter announcing the death. The official notification, however, arrived a few days later.

The letter which Private Dean wrote to his brother on the 9th February said that he had received his welcome letter that morning; that he was very pleased to hear from him, and also pleased to inform him that he was quite well. The weather where he was stationed was not very warm, but in the course of a few weeks they might expect good weather. It was a very nice country in summertime, judging from what he saw and experienced last summer. He had been in the trenches for 5 days, and they were expecting to leave there on the Friday of the same week – if they had luck. The letter, and the following, was received by his brother in Widnes:

> SIR,– This letter was sent by Private S. Dean to you on the 9th inst., and he was killed whilst on trench duty on the 10th inst., and I thought the least I could do was to inform you of his death, and his comrades feel for you in your great trouble. And you all have our sympathy.
>
> Yours sincerely,
>
> H.O. BRITTEN, C.S.M.

Private Dean, who was more popularly known amongst the Flintonians as 'Sammy Dean', enlisted in the King's Own Scottish Borderers when he was at Ashton-in-Makerfield, and was immediately sent to the Battalion in the Edinburgh district. After some months' training in military work he left with the Battalion for France, and July last year he was admitted into one of the Belgian Hospitals, where he said he was treated for an attack of pneumonia. When he had sufficiently recovered to be removed he was conveyed to England, where he was sent to hospitals, one of which was at Ipswich. He subsequently paid a visit to his friends in November 1915 in Flint, and left for Lancashire in order to see his friends there, leaving for France again a fortnight before Christmas. In his younger days Dean had been employed at the Chemical Yard, and when the chemical industry was reputed to be in an exceedingly flourishing condition. In the mid-1890s Sammy Dean was considered to be one of the most expert centre half-backs of the Association Code in Wales. He learned his football in the Borough, and played several seasons with the Flint Town Football Club team. In those days the Association game was increasing in importance in Flint; and Dean was always a great favourite amongst the home spectators and many of whom travelled miles to witness his prowess in leading his side to victory. Though the matches were often invested with much excitement, and the work of players conducted with fearless vigour, Sammy was classed as a clean exponent of the game. The team was known to be one of the best on the North Wales Coast, and frequently took part in the Welsh and English Cup Ties. His services were often hunted after by other clubs, but he remained faithful to his team, and upon one occasion he played in a match of picked 11s representing Wales in the South Wales area. His abilities as a half-back were not ignored by the Welsh Association.

Eventually, Dean left Flint for the mining locality of Ashton-in-Makerfield, near Wigan, for employment; and then he became associated with the team of that town, figuring in matches for the team, and others, throughout Lancashire. The information

A newspaper photo of Private Thomas Dean

before mentioned in the letter from his Company Sergeant Major indicates that he has manfully played his last game as a true patriot of his King and Country on the battlefield; and his memory will be revered by all those who were acquainted with him.

Sammy's brother Thomas had a son, also named Thomas, who was born in Flint in 1897, and the family moved to live at 5, Wood Street, Widnes. Thomas junior served in the war as a Private, No. 41466, with the 1/7th Battalion, the Worcester Regiment (Territorial Force). He was killed in action at the Battle of Passchendaele, Belgium on 26th August, 1917 aged 19.

In addition to official notice the following letter has been received by the deceased's aunt, from her husband, who was in the same company as Private Dean.

> I am upset about poor Tommy Dean. As he said to me before going over the top he wished me the best of luck, and I wished him the same, but poor little fellow – it was through trying to save his mate's life (a St Helen's soldier) that they both got killed together. His mate, from what I can make out, was on fire. All his ammunition was burning, and he (the deceased) went to get them off, when they both got shot.

Private Dean was called to the colours in February 1917, and was drafted to France in the following July. He was in civil life employed at the Hutchinson Works. As a boy he attended Simm's Cross School, and was a member of the Boy Scouts. He attended St Ambrose Church.

He is commemorated on the Tyne Cot Memorial, Belgium on Panels 75 to 77, Widnes war memorial and St Ambrose Parish Church, Widnes.

IN MEMORIAM

Sleep on, dear brother, in a foreign grave,
Your life for your country you nobly gave;
No loved one beside you to say goodbye,
But safe in God's keeping now you lie.

Fondly remembered by his Brother and Sister, R and K Jones. Duke Street, Flint.
(County Herald, 9th February, 1917)

He has gone to his last commission,
To the beautiful land called rest.

From his brother and sister, R and K. Jones. 74, Duke Street, Flint.
(County Herald, 15th February, 1918)

SERGEANT
GEORGE ROBERT DENTON

19112, 16th (Service) Battalion
Royal Welsh Fusiliers

George Robert Denton was born on 13th July, 1892 at Dee Bank Cottages, Halkyn, and the youngest of two children to James Arthur Denton and Mary Sarah (Davies).

The Denton family lived for some years in Halkyn, then moved to 2, Bennett's Row, Oakenholt.

George worked for seven years in the offices of the United Alkali Company, Flint, as a commercial clerk, then in 1912 went to reside at Oldham and became an employee of the well-known Platt's Works who manufactured textile machinery.

He married Edith Wrigley in 1913, at St John's Parish Church, Oldham and came to live with his parents in Flint at Moorings, Chester Road. They had a son named James Arthur who was born in Flint in 1914, married Gertrude Stott in Oldham, in 1937, and died in Rickmansworth, Hertfordshire in 2003.

Sergeant Denton with his wife Edith and son James Arthur

Before the war George had served for four years with the Territorial Army. He enlisted in Flint on 28th December, 1914 and landed in France in December 1915.

Sergeant Denton died in France on 8th March, 1916 as a result of a gunshot wound in the head from a German sniper's rifle. He was buried in the Bethune Town Cemetery, Pas de Calais, France, (Plot V, Row A, Grave 87).

After her husband's death, Edith returned to Oldham with son James to live with her parents at 47, Worcester Street (which was later named Halkyn House).

Sergeant Denton is remembered on three war memorials: Flint Town, St David's Parish Church, Oakenholt and Oddfellows Hall, Flint. He is also commemorated on the North Wales Heroes' Memorial Arch, Bangor. He was awarded the 1914–15 Star, British War Medal and Victory Medal.

George was regarded as an intelligent young man and, whilst living in Oldham, attended the services at the Hollinwood Congregational Church, Manchester Road with his wife and friends.

His abilities extended in the direction of music, and it is stated that when he lived at home in Oakenholt he had officiated occasionally as organist in the St David's Church Sunday School, and also at the Church.

For his intelligence in his military duties Sergeant Denton secured well-deserved promotions, and it was said that it was only shortly before he met with his fatal wound he had been promoted to the rank of Sergeant. Amiable of disposition, and ever ready to do his duty, he was much respected by his comrades, who felt his loss most keenly.

It is believed that he met with his fatal wound when on duty at Levantie, on the Le Bassee Road. Mrs Denton, his widow, received the official notification of his death, which stated that he died at a clearing station in France from the effects of a "gunshot wound in the head received in action." The bullet penetrated the lower portion of the back of the head and passed through the neck. The following Sunday morning, at the St David's Church, a special memorial service was held, and was attended by a sympathetic congregation. The Reverend Humphrey Lloyd delivered a very appropriate discourse, in which he paid special tribute to the memory of the deceased soldier who, he stated, had been an organist in their Sunday School. He had been of much assistance to the work connected with that church when he resided in the district; they missed him very much, and he was sure that the residents of the whole of the neighbourhood were in deep sympathy with the family. The service was of an impressive character, and the following hymns were sung: Thy Ways, Not Mine, O Lord, Rock of Ages, When Our Heads are Bowed with Woe. At the evening service the hymns were: Onward Christian

Soldiers, Eternal Father, Lead, Kindly Light, and Nearer my God to Thee. Sergeant Denton was a member of the Loyal Flint Castle Lodge of Independent Order of Oddfellows (Manchester Unity).

By early 1918 Oldham born Edith was living at 52, Oxford Street, Werneth, Oldham, where she died in 1958, aged 67.

George's father, James Arthur, was born in Meliden and died 29th December, 1938, aged 79, at his home, Ivy Cottage, 335, Chester Road, Flint, and buried in the Northop Road Cemetery.

Mr Denton came to Flint in the 1880s as an employee of the old United Alkali Company, with whom he had rose to the position of traffic foreman, which post he held for over 40 years. When the company left Flint he retired and became one of the firm's pensioners. He was a staunch churchman and member of the St David's Church, Oakenholt, where for many years he was a Sunday School teacher and also Sunday School Superintendent. In politics he was a Conservative and was formerly a member of the Flint Conservative Club, where at one time he served on the committee. He was a member of the Flint Castle Lodge of Oddfellows.

George's mother, Mary Sarah was born in Northop and died 21st May, 1949, aged 83, and buried with her husband. She was a member of the St David's Church, Oakenholt, and was a former member of the British Legion.

Edith and James Arthur

ROLL OF HONOUR

Not dead to me, I loved him dear,
Not lost but gone before;
He lives with me in memory still,
And will for ever more.
Sleep on, dear George in a soldiers grave,
Your life for your country you nobly gave,
No one stood near you to bid you goodbye,
But safe in God's keeping now you lie.
Dear Dada, how I wish your grave was here,
I would take such lovely flowers;
But angels, dear Dada, will guard you there
Through all the darkest hours.
His ever sorrowing widow (Edith) and baby (Jim).
Halkyn House, Worcester Street, Werneth, Oldham.
(County Herald, 9th March, 1917)

Sleep on, dear son, in a soldier's grave,
A grave we shall never see;
But as long as life and memory last
We shall still remember thee.
Sadly missed by his Father and Mother, Brother and Sister. Moorings, Flint.
(County Herald, 9th March, 1917)

Man's inhumanity to man
Makes countless thousands mourn.
His dear brother Charlie in France.
(County Herald, 8th March, 1918)

He bravely answered duty's call,
He bravely fought and fell;
He did his best for one and all,
And for those who loved him well.
Oft I think of you, dear George,
And my heart is sad with pain,
Oh, this world would be all Heaven
Could I have you back again.
Ever sorrowing widow (Edith).
(County Herald, 10th March, 1922)

Sometime, someday in a better land,
My daddy and I will meet and understand.
Ever sorrowing son (Jim). 52, Oxford Street, Werneth, Oldham.
(County Herald, 10th March, 1922)

The Widow and Son of the late Sergeant G R Denton wish it
to be known that owing to them not being notified that a war
memorial was being erected in Flint,
that is the reason no wreath was laid on the Cenotaph from them at
the official ceremony.
Sorrowing Widow and Son, Edith and Jim, 52, Oxford Street,
Oldham.
(County Herald, 15th October, 1926)

PRIVATE
JOHN DODD

**12449, 8th (Service) Battalion
Royal Welsh Fusiliers**

John Dodd was born in 1890 in Eastham, Chester, and the fourth of six children to John Dodd and Sarah (Foster).

John's parents were both born in Little Sutton, Wirral; John, who was a Master Mariner in the Merchant Service, in c.1855 and Sarah in c.1857.

Soon after John junior was born the family moved to Chester Road, Little Sutton, Wirral and the 1901 census found them living at 13, Harrison's Terrace, Little Sutton.

A newspaper photo of Private Dodd

John married Susan Smith at the English Presbyterian Chapel, Chester Road, Flint, on 18th December, 1910. She was born in Flint and a daughter of William Henry Smith, a mariner's mate in the Merchant Service, and his wife Caroline (c1861–1947). Caroline was employed as a domestic servant at Huntley Lodge, Flint, and resided at 191, Chester Road, Flint.

The 1911 census revealed John Junior to be living at Broad Oak, Northop, the home of farmer John Cheers Waight, where he was employed as a farm labour. It is not known where his wife Susan was at this time, but John parents were now living at 24, Black Brook Street, Chester. It is not known what became of them after this date.

John and Susan had two children: John Henry (1911–1944) and Richard (1914–?). They set up home at 9, Queen Street, Flint, and John changed jobs to work as an ironworker at the Hawarden Bridge Ironworks, Shotton.

He enlisted in Shotton on 28th August, 1914 and served as a dispatch rider. He landed at Gallipoli circa June 1915.

He died in Malta on 19th October, 1915 from the effects of pneumonia and was buried in the Pieta Military Cemetery, Malta (Plot A, Row XV, Grave 6).

He is remembered on two war memorials: Flint Town and the English Presbyterian Chapel, Chester Road, Flint, and was awarded the 1914–15 Star, British War Medal and Victory Medal. He is also commemorated on the North Wales Heroes' Memorial Arch, Bangor.

Private Dodd's last letter home was dated 2nd October, 1915. He wrote informing people that he was in good health. He was well-known and very popular among his comrades in Flint.

Susan re-married in 1919 to Reginald Dennis Blakemore (1890–1980) and they had five children – Elizabeth, William Joseph, Lilian May, Sheila and Reginald Dennis.

John and Susan's eldest son, John Henry, served in World War 2 as a Trooper with the 3rd King's Own Hussars, Royal Armoured Corps, No. 4193804, and died in Italy on 26th May, 1944 and buried in Cassino War Cemetery, Italy (Plot XI, Row J, Grave 9). He married Eva Hough of Flint in 1935.

Susan with two children from her second marriage

Susan died 17th January 1951, aged 60, after a short illness, at her home, 187, Chester Road, Flint, and buried in the Old London Road Cemetery with second husband, Reginald. She was a member of the English Presbyterian Church.

PRIVATE
JOHN WILLIAM ECCLES

32490, 2nd Battalion Lancashire Fusiliers

John William (Willie) Eccles was born on 13th September, 1897 at 4, Gardeners Row, Oakenholt and baptised on 24th October, 1897 at St Mary's Parish Church, Flint. He was the illegitimate son of Elizabeth Eccles. In the 1901 census Willie and his mother were living at 4, Gardeners Row with her parents, William and Mary Eccles, and her brothers Willie and Joseph, and sisters Florrie, Edith and Mabel.

In 1902 Elizabeth married Robert William Jones in Chester and they had seven children and first lived at 5, Queen Street, and much later at 63, Woodfield Avenue. Willie, however, continued to live with his grandparents William and Mary who had moved to 1, Gardeners Row. Willie was employed by the North Wales Paper Mill, Oakenholt, and was unmarried.

He enlisted in Flint on 17th September. 1916 with the Royal Field Artillery, No. 160712, but it is not known when he transferred to the Lancashire Fusiliers.

He was killed in action in France on 3rd May, 1917 and buried in the Brown's Copse Cemetery, Roeux, France (Plot III, Row E, Grave 5).

He is remembered on two war memorials – Flint Town and St David's Parish Church, Oakenholt, and was awarded the British War Medal and Victory Medal.

He is also commemorated on the North Wales Heroes' Memorial Arch, Bangor.

Willie's mother, Elizabeth, died at Flint Cottage Hospital, following an operation, on Thursday, 21st May, 1943, aged 63. An inquest was held the following day where Dr Bateman said Mrs Jones suffered from a strangulated hernia and he suggested that she undergo an operation. He thought that if she did not have an operation Mrs Jones would have died within a few hours. The coroner, Mr H Llewelhyn Jones, returned a verdict that Mrs Jones died from "post operational shock following an operation for strangulated hernia." Mrs Jones was born in Flint and in her early days was employed as a domestic servant. She was well known and held in high esteem, and was a member of the Parish Church. She had been an invalid for some years. She is buried in the Old London Road Cemetery with her husband and son Robert William.

The grave of Willie's mother and stepfather

IN MEMORIAM

In memory of William Eccles

A light is from our household gone,
A voice we loved is stilled,
A place is vacant in our home,
Which can never be filled.
Gone, but not forgotten.
From his sorrowing Mother
(County Herald, 11th August, 1916)

PRIVATE
ROBERT THOMAS EDWARDS

241604, 1/5th (Flintshire) Battalion Royal Welsh Fusiliers

Robert Thomas (Tommy) Edwards was born on 16th August, 1882 in Mold and the youngest of four children to Edward and Ann Edwards.

Tommy's parents were both born in Ysceifiog and continued to live there until Tommy was born and by 1891 had moved to 5, Halkyn Street, Flint. Mr Edwards was employed as an assistant superintendant for the Prudential Insurance Company. He was born in c1845 and died before 1901. By the 1901 census his widow Ann and children had moved to 52, Halkyn Street in a row known as Foundry Villas.

Also living with them was Tommy's sister, Maria Ellen, and her husband, Mr Isaac Peers Davies, who was in business as a grocer and provision dealer in Church Street, Flint, and who had employed Tommy as his assistant.

Tommy remained there until he joined the army and he never married.

He enlisted in Flint on 11th April, 1916 and his service record is as follows:- Home base until 10th December, 1916; embarked Southampton, 11th December, 1916; disembarked from His Majesty's Troopship, Kalyan, in Alexandria, on 26th December, 1916; joined battalion for duty In the Field, 31st December, 1916; on enlistment he was 5 ft 4 in, chest 34½ in, weighed 113lb and his physical development was good.

He was killed in action at the Battle of Gaza, Palestine, on 26th March, 1917. He has no known grave but is commemorated on the Jerusalem Memorial, Israel, on Panels 20 to 22.

He is remembered on the Flint Town war memorial and was awarded the British War Medal and Victory Medal. He is also commemorated on the North Wales Heroes' Memorial Arch, Bangor.

Tommy was a member of the Welsh Baptist Church, and very well known and much respected by a large number of the people. During his experience at the Front he forwarded exceedingly interesting letters home. He was for several seasons a member of the Flint Liberal Club billiard team and was regarded as one of the brilliant cueists of Flintshire.

Tommy's mother, Ann, was born in Ysceifiog c.1846 and was still alive in May 1922.

IN MEMORIAM

*In loving birthday remembrance.
Oh blessed hope, beyond the hope
That lies beneath the sod,
That gallant lads we love and lose
Go home to be with God!*

*"For greater love hath none," Christ said,
"Than he who for a friend lies dead."*
Mother, Sister and Brother.
Halkyn Street, Flint.
(County Herald, 17th August, 1917)

❧

*Sweet be your rest, dear brother,
'Tis sweet to breathe your name,
In life we loved you very dear,
In death we do the same.*
Sadly missed by all at Foundry Villa, Flint.
(County Herald, 28th March, 1919)

❧

*When last we saw his smiling face,
He looked so young and brave,
We little thought how soon he'd be
Laid in a soldier's grave.*
Never forgotten by his loving brother and sister-in-law,
John and Ada; also Louie and Eveline.
(County Herald, 28th March 1919)

❧

*Dear brother in our hearts you still have a place,
Our home is so lonely without your dear face,
We think of you always and oft breathe your name,
We cannot forget you, love will always remain.*
From his loving Brother and Sister-in-law
John and Ada, and Nieces.
67, Partington Street, Castleton, Lancs.
(County Herald, 26th March, 1920)

PRIVATE
ARTHUR ELLIS

2233, 2/5th (Flintshire) Battalion Royal Welsh Fusiliers

Arthur Ellis was born in Flint in 1896 and baptised on 9th September, 1896 at St Mary's Parish Church, Flint. He was the fourth or fifth (he had a twin sister) of nine children to John (Jack) Ellis and Mary Ellen (Edwards).

When Arthur was a boy the Ellis family lived at 36, Earl Street, Flint, then by 1911 had settled at 72, Earl Street.

Arthur's eldest brother, Robert Edward, was one of the most promising young men in the town, and was very highly respected. He took a most prominent part in much of the social and religious life of Flint. Amongst the many offices he held were those of secretary to the Church of England Men's Society, assistant secretary to the local branch of Oddfellows, referee in the Chester and District Football league, etc. He was a member of the Parish Church choir, a bell ringer, a member of the Conservative Club, and a teacher of shorthand. Employed as a clerk at the United Alkali Works, Flint, he worked up to Monday 22nd December, 1910 when he had to take to his bed after an attack of pneumonia and died two days later aged just 21. The flags at the Conservative Club and Oddfellows Hall were flown at half-mast. The funeral, which took place on the Saturday afternoon, was extremely impressive. Over 800 representatives of various societies joined the procession from the house to the Welsh church, and again to the cemetery, a remarkable testimony to the popularity of the deceased. Two of the bearers were Sergeant George Robert Denton (see page 111), and Lieutenant Hugh Osborne Williams (see Volume Two).

Cambridge Military Hospital, where Private Ellis died

Arthur, who was never married, was employed in the Offices of the United Alkali Company's Works in Flint, and before the war had served with the Territorial Army. He enlisted in Flint in circa August 1914 and served in Egypt.

He died after a brief illness at Cambridge Military Hospital on 2nd July, 1916 and was buried in the Northop Road Cemetery, Flint (Grave 3, Line 7, South Side) with his sister, Sarah, who died in May, 1900, aged 3 weeks, and brother Robert Edward.

He is remembered on three war memorials: Flint Town, St Mary's Parish Church, Flint and Oddfellows Hall, Flint. He is also commemorated on the North Wales Heroes' Memorial Arch, Bangor. It is not known if he was awarded any medals as his medal card cannot be traced, although it is almost certain he would have been awarded the usual British War Medal and Victory Medal.

The funeral of Private Ellis took place on the afternoon of Saturday 8th July 1916 amid manifestations of deep and respectful mourning. He was exceedingly popular amongst his soldier comrades in the 2/5th Battalion of the Royal Welsh Fusiliers, and in the Infantry Brigade Offices at Bedford. He died after a brief illness in a hospital at Cambridge, with his parents present, whither he had been removed for special treatment, the previous Sunday evening; and his remains were conveyed by rail to Flint on Wednesday, where they arrived in the evening. The inhabitants of the Borough never failed to honour the memory of any of its native departed soldiers, and at the funeral they were, in a large degree, sorrowing with the bereaved parents and relatives of the young soldier and though only 19 years of age had been in the army a considerable time serving his King and country faithfully.

Shortly before half-past three o'clock in the afternoon a large number of general mourners assembled at the Ellis residence in Earl Street, and as it was decided to accord the deceased full military honours a detachment of the 5th Territorials Welsh Regiment were in attendance from their military quarters of Queensferry Government Factory, together with a number of men from the Castle Headquarters, under the command of Lieutenant Brook. The massive coffin, which was covered with the Union Jack, and upon which were placed the cap and belt of the deceased, with a profusion of beautiful floral tributes, was brought from the interior of the house, whereupon the opening prayers of the burial office were read by the Reverend Canon W Llewelhyn Nicholas, MA, RD (Rector), who was accompanied by the Reverend R E Jones, MA (senior curate). The cortege was then formed, with the members of the Welsh Regiment leading as

The grave of Private Ellis and his brother, Robert Edward, and sister, Sarah

the firing party with reversed arms; then came a numerous attendance of members of the Loyal Flint Castle Lodge of Independent Order of Oddfellows (Manchester Unity), each wearing the mourning sash, and carrying sprigs of flowering thyme; and then there came the remains, borne by members of the local headquarters of the Royal Welsh Fusiliers The chief mourners followed immediately behind the remains, and the long procession afterwards comprised chiefly employees of the United Alkali Company's various departments of the Works. The procession having arrived at the Welsh (St. Catherine's) Church, the remains were placed near the choir stalls, the organist (Mr Pryce Jones) meanwhile discoursing one of Battersill's funeral compositions.

The interior of the church was nearly crowded with people who were paying their last tributes of respect to the deceased, and it was noticeable that included in the congregation were parents of soldiers who had been wounded recently and were lying in hospitals; Lieutenant Lionel Williams, Sergeant J A Edwards, and other soldiers who were on leave of absence from their Battalions at home. There were also present several tradespeople, and members of the Conservative Club. The Reverend Canon Nicholas (Lieutenant Colonel Chaplain) read the service, and the hymns "For ever with the Lord," and "Brief life is here our portion," were feelingly sung. As the remains were being conveyed from the church the organist played the "Dead March" (Saul), and the funeral procession having been re-formed, it went to the Cemetery, where in a new portion of the "hallowed acre" the remains were reverently consigned to their last resting place. The solemnity of the occasion was characterized by much impressiveness, for there, in the exhilarating breezes of the early evening, a large concourse of people had gathered to honour the departed. The Reverend R E Jones read the committal lines, after which the usual volleys were discharged over the grave, and the Last Post sounded. There yet remained another honour to be paid to the deceased, and that by the Oddfellows, whose solemn funeral ritual took place. The members of the Lodge, of which the deceased was a member, congregated round the grave, and Brother John Owen Jones, who is the present Grandmaster of the District comprising the whole of the Lodges connected with Flintshire, read the service, which was listened to by all the mourners; and as the members of the Lodge took their last leave they deposited on the coffin in the grave the sprigs of thyme, which is emblematic of one of the phases of the true brotherhood of Oddfellowship.

Of the many magnificent wreaths placed on the grave one was particularly significant: "With deepest regret" from Private William Parry (see Volume Two), 1/5th Royal Welsh Fusiliers, Egypt.

Arthur's mother, Mary Ellen, was born in Liverpool and died 2nd December, 1919, aged 53. At the funeral the Rector of Flint (Reverend Canon Nicholas) officiated at the house and conducted the service in St Catherine's Church and at the graveside in the Northop Road Cemetery. In addition to the family, representatives of the Foresters, the Conservative Club, and many other prominent townspeople, attended the funeral.

Jack and Mary Ellen's youngest child, Samuel, died on 9th October, 1923 aged 20. He was an apprenticed fitter at the United Alkali Company's works at Flint and was afterwards transferred to Weston Point to complete his apprenticeship. He was of a studious nature, and regularly attended the evening technical classes. He was a popular playing member of the Helsby Football Club , and was a promising footballer. He came home on Friday, 5th October complaining of pains in his head and died four days later. He was a member of the Flint Castle Lodge of Oddfellows, and also a member of the

Flint Conservative Club, and the flags of the latter institute were hoisted half-mast out of respect. The funeral took place on Saturday the 13th in the presence of a large gathering of relatives and friends, and he was buried with his mother.

Arthur's father Jack was born in Hanley, Staffordshire and died on 2nd March 1932, aged 66, at his home, 72, Earl Street, and was buried with his wife and son Samuel.

Mr Ellis was educated at Flint Church School, after which he entered the employment of Messrs Muspratt Brothers and Huntley at their Chemical Works at Flint, and when the works were taken over by the United Alkali Company he was employed by them as the chief shipping clerk, continuing in that post until the works closed down. Then he entered the service of Messrs Courtaulds and for many years was a gatekeeper at the Castle Works. He was a prominent member of the Flint Conservative Club, where he served on the committee, and when he died the flag at the club was flown at half-mast as a token of respect. He was a great lover of all sport, and in his younger days he was a well-known cricketer playing for Flint and the Flintshire County teams. In the old days of the Flint Town Football Club – in the 1890s – he was a member of the committee at a time when his brother, Mr E A Ellis, then played at right half for the town team. He was also a great bowling enthusiast and a good player, being a valuable member of the Flint Conservative Club Bowling team. In 1927, he won the Ashton Cup for bowling, the competition taking place at Prestatyn. His eldest son, Mr Jack Ellis, Rhos, was a right full back for Tranmere Rovers and Wrexham, and later a member of the Wrexham Rural District Council, chairman of the Rhos Branch of the British Legion, and chairman of the Rhos Charitable Association. His second son, Mr R T Ellis, was with the Castner-Kellner Imperial Chemical Industries, and his third son, Mr Albert Ellis, was employed by Messrs Courtaulds at their Castle Works. Mr Ellis was a member of the Ancient Order of Foresters for 50 years, and a member of St Mary's Parish Church, Flint where, at one time, he was a sidesman there.

PRIVATE
ARTHUR LESLIE EVANS

15776, 17th (Service) Battalion (1st City) The King's (Liverpool Regiment)

Arthur Leslie Evans was born in Flint on 24th December, 1893 and baptised on 7th January, 1894 at St Mary's Parish Church, Flint. He was the youngest of seven children to Joseph Wood Massey Evans Justice of the Peace, County Councillor, and Mary (Foulkes) of Pendre, Church Street, Flint.

Arthur Leslie was a godson of the Reverend Canon Llewelhyn Nicholas, rector of St Mary's Parish Church.

Arthur's sister, Sarah Olive (1884–1965), married Otto Charles Kahn (son of physician Dr Herman Kahn) at St Mary's Parish Church on Flint on 30th June, 1909. A resident of Rochelle, New York, he was Departmental Manager of the Union Pacific Railway. Their engagement was announced in the New York Times on 22nd June, 1909.

Another sister, Mai (1882–1976), married Otto's brother, Joseph Henry (1884–1946), also at St Mary's Parish Church, on 30th April, 1913. He was a merchant, of Moffel Bay, South Africa, but later resided in Sutton, Surrey. He fought for the English in the South African Campaign (1899–1902).

Their youngest sister, Nina (1889–1964), married Reginald Elsenham Montgomery Moore (1892–1926) at All Saints' Church, Sydenham, London, on 19th June, 1920, and they resided in Prestatyn. He was the son of the late Dr William Holmes Moore, of Charters Towers, Queensland, and Mrs Moore of Sydenham, London.

Arthur, who never married, was an Apprentice clerk with Messrs J Blythe and Sons Corn Merchants, Bootle, Merseyside. He enlisted in Liverpool on 1st September, 1914 and his service record is as follows: Belton Camp, Grantham, 29th November, 1914; Whiston Hospital with influenza, 8th January, 1915 to 13th January, 1915; Rain Hill Hospital after vaccination, 24th February, 1915 to 3rd March, 1915; Larkhill Camp, Salisbury, 5th September, 1915; embarked Southampton, 6th November, 1915; landed at Boulogne, 7th November, 1915; granted 1st Good Conduct Badge on completion of 2 years' service, 1st September, 1916; leave to UK, 4th – 14th February, 1917. His personal belongings were sent to Mr Alfred Harvey Blake, 8, Seafield Drive, New Brighton, Cheshire and were: identity disc, photographs, safety razor, fountain pen, scissors, leather purse, 2 pocket mirrors in case, knife and a half-Franc note (defaced) souvenir. On enlistment he was 5 ft 10½ in, weighed 143lb, chest 34½ in, had dark complexion, brown eyes, black hair, scar on back of neck, and his physical development and vision were good.

He died on 6th December, 1917 at the No. 53, Casualty Clearing Station, Bailleul, France, from gunshot wounds in the chest and left thigh. He was buried in the Bailleul Communal Cemetery Extension (Nord), France (Plot III, Row E, Grave 40).

He is remembered on two war memorials: Flint House and St Mary's Parish Church, Flint. He is also commemorated on the North Wales Heroes' Memorial Arch, Bangor.

He is also remembered on his parents' headstone in the Old Ground of the Northop Road Cemetery, Flint, and was awarded the 1914–15 Star, British War Medal and Victory Medal.

On Monday the 10th December, 1917 Mr and Mrs Evans received a communication in a letter, and unofficially, that their youngest son, Private Arthur Leslie Evans, had been wounded; and further information was anxiously awaited.

Another letter was to hand from the Liverpool district on Tuesday morning corroborative of the information, and stating that Private Evans had sustained wounds while pursuing his duties. He was conveyed as speedily as possible to a dressing station so that his injuries should have the necessary attention.

Hopes were entertained by those who were with him that there would be a favourable turn in his condition, and Alderman Evans and his family were also somewhat buoyed up; but, early on Tuesday afternoon an official telegram arrived conveying the sad intelligence that Private Evans had died the following day. He would have been 24 years of age on the Monday next. He patriotically answered the call of his country and joined the army, and had been over two years at the Front. He was home on leave from the Front in February last. He was greatly respected by his soldier comrades, and beloved by all those who shared his acquaintance in his home surroundings.

A few days later Mr Evans received the following letter from Arthur's Commanding Officer.

3, King's Mount
Birkenhead

13/12/17

My dear Mr. Evans,

I am Transport Officer of the 17th King's and am at present home on leave, and only heard to-day the sad news of Leslie's death. I had a letter 3 days ago from my Assistant telling me Leslie and another man had been wounded and I had hoped for the best, but a rumour I heard last night caused me to look up A. H. Blake, who, of course told me of the calamity.

I have been his officer since June 1915, and may say it is entirely due to men of his stamp that I have one of the best Transports in France. He was devoted to his horses and his turn-out was a credit to himself and to the Battalion. His conduct was exemplary during the whole time he was with me, and his cheerful disposition enabled him to rise superior to the wretchedest surroundings. I never knew a kinder boy with animals, or a more trustworthy and I cannot adequately replace him. I feel the deepest sympathy with you all in your great loss, as it was easy to see from his letters home how close the family ties were.

Well, the poor boy has paid the greatest of all sacrifices, and we shall hope not in vain, but take consolation that he died as a soldier should, doing his duty cheerfully and bravely. His memory will always be with us, "as one of the best" and could any man have a better epitaph?

If there is anything I can do, Mr. Evans, to help you in any way, please do not hesitate to let me know, and in the meantime,

I am, Yours with deepest sympathy,
(Signed)

C. W. Marshall, Capt.

This verse, about life at Larkhill Camp, Salisbury, where Private Evans was stationed from 5th September, 1915 to 6th November, 1915, emphasises the importance of infantry training, and highlights the difficulties.

LARKHILL CAMP

There's an isolated desolate spot that I'd like to mention
Where all you hear is 'Stand at ease,' 'Slope arms,' 'Quick march,' 'Attention,'
'Slope arms,' 'Fix bayonets,' then 'Present,' they don't half put you through it
And as you stagger to your hut, the Sergeant shouts 'Jump to it.'
It's miles away from anywhere, by gad it's hard to have fun,
A bloke lived there for 50 years and never saw a woman.
There's only 2 lamps in the place, so tell it to your Mother
The postman always carries one, the policeman has the other
And if you want a jolly night and you don't care a jot
Just take a ride inside the car, the car they haven't got.
Lots and lots of tiny huts are dotted everywhere
For those who have to live in them, let's offer up a prayer
The soldiers live inside the huts, it fills my heart with sorrow
With tear stained eyes they say to us it's Lark Hill again tomorrow.
Inside the huts there's great big rats, as big as nanny goats
Just last night a soldier saw one, trying on his greatcoat.
For breakfast every morning it's like Old Mother Hubbard
You double round the hat three times and jump up at the cupboard.
Sometimes they give you bacon, sometimes they give you cheese
It forms platoons upon your plate, Orders Arms and Stands at Ease.
Every night you sleep on boards, just like a lot of cattle
and when you turn from left to right, your bones begin to rattle.
and when the bugle blasts at morn it drives you off your noodle
you knock the icebergs off your feet and damn and blast the bugle.

Anon

Arthur's older brother, Edward Nevylle (1879–1965), served in the war for 4½ years with the 17th King's (Liverpool Regiment) attaining the rank of Lieutenant. He served in France and Italy and was awarded the Military Cross in 1917 and the Edinburgh Gazette of 19th April, 1917 reported: "For conspicuous gallantry and devotion to duty. Accompanied by one man, he succeeded in capturing his enemy's position together with six prisoners. Later, he took command of his company and drove off an enemy counter-attack." It was reported he had experienced a number of miraculous escapes from serious injuries.

Joseph Wood Massey Evans was born on 3rd January, 1846 at Pendre in Church Street and died there on 30th October, 1929 and buried in the family plot in the Northop Road Cemetery.

Mr J W M Evans was a native of Flint, and extremely well known and highly respected in the town. He was born in the house in which he died, and was probably one of the oldest residents of the borough. He was the son of the late Mr and Mrs Joseph Evans. Mr Jos Evans conducted a general store known as Pendre Stores, and the late Mr Evans entered into business with his father when he was 18 years of age. After his father's death he carried on the business of Corn Miller at the Bryn Mill, which he visited five days before he died. He contracted a chill and was taken worse two days later, when Dr Dobey, Chester, was called in consultation with Drs J Humphry Williams and Bateman, but he gradually became weaker and passed away in the early hours of Wednesday morning.

In his younger days Mr Evans had been a prominent and popular public man. He served on the Flint Town Council in the late 1870s, and was also an alderman of the Flintshire County Council for some time. He was responsible for the planting of trees in Church Street to commemorate Queen Victoria's Diamond Jubilee in 1898. His name was enrolled on the Commission of the Peace in 1909. He was a staunch Conservative, and was president of the Flint Conservative Club for many years. He was also an ardent churchman and was a faithful member of St Mary's Parish Church, Flint, where at different times he occupied various offices, including those of warden and sidesman. Mr and Mrs Evans celebrated their golden wedding in June, 1928 when they were the recipients of many congratulatory messages. At the Parish Church on the Sunday morning following the funeral, the Rector (Reverend T J Davies, Bachelor of Arts) referred in sympathetic terms to the late Mr J W M Evans, and said that he had been greatly interested in Church work during his life, and had also been very active in public affairs. The Rector reminded the congregation that the late Mr Evans was baptised at the opening of the present Parish Church in 1848.

A 1922 newspaper advertisement for Mr Evans' business

The Evans' family vault

Joseph's wife, Mary, was born in Bagillt on 23rd July, 1851 and died at Pendre, after a long illness, on 7th June, 1935. She was buried with her husband and their daughters, Dorothy Vois (1886–1890) and Gladys Marie (1880–1933). Also in this grave are the parents of Mr J W M Evans – Joseph (1808–1863) and Maria Matilda (1814–1867), and their only daughter Annie Matilda, Justice of the Peace (1843–1933).

Mrs Evans, who was of a quiet disposition, was greatly attached to St Mary's Parish Church, and was well known and highly esteemed in Flint and district.

PRIVATE
JOHN EVANS

573, 1/5th (Flintshire) Battalion Royal Welsh Fusiliers

John Evans was born on 6th March, 1888 at 7, Princes Street, Flint and baptised as John Cullen Evans on 29th April, 1888 at St Mary's Parish Church, Flint. He was the youngest of seven children to John Evans and Harriet (Jones) and an uncle to Articifer William Arthur Evans (page 131).

John Senior was born in Flint and worked as a chemical labourer. He died at his home at 7, Princes Street on 21st November, 1903, aged 62, and was buried in the Northop Road Cemetery with his daughter Ann Jane, who died in 1892, aged 23. The 1911 census revealed John was employed as a chemical labourer and living with his widowed mother and older sister at 29, Feathers Street.

His mother, Harriet, who was also born in Flint, died in December, 1912 and is buried with her husband and daughter.

Before joining the army, John, who never married, had moved to 56, Chester Street, Flint and was now employed as an ironworker. He enlisted in Flint, but it is not known when, and landed at Gallipoli in August, 1915. He was killed in action at Gallipoli on 13th September, 1915. He has no known grave but is commemorated on the Helles Memorial, Turkey, on Panels 77 to 80

He is remembered on two war memorials: Flint House and St Mary's Parish Church, Flint, and was awarded the 1914–15 Star, British War Medal and Victory Medal. He is also commemorated on the North Wales Heroes' Memorial Arch, Bangor.

PRIVATE
PETER EVANS

15720, 10th (Service) Battalion Royal Welsh Fusiliers

Peter Evans was born in Flint in 1894 and baptised 20th July 1894 at St Mary's Parish Church, Flint, and was the third of six children to Edwin Evans and Gertrude (Cooper). He was a brother to Private Thomas Evans (page 128).

The Evans family were living at Leadbrook Cottage, Oakenholt when Peter's Liverpool born mother, Gertrude, died after a short illness in August 1902, aged just 34. She was buried in the Northop Road Cemetery. By the 1911 census widower Edwin had moved the family to 4, Bennetts Row, Oakenholt, and Peter, who never married, was employed as a silk worker, however on joining the army he was employed by the British Glanzstoff Manufacturing Company, Flint.

He enlisted in Flint on 26th September, 1914, joined at Wrexham and landed at Boulogne, France, on 27th September, 1915. He was killed in action by shrapnel in France on 20th July, 1916. He has no known grave but is commemorated on the Thiepval Memorial, France (Pier and Face 4A).

He is remembered on two war memorials: Flint Town and St David's Parish Church, Oakenholt and was awarded the 1914–15 Star, British War Medal and Victory Medal. He is also commemorated on the North Wales Heroes' Memorial Arch, Bangor. For his memorial service at St David's Church see Corporal John Bellis (page 15).

In late July, 1916 it was stated in various sources in the Borough that Private Evans had met with his death through wounds sustained on the battlefield in France. Evans, who was well known and respected in the Oakenholt locality, as well as by a number of residents in the town, was one of the first batches of young men of the Borough who left to join the Forces at Wrexham after which he was drafted into one of Lord Kitchener's Battalions of the Royal Welsh Fusiliers. He was very popular amongst his co-workers at the British Glanzstoff Manufacturing Company's Works, and his friends were exceedingly sorry to learn of his death.

The intelligence respecting the death of Evans was soon verified, and a letter had been received by his father from his Officer, who stated that he was wounded so seriously with shrapnel that death was instantaneous.

Peter's father, Edwin, was born in Wrexham and died on 5th January, 1929, aged 62, at his home, 3, Gardeners Row, Oakenholt, and is buried with his wife. Mr Evans was employed for many years by the North Wales Paper Company, Oakenholt. He was of a kind and generous disposition, and was well known and highly esteemed in the neighbourhood.

Mrs Gertrude Evans and Mr Edwin Evans, the mother and father of Private Peter Evans and Private Thomas Evans (below)

PRIVATE
THOMAS EVANS

241471, 1/5th (Flintshire) Battalion Royal Welsh Fusiliers

Thomas (Tom) Evans was born in Flint in March, 1897, and baptised on 2nd April, 1897 at St Mary's Parish Church, Flint, and the fourth of six children to Edwin Evans and Gertrude (Cooper). He was a brother to Private Peter Evans (see above for details of his parents).

The 1911 census revealed Thomas was employed as a shop boy and living at 3, Gardeners, Row, Oakenholt. He never married before joining the army was working as a spinner.

He enlisted in Flint on 22nd February, 1916 with the 3/5th Royal Welsh Fusiliers (RWF), No. 3742.

He was medically examined in Flint by Dr Twemlow of 33, Church Street. He was 5 ft 4 in, weighed 8st 8lb, chest 35 in, and his physical development was good as was his vision.

His service record is as follows: home based from 22nd February, 1916 to 26th June, 1916; embarked on His Majesty's Troopship, Northland, at Devonport, 27th June, 1916; disembarked at Alexandria, on 9th July, 1916; joined at Base Depot, Alexandra, on 9th July, 1916; joined for duty at 1/5th RWF in Ismailia, 14th July, 1916; entered hospital at 3rd Highland Field Ambulance with "scabies," 13th January, 1917; 2 Australian Stat Hospital with "scabies," 19th January, 1917; 24th Stationary Hospital with "scabies," 1st March, 1917; 31st General Hospital at Port Said with "scabies," 3rd March, 1917; rejoined Battalion for duty in the field, 12th May, 1917; Posted to 5/6th RWF, on 2nd August, 1918.

Gertrude, Private Peter Evans' (page 127) and Private Thomas Evans' mother.

Private Evans accidentally received a gunshot wound in the right pelvis on 20th September, 1918 and taken to No. 74 Casualty Clearing Station, Egypt, where it was reported he was dangerously ill. He died there on 28th September.

A Court of Inquiry assembled in the Field on the 30th September, 1918, by order of Major T H Parry Distinguished Service Order Commanding 5/6th Royal Welsh Fusiliers for the purpose of inquiring into the circumstances under which 241471 Private T Evans "C" Company 5/6th RWF was injured.

In the presence of Captain A K Richardson 3rd RWF (President) and Lieutenant W Marshall 5/6th RWF & 2nd Lieutenant W N Roberts 1/6th RWF (Members). The Court having assembled pursuant to order, proceed to take evidence.

<u>1st witness: Captain J B Marsden Commanding Officer 'C' Company 5/6th RWF</u>
I was in action with my Company and about midnight I noticed two figures silhouetted in the moonlight approaching my right rear. I ordered my acting Company sergeant major to halt & challenge them. He picked up a rifle and moved towards them. They appeared to be moving in what I considered to be a suspicious manner. The acting sergeant major challenged them three times. On the third time one appeared to double off back. The acting sergeant major then fired his rifle and I afterwards found my servant No 241471 Pte T Evans RWF had been wounded. I should say they were between 50 and 60 yards away. Stretcher-bearers were detailed to convey the injured man to Battalion Headquarters. These men had received no orders from me to be wandering about.

<u>2nd witness: 240863 Private Williams, J 5/6th RWF</u>

On 19th September at about midnight Pte Evans T (No 241471) and I were going to Company Headquarters to fetch our water bottle. We were challenged by the acting Company sergeant major twice. Pte Evans answered the challenge twice: "Officers servant" and I shouted "Friend" once. Then the acting sergeant major & I observed that No 241471 Pte Evans had been hit in the hip. We were roughly 30 yards away when the sergeant major challenged. I went to Pte Evans assistance.

<u>3rd witness: 240575 Sergeant Hession "C" Company 5/6th RWF</u>

I was with Capt Marsden OC "C" Coy when he saw two men approaching from our right flank rear and asked me to challenge. I called loudly: "Halt! Who goes there?" There was no reply. I advanced 5 or 6 paces and repeated the challenge. Again there was no response. I advanced further and again repeated the challenge. The men then halted but did not reply. I then ordered them to advance to be recognised. The man in rear appeared to turn about & move in the direction from which he had come. I then fired and immediately after one of the men called out: "Sergeant Hession." The man who had moved away came back and I found that Pte Evans had been wounded. Neither of these two men had to my knowledge received orders to leave the position in the line.

<u>4th witness: 62552 Private Bradbury, W V "C" Company 5/6th RWF</u>

On the night of the 19th September about midnight I was in Company with Captain Marsden and Coy Sergeant major Hession at Coy Headquarters. I heard Coy Sergeant major Hession challenge two figures in a crouching position moving in the direction of our rear right flank. I heard no reply to the challenges. I afterwards learnt that Pte T Evans had been wounded in the hip. The two figures appeared to be between 50 and 60 yards away.

<u>5th witness: Captain Harding Roberts 5/6th RWF "C" Company</u>

I heard someone shout: "Halt! Who goes there?" and immediately afterwards I heard someone shout out: "Oh my leg." I had heard no reply to the challenge. I phoned through to OC "C" Coy and asked him what had happened where after I was informed that Pte T Evans had been hit.

<u>T H Parry Major Commanding 5/6th RWF in the field — 2nd October, 1918</u>

I am of opinion that acting sergeant major Hession acted quite properly in firing when he did, as he took every precaution by way of challenging prior to doing. Pte Williams states in his evidence that both Pte Evans & himself heard the challenge and both replied to same. A/S M Hession must have been prevented from hearing the responses to his challenges owing to the firing that was going on at the time, and the distance at which Pte Evans and Pte Williams were from him. Taking into consideration all the circumstances I have come to the conclusion that the occurrence was accidental, and that no blame can be attached to anyone for it.

Private Evans was buried in the Jerusalem War Cemetery, Israel (Plot L, Grave 59). He is remembered on two war memorials:- Flint House and St David's Parish Church, Oakenholt, and was awarded the British War Medal and Victory Medal.

He is also commemorated on the North Wales Heroes' Memorial Arch, Bangor.

ARTICIFER
WILLIAM ARTHUR EVANS

M/749, Engine Room Artificer 4th Class Royal Navy

William Arthur Evans was born in Flint on 13th May, 1893 and baptised on 31st May, 1893 at St Mary's Parish Church, Flint. He was the eldest of three children to Captain William John Evans and Mary Florence (Eaton). He was a nephew to Private John Evans (page 127).

By 1901 the Evans family had moved to live at 33, Park Road, Dover, Kent, and by 1911 were living at 59, Buckland Avenue, Dover.

William Arthur never married and joined the Royal Navy straight from school and began as a Boy Artificer Engineer.

He enlisted in Chatham, Kent on 13th May, 1911 for 12 years and his service record is as follows: on enlistment he was 5 ft 7 in, chest 34 in, auburn hair, blue eyes, fresh complexion with freckles, and had a horizontal scar below the right knee. Served on the following ships: Tenedos, as a Boy Articifer, 1st January, 1909 to 15th July, 1910; Indus, 16th July, 1910 to 3rd January, 1912; Vivid II, 4th January, 1913 to 23rd March, 1913 – warned for inadequate progress and workmanship; Lord Nelson, 24th March, 1913 to 8th April, 1914; Pembroke II, 9th April, 1914 to 19th May, 1914; Queen, 20th May, 1914 to 2nd June, 1914; Pembroke II, 3rd June, 1914 to 5th June, 1914; Implacable, 6th June, 1914 to 1st August, 1914; Pembroke II, 2nd August, 1914 to 24th October, 1914; Recruit, 25th October, 1914 to 1st May, 1915; his conduct was described as very good throughout his career.

He was drowned at sea on 1st May, 1915 after his ship, His Majesty's Ship (HMS) Recruit, was blown up by a German submarine.

HMS Recruit was a "C" Class Destroyer launched by J & G. Thomson, Clydebank, yard No. 290, on 22nd August, 1896 and sunk on her first patrol 1st May, 1915, in the southern North Sea, 30 miles southwest from Galloper Light Vessel, off the Thames Estuary, Southeast England - torpedoed, probably by German "U 6" or "UB 6." The Recruit and sister-ship, Brazen were on patrol off Galloper when the Recruit was torpedoed. She was cut in two and sank around 11:20 hours. Brazen attacked the U-boat without success. Some 39 men were lost, but a Dutch steamship saved four officers and 22 ratings. Sources vary on the identity of the attacker and include U 6, U 66, UB 6 and UB 16.

His Majesty's Ship, Recruit

William Arthur's body was not recovered but he is commemorated on the Chatham Naval Memorial, on Panel 11. He is also remembered on the memorial at St Mary's Parish Church, Flint. It is not known if he was awarded any medals.

William Arthur's father, William John, was born in Flint and died in Dover in 1939, aged 73. He was Trinity House Pilot and a well-known navigator, who was for some time employed in bringing vessels from different Ports for Government purposes. He was an older brother to Private John Evans (page 127), and before his marriage resided at 7, Princes Street, Flint.

His mother, Mary Florence, also born in Flint, died in Folkestone in 1957, aged 85. She was a daughter of Thomas Eaton (c.1825–1891), licensed victualler of the Ship and Anchor Inn, Holywell Road, Flint, and his wife Bridget (c.1830–1887).

Chatham Naval Memorial

PRIVATE
THOMAS FERGUSON

3670, 1st Battalion Royal Welsh Fusiliers

Thomas (Tommy) Ferguson was born in Flint on 30th November, 1888 and baptised on 23rd December, 1888 at St Mary's Catholic Church, Flint. He was the fifth of nine children to Thomas Ferguson and Alice (Metcalfe). They lived at 26, Castle Street before settling at No. 35.

Tommy's mother, Alice, was born in Holywell and died 2nd March, 1900, aged 41, at her home in Castle Street, Flint, just three days after giving birth to a son named William, who himself died five days later. She was probably buried in Pantasaph Cemetery.

Thomas Senior was born in Holywell and died in June, 1907, aged 48, after a lingering illness and buried in Pantasaph Cemetery. He was a brickyard labourer and formerly a chemical labourer and fish dealer.

Tommy enlisted in Flint in August, 1914 and landed at Zeebrugge on 7th October, 1914.

He was killed in action in the Battle of Festubert, France, along with Corporal Thomas Henry Roberts and Lance-Corporal Charles Videon Williams (see Volume Two for both), on 16th May, 1915.

He has no known grave but is remembered on the Le Touret Memorial, France on Panels 13 and 14.

He is remembered on three war memorials: St Mary's Catholic Church, Flint, Bagillt Village and St Mary's Parish Church, Bagillt.

He was awarded the 1914–15 Star, British War Medal and Victory Medal.

It was reported that Tommy was married, and that his wife resided at Pentre Bach, Bagillt, but no record of this marriage could be found. His occupation is unknown.

The news reached Flint on Thursday morning 27th May, 1915 about the gallant work done by the Royal Welsh Fusiliers in the storming of a portion of the enemy's line in France, but unfortunately at a severe cost, and the sad news was contained in a letter sent home by Private Laurence Ferguson of the death in action of three local lads who were all from the same regiment: Corporal Tom Roberts, Lance-Corporal Charles V Williams and Private Thomas Ferguson.

The letter containing the sad news, which had not been officially confirmed, was received by Mrs T Campbell, 75, Mumforth Street, from her brother, Private Lawrence Ferguson. He wrote that he supposed she had heard of the death of their brother, Tom Ferguson, who although a member of the 3rd Battalion, was attached to the 1st Battalion in France. He wrote:

> Well, don't worry, he died for his King and country, and we must be proud of him. His name will now appear in the Roll of Honour as one of our gallant heroes who died for a great cause. There was many a mother's son who fell on Sunday, the 16th May . . . My regiment has covered itself with glory. We were first to take the enemy's trenches, and, my God, the devils who were spared on the other side will have cause to remember the gallant charge of the 1st Royal Welsh Fusiliers. We never looked behind, but went straight to the heart of the enemy. I am sorry to say Corporal Tom Roberts and Corporal C Williams were also killed in action on Sunday. Sergeant Jones was wounded. I put a bandage round the wound, but he bore up gallantly. We were under very heavy shell fire for three whole days. Our General spoke to the remains of the regiment this morning and thanked us for the gallant work which we had done by heading the attack of the Divisions.

Private Lawrence Ferguson concluded that there were some awful sights on the battlefield, which he would never forget. He further stated that the Royal Welsh Fusiliers performed a gallant deed in the battle, and were engaged in a desperate bayonet charge and that when the call came the charge was made; there was no lagging behind; and the result was that the regiment made its mark.

Mrs T Campbell received another letter from her brother Private Lawrence Ferguson, who was with the Machine Gun Section of the 1st Royal Welsh Fusilier's Battalion. Private Ferguson's letter was couched in endearing terms to his sister, and in tragic and pathetic terms respecting the death of his brother Private Thomas Ferguson, and other Flint comrades who fell in a great charge in Flanders. The particulars in the letter assisted in elucidating somewhat a mystery in respect of the statements as to Corporal Tom Roberts and Lance Corporal C Williams of Flint, who were reported by the War Office as having been killed in the battle referred to. Ferguson commenced his letter in thanking his sisters for their kindness in sending him weekly the "good old County Herald," and he received a letter and a paper on the 30th May. The last he saw of his brother, Private T Ferguson, was on the evening before the great charge, when "he came to my billet and shook hands with me and said he hoped we would both come through to-morrow's battle safe and sound. But a great chum of Tommy brought me the news of how Tommy met his death". He continued:

> God bless them; they died for a great cause – their King and country. When you write again I would thank you for a little news as to the welfare of Sergeant J Jones, of Flint, whom I bandaged during the attack. I sincerely hope he is in the pink; poor chap, he had a nasty wound. I agree with the letter in the "County Herald" from Private J Jones, in which he says that the Germans are a lot of pigs. I was myself present on the parade when the General spoke of the Welsh Fusiliers; and I also witnessed the white flag trick which the Germans so often use, with their cries of "Mercy" and "Comrade;" but all those things did not work with the boys of the Gallant 23rd. If they had left it to the boys there would not have been left one German to tell the tale; but those who were left or spared in that battle will, I am sure, have cause to remember the boys of the Gallant 1st RWF, who went for them "hell-for-leather." Such gallant deeds have never before been known. We took a parapet that morning, in the highest spirits – quite undaunted of any fears

Mrs Ferguson, widow of Private T Ferguson, received a sympathetic letter from Private Lawrence Ferguson, saying he is in the pink of condition.

> My dear brother died fighting for his King and country, and moreover, I am pleased to say he died the death of a hero. It so happened that on the Sunday morning my regiment were ordered to take up positions and make an attack upon the enemy, which we did in gallant style, driving the German devils hell for leather from trench to trench and showing no quarter. The boys of the RWF have left their mark on that portion of the enemy in that never to be forgotten charge. I am pleased to say I came out of that charge myself without a scratch, and I am now prepared for the next. The more we strike the quicker the end.
> It is all for a good cause. My regiment suffered heavy losses, but the gain was great.

Tommy's brother, Laurence, served in the army for eight years from 9th March, 1911 to 16th March, 1919, as a Private, first with the RWF, and ended his service with the Machine Gun Corps, No. 19190. During the war he was awarded the Mons Star. He married Sarah Wiggins (c.1895–1942), widow of Private Reuben Wiggins (see Volume Two), and died in 1958, aged 65.

PRIVATE
WILLIAM FORRESTER

93570, 17th (Service) Battalion Royal Welsh Fusiliers (2nd North Wales)

William (Willie) Forrester was born in Marchwiel, Wrexham on 23rd July, 1897 and was the sixth of seven children to William Henry Forrester and Caroline (Chapman).

Willie's mother, who was born in West Bromwich, died at Abenbury, near Wrexham, in September 1900, aged 36, and was buried in St Marcella's Churchyard, Marchwiel.

At the time of the 1901 census, the family were living at 17, Palmer Street, Wrexham, then a few months later Mr Forrester married spinster Elizabeth Ann Conway and they had a son, Berty Conway, who was born and died in 1902, and a daughter Mabel Agnes (1906–1999).

The Yacht Inn, Oakenholt

The 1911 census found William Henry as Proprietor of the Royal Oak Inn, Bagillt with wife Elizabeth as "Assisting in Business," and by the time the war began they had moved to the Yacht Inn, Oakenholt.

Willie's brother, Thomas Henry, served with the 8th Battalion Royal Welsh Fusiliers as Private No. 12582, from 31st August, 1914 to March, 1919, and was mentioned in a letter home, dated 12th February, 1916, by Corporal John Bellis (page 15), also of the 8th RWF.

Dear Sister & Bro

Just a few lines in answer to your letter I received safe but I have not seen anything of the parcel which you say you sent along with the fiths? But all the mails were held back Christmas time owing to the evacuations of the Peninsula. I was in the both evacuations of Suvla Bay & Cape Helles as our division made a success @ Suvla we had to go to Cape Helles to do the evacuation there and we got a rough time of it too.

We are now in Egypt and out of danger at present. I don't know for how long but I believe we are out for a good spell this time. There is talk of us going to do garrison duty. I had a letter from H Forrester last week the first we had heard of him since last August he has been at hospital at Cairo with scarlet fever. he is now waiting for new teeth. It is very hot here in the day. Hulley & Co are all doing well.

I now conclude hope you are all quite well as it leaves me.

Your Affec Bro
Jack

The "Hulley" he referred to was Private Joseph Albert Hulley (page 192). Willie never married and his occupation is unknown.

He enlisted in Wrexham on 23rd February, 1918 with the South Wales Borderers, No. 48633, but it is not known when he was transferred to the RWF.

He was killed in action in France on 4th September, 1918 and buried in the Guards' Cemetery, Lesboeufs, France (Plot VII, Row R, Grave 4).

He is remembered on two war memorials: Flint Town and St David's Parish Church, Oakenholt. He is also remembered on his parents' headstone in the Northop Road Cemetery, Flint (Grave 10, Line 37, South Side). He is also commemorated on the North Wales Heroes' Memorial Arch, Bangor. He was awarded the British War Medal and Victory Medal.

The grave of William Henry and Elizabeth Forrester on which Willie is remembered

Willie's father, William Henry, was born in Ruabon and died 31st December, 1918, aged 56, after a long illness, at the Yacht Inn, Oakenholt.

Mr Forrester was of a most genial and generous disposition, and was well known and highly respected in the neighbourhood. Before moving to Flint he was a farmer in Five Fords, Marchweil. Apart from William his three other sons also served their King and country in the war.

His second wife, Elizabeth Ann, was a native of Bagillt and had lived in the Village nearly all her life. Mrs Forrester was an active member of St Mary's Parish Church, a member of the Mothers' Union, and a member of the women's section of the British Legion. She died on 23rd December, 1945, aged 67, at her home, 10, Hanmer Terrace, Bagillt, and buried with her husband.

IN MEMORIAM

In loving 22nd Birthday remembrance
(July 23rd).
When last we saw his smiling face,
He looked so young and brave,
We little thought how soon he'd be
Laid in a soldier's grave.
Ever remembered by Mam, Harry and Agnes.
(County Herald, 25th July, 1919)
His kindly ways and happy smile,

Are pleasant to recall,
He nobly did his duty
And was beloved by all.
For Honour, Liberty and Truth,
He sacrificed his glorious youth.
Sadly missed
by Mother,
Brothers and Sisters.
(County Herald, 5th September. 1919)

PRIVATE
PETER FOX

20565, 14th (Service) Battalion Royal Welsh Fusiliers

Peter Fox was born in Flint on 27th December, 1881 and baptised on 28th January, 1882 at St Mary's Catholic Church, Flint He was the youngest of six children to John Fox and Maria (Durnine).

Peter grew up at 10, Swan Street, where the family had lived for many years, and at the age of 20 he was employed as a navvy. Then tragedy was to befall the Fox family in two short years. Their mother died at her home on 13th February, 1902, aged 63, and was buried in the Northop Road Cemetery. She was born in Dublin, Ireland and had been blind from about 1887.

Then on 9th August, 1904, also at his home, their father died, aged 64, and was buried with his wife. He was a labourer at the chemical works.

The memorial commemorating the fallen in the First World War at Anfield Cemetery, Liverpool

The 1911 census found Peter a lodger at the home of a Mr and Mrs Murray of 39, Sydney Street, Flint and he was employed as a labourer and unmarried.

The 14th Battalion Royal Welsh Fusiliers (RWF) Embarkation Roll for 1st December, 1915 states that Private Fox was resident at 10, Albert Place, Llanrwst, Denbighshire, but his death report in the Flintshire County Herald gave his address as 35, Mumforth Street, Flint, the home of a Mrs Welsh, whereas his death certificate stated 72, Henry Street, Manchester.

He enlisted in Flint and landed in France in December, 1915; he was reported wounded in August, 1916.

He died on 16th July, 1917 at Highfield Military Hospital, Knotty Ash, Liverpool (now Broad Green Hospital), due to a shrapnel wound to the right lung that caused an abscess.

The funeral was of a military character, several soldiers who had taken part in the battles with him attended and floral tributes were placed on the grave. His obituary stated that before his enlistment he was employed at the Hawarden Bridge Ironworks, Shotton.

He is buried in an unmarked grave in Anfield Cemetery, Liverpool (Section 5 [Roman Catholic], Grave 1797).

The Screen Wall (North), where Private Fox is remembered. His grave is right in front of the wall, to the left

He is remembered on two war memorials: Anfield Cemetery, Liverpool, on the Screen Wall (North) and St Mary's Catholic Church, Flint.

He was awarded the 1914–15 Star, British War Medal and Victory Medal.

PRIVATE
GEOFFREY GEORGE

240709, 1/5th (Flintshire) Battalion Royal Welsh Fusiliers

Geoffrey George was born in 1896 at Bryn y Garreg, Flint Mountain, and was the third of eight children to Edward George and Elizabeth (Ball).

Geoffrey lived at Woodleigh, Bryn y Garreg all his life and at the age of 14 was employed as a dyer. Before joining the army he was working as an ironworker and was unmarried.

His mother, who was born in Chorlton, Cheshire, died at Bryn y Garreg on 22nd February, 1914 and is buried in the Northop Road Cemetery. Mrs George, who was 51 years of age, had been indisposed for some time and, her illness assuming a very serious aspect, she became worse and died on a Sunday afternoon, when several of her family were attending the service at St Thomas's Church, Flint Mountain. She had been a worshipper at the church.

Geoffrey enlisted in Flint on 6th October, 1914 aged 18 years and 11 months. He was 5 ft 4 in, chest 34½ in, and his vision and physical development were good.

His service record details are as follows: 4 days confined to barracks for not complying with an order on 28th April, 1915; 5 days confined to barracks for irregular conduct on the march, not complying with an order and being absent from the orderly room on 5th May, 1915; 6 days confined to camp for disobedience of orders (smoking cigarettes during prohibited hours) on 26th June, 1915; embarked on His Majesty's Troopship Caledonia at Devonport for Gallipoli, 14th July, 1915; 72 hours' Field Punishment No. 1 for disobedience of orders (urinating in Company lines) on 29th July, 1915; hospital (exposure) in Gallipoli, 30th November, 1915; hospital (debility) and sent to Malta, 6th December, 1915; 7 days' Field Punishment No. 2 for failing to comply with an order and using obscene language on the 8th & 9th February, 1916; rejoined battalion for duty at Khatatbah, 23rd February, 1916; hospital in Khatatbah, 6th March, 1916; joined Class "B" at Cairo, 7th March, 1916; joined at Alexandria, 7th April, 1916; rejoined battalion for duty at Wadi Natrun, 24th April, 1916; 5 days confined to camp for being absent from 1700 parade on 14th July, 1916; attached to 156th Brigade Headquarters at Ismailia, 22nd July 1916; rejoined battalion from 156th Brigade Headquarters at Egypt, 23rd July, 1916; attached to 155th Brigade Headquarters at Egypt, 23rd July 1916; 1/1st Field Ambulance hospital ex 155th Brigade Headquarters at Egypt, 3rd August, 1916; hospital (diphtheria) in Egypt, 3rd August, 1916; 31st General Hospital (diphtheria) in Port Said, 20th August, 1916; rejoined battalion for duty In the Field, 30th August, 1916; granted Class 2 Proficiency Pay, 6th October, 1916; wounded in action at Gaza (gunshot in right foot), 26th March 1917 and in Cairo hospital until 4th April, 1917; joined ex hospital In the Field, 12th May, 1917; rejoined battalion 24th May, 1917; confined to camp for being late to parade at 0530 on 16th June, 1917; granted Class 1 Proficiency Pay, 1st July, 1917.

Private Geoffrey George

IN MEMORIAM

In loving memory of my dear friend Geoffrey.
*In the bloom of life death claimed him,
In the pride of his manhood days,
None knew him but to love him,
None mentioned his name but with praise.*

*There is a link death cannot sever,
Fond remembrance last for ever.*
From his dear friend Tom Hughes,
12, Mumforth Street, Flint.
(County Herald, 7th March, 1919)

He was killed in action in Palestine on 9th March, 1918 and buried in the Jerusalem War Cemetery, Israel (Plot M, Grave 76).

Family legend has it that Geoffrey was shot while standing up in the trenches.

He is remembered on two war memorials: Flint House and St Mary's Parish Church, Flint, and was awarded the 1914–15 Star, British War Medal and Victory Medal. He is also commemorated on the North Wales Heroes' Memorial Arch, Bangor.

Geoffrey's father, who was born at Bryn y Garreg, died in April 1939, aged 83, and is buried with his wife.

Mr George was a native of Flint Mountain, being a son of Mr and Mrs William George, farmers, and had lived at Woodleigh since 1865. He was employed as a collier but carried on the small farm after the death of his parents, which was a small holding on the estate of Sir John Bankes in the locality of Bryn y Garreg. He was a member of St Thomas's Church.

PRIVATE
ALBERT LOWTHER GILLOTT

33919, 4th Battalion South Wales Borderers

Albert Lowther Gillott was on 5th February, 1887 at Burton Leonard, Knaresborough, Yorkshire, and was the seventh of eight children to Thomas William Gillott and Jane (Lowther).

The Gillott family had resided at Burton House, Knaresborough and Ripon, Yorkshire before settling in Flint at 104, Mount Pleasant, Northop Road.

He married Helen Reay at the Register Office, Chester, on 11th March, 1914. Helen was born c.1893 and a daughter of Robert Reay, a chauffeur. On the marriage certificate Albert's address was given as 33, Cuppin Street, Chester. He was employed by The Co-operative Society, Bootle, Liverpool, and was formerly a grocer's assistant. It is not known if they had children.

Albert's mother, Jane, was born in Low Catton, Yorkshire and died 19th June, 1914, aged 64, at her home, 104, Mount Pleasant, Northop Road, Flint, and was buried in the Northop Road Cemetery. With the exception of a brief illness she had apparently been in the enjoyment of ordinary health, and in the course of her daily household duties she also engaged in the rearing of poultry, etc., on the land adjoining her residence. About eight o'clock the previous Friday morning she was in the garden at the rear of the house attending to the poultry and conversing with a neighbour in a friendly manner. A few moments afterwards she was suddenly seized with illness, and her collapse being quickly observed she was carried into the kitchen and placed upon the sofa, where she expired almost immediately, much to the poignant grief of her husband and daughters, and other members of the family. She was employed in the offices of Messrs Hughes and Hughes, solicitors, and a worshipper at the Parish Church and was highly respected by a number of the residents.

Albert enlisted in Chester and was killed in action at Mesopotamia on 15th February, 1917.

He has no known grave but is remembered on the Basra Memorial, Iraq (Panels 16 and 62).

He is remembered on the war memorial in St Mary's Parish Church, Flint and was awarded the British War Medal and Victory Medal.

It is not known what became of Albert's wife Helen after his death.

Albert's father, Thomas, was born in Aldecar, Derbyshire. He died on 29th March, 1920, aged 67, and was buried with his wife. He was a senior clerk in the employ of Messrs Hughes and Hughes, solicitors, Flint and Connah's Quay.

The grave of Thomas and Jane Gillott

PRIVATE
HARRY GLOYNE

85267, 18th (Service) Battalion (2nd City) The King's (Liverpool Regiment)

Henry (Harry) Edward Gloyne was born in Flint on 11th February, 1892 and baptised 6th March, 1892 at St Mary's Catholic Church, Flint. He was the eighth of nine children to Archibald Gloyne and Catherine (Jones).

After Harry was born the Gloyne family lived at 12, Salisbury Street, then in 1901 were living at 27, Mumforth Street, then eventually settled at 41, Mumforth Street. Harry was employed at the local chemical works.

He married Harriet Williams on 19th February, 1918 at St Winifride's Catholic Church, Well Street, Holywell.

At the time of their marriage Harry was based at Park Hall Camp, Oswestry.

They had no children but Harriet had an illegitimate son in 1920, named Henry Edward, who died in 1999.

He enlisted in Flint with the 9th Battalion Royal Welsh Fusiliers (RWF), No. 13535. He was wounded in action, whilst still with the RWF, on the 2nd July, 1916, and was also suffering from shell shock.

He was killed in action in France on 10th October, 1918 and buried in the Montay Communal Cemetery, France (Grave 5).

He is remembered on two war memorials: Flint House and St Mary's Catholic Church, Flint, and was awarded the British War Medal and Victory Medal.

> **IN MEMORIAM**
>
> *He has fallen with others so noble and brave,*
> *And to-night he is sleeping in a hero's grave;*
> *Only sad memories forever will stay*
> *Of the one who sleeps in that grave far away.*
> Fondly remembered by
> his Wife and Child and all
> at 6, Davies Square, New Road, Holywell
> (County Herald, 8th October, 1920)

Harriet was born in Holywell in 1894 and during the war she was a munitions worker. Whilst Harry was in the army she went to live with her widowed mother in 6, Davies Square, New Road, Holywell. In 1925 she remarried in Wrexham to a John H Jones, but it is not known what became of her after that date.

Harry's father, Archibald, was born in Dover, Kent and died 25th January, 1933, aged 77, at his home in 41, Mumforth Street and was buried in the Northop Road Cemetery. Mr Gloyne had resided in Flint for over 40 years, and was well known and highly respected in the town. For many years he was in the employ of the United Alkali Company as a fireman. He was a member of the Flint Conservative Club and also of the Flint Castle Lodge of Oddfellows, and when he died the flag was flown at half-mast at the headquarters of both organisations. He was a faithful member of St Mary's Catholic Church, Flint. In August 1932 Mr and Mrs Gloyne celebrated their diamond wedding.

Archibald's wife, Catherine, was born in Flint and also died 41, Mumforth Street on 9th August, 1934, aged 81, and was buried with her husband in an unmarked grave. Like her husband, Mrs Gloyne was well known and highly esteemed and was also a member of St Mary's Catholic Church.

PRIVATE
HERBERT HAYES GUNNING

5217, 1/10th (Scottish) Battalion The King's (Liverpool Regiment)

Herbert Hayes Gunning was born in 1895 in Southport, Merseyside, and he was the only child of John Edward Gunning and Mary Alice (Hayes).

On 23rd August, 1897, when Herbert was just under two years old, his mother Mary Alice, who was born in Runcorn and known as 'Lallie', died at the age of 27. She was buried in Duke Street Cemetery, Southport in the grave of her father-in-law William.

Mr Gunning married again at Ormskirk in 1900 to Bertha Hardman. At this time they were living at 34, Maple Street, Southport, and Mr Gunning was employed as a letterpress printer.

In about 1902 Mr Gunning and his family had moved to Flint, where he was conducting a successful business as a newsagent and stationer, and as a printer at the Borough Printing Works in Church Street. Their residence was next door at Avondale, 17, Church Street.

Herbert was educated at Holywell County School and on leaving became a Printer and typograph operator in the employ of his father. He was unmarried.

Mr Gunning's printing shop and home on the right

He enlisted in Liverpool on 10th September, 1915 and his service record is as follows: he was 5 ft 11 in, 148lb, chest 34 in and his vision and physical development were good. Home base, 10th September, 1915 to 1st March, 1916; embarked Southampton, 2nd March, 1916; disembarked Rouen, 3rd March, 1916; joined unit 16th March, 1916; hospital (measles) and transferred to Isolation Hospital, 22nd March, 1916; Meerut British General Hospital, 27th March, 1916; 55 Division Base Depot, 6th April, 1916; joined unit, 14th May, 1916; his personal items sent home which his father received on 1st February, 1917 were: 1 wallet containing letters, cards & photos, 1 testament, 1 metal wrist watch in case.

In April 1916, at a Military hearing at the Town Hall, Flint, Mr Gunning asked for absolute exemption to be granted Edgar Vaughan Jones, 26, married with two children, residing in Hill Street, Flint, and who was in his employ as a printer and typograph operator. Jones was an attested man, and he was the only man he had left in his employ. His son Herbert was the operator before he enlisted in the army, and much of the work on the premises was for important establishments in the district. His son would have joined the army earlier but for the fact he had to train Jones in the use of the typograph machine. In his defence Mr Gunning said: "The work which I am doing is really indispensable and essential for the community," and added, "The work was chiefly for the factories, and as the printing trade was upset throughout the whole country it was impossible to obtain another typograph operator. If Jones went he would require two other men to carry on the work and it would be really impossible to obtain them." The Tribunal granted six months' conditional exemption, dating from that day. The exemption was granted conditionally that Jones remained at that trade.

Herbert was killed in action by a shell in France on 3rd September, 1916. He has no known grave but is commemorated on the Thiepval Memorial, France (Pier and Face 1 D, 8 B and 8 C).

He is remembered on four war memorials: Flint Town, the English Presbyterian Chapel, Chester Road, Flint, Holywell County School and Southport Town. He is also remembered on his parents' headstone at Duke Street Cemetery, Southport (Grave 473, Section 2) and is commemorated on the North Wales Heroes' Memorial Arch, Bangor. He was awarded the British War Medal and Victory Medal.

On Sunday, 10th September information reached the Borough, through the source of a letter, to the effect that Private Gunning had been killed in action. A member of the same regiment, and who knew Private Gunning, had forwarded the base information to a friend and his mother, but regretted he was unable to send details of the announcement. Much anxiety had, therefore, been experienced by Mr and Mrs Gunning. From Monday morning almost every possible means had been resorted to for the purposes of securing more intelligence from the Battalion officials, but up to Wednesday afternoon nothing of a definite character from that quarter could be ascertained. To add to the anxiety of the parents and friends it would appear that no letters had been received from Private Gunning for some time, and that had he been with the Battalion, or even a prisoner in the hands of the enemy, there would have been probably tidings of his whereabouts before this. No communication had been received from any of the officers or the chaplain to the Battalion, and consequently further news of Private Gunning was anxiously awaited.

The Gunning grave in Duke Street Cemetery, Southport where Private Gunning is remembered

On Friday morning, a letter was received from a friend in the Birkenhead locality in which there was an intimation from another source referring in touching terms to rumours or statements concerning Private Gunning. However, about noon of the same day a telegraphic message was received by Mr Gunning from the officer commanding Private Gunning's regiment communicating the assurance that the Private had been killed by a shell on the date named, and that his remains had been interred. The message concluded: "Please accept assurance of respectful sympathy."

Thus, another youthful and promising young life of the Borough had been sacrificed on the battlefield, for King and country. Private Gunning, sometime after the commencement of the war, when there was proceeding a depletion of the young men's circles of the Borough owing to the pressing claims of the army, combined with the patriotic waves, expressed the feeling that he would be prepared to join the military forces. Time advanced, and eventually he became a member of the said regiment, and after training he left for the Front.

For a long period he officiated as organist of the English Presbyterian Church and Sunday School, and was the honorary secretary of the Library and Debating Society connected with that church. In everything that tended to progress of the church he was associated with his parents; and he was not only esteemed for his kindliness of disposition by the members and friends of the church and Sunday School but by a large circle of intimate friends in the Borough, and by whom his death is lamented. When he was last seen in the Borough he presented a fine, soldierly appearance.

When Mr Gunning retired in 1919 it was reported he did so solely on account of his health and after resting in Flint for about a month he and his wife left to live in Southport. The business was disposed of, and was formerly transferred to Mr Edwin Williams, The Cross, Mold. Whilst living in Flint he was a prominent and active member of the Chester Road English Presbyterian Church. Mr Gunning was a staunch Liberal in politics. Born in Liverpool, he died on 10th March, 1936, aged 69, at his home, 23, Pilkington Road, Southport, and is buried with his first wife.

When Mr Gunning retired, Edgar Vaughan Jones (brother of Corporal Harold Jones – see Volume Two) set himself up in business as a printer in a shop situated at the rear of the Royal Oak Hotel, which can still be seen today. When Mr Jones retired, it was his son, Edgar Vaughan junior who inherited the business which, for many years, was run from the old Baptist Chapel at the top of Church Street.

Mr Gunning's second wife, Bertha, died in 1944, aged 72, at a Southport Nursing Home, and was buried with her husband.

PRIVATE
ARCHIBALD GUNTHER

714, 1/5th (Flintshire) Battalion Royal Welsh Fusiliers

Archibald (Archie) Gunther was born on 25th June, 1886 and baptised 4th July, 1886 at St Mary's Catholic Church, Flint and was the eleventh of 16 children to Charles (Karl) Gunther and Mary Ann (Gittins). He was a brother to Donkeyman Robert Henry Gunther (page 151).

At the time of the 1891 census, Charles and Mary Ann, with nine of their children and two lodgers, were living at 31, Castle Street, Flint.

Charles Gunther was born in Basel, Switzerland and died of heart disease on 24th February, 1896, aged about 60, at his home in Castle Street, and buried in the Northop Road Cemetery. He was a Chelsea Pensioner, having served in the 4th Battalion Rifle Brigade, in Malta, Gibraltar (where he received a Good Conduct badge meriting additional pay of a penny a day) and Montreal, Canada. He was discharged

Mary Ann Gunther and a drawing of Charles (Karl) Gunther, her husband from an original photo, by Charles Evans-Gunther

on 30th March, 1869, after 10 years and 1 month service, in consequence of "Chronic rheumatism and palpitation." He was awarded a pension of 7d per day. In Flint he was employed as a chemical labourer, eventually setting himself up in business as a greengrocer.

The 1901 census found the Gunthers, living at 25, 27 and 29 Castle Street, listed as the Common Lodging House, and 10 years later they were occupying No. 29 only, but without Archie. It is not known where he was on census night in 1911 but there is reason to believe he had been serving in the army since about 1908 so may well have been overseas.

A boxing tournament was held at the Drill Hall, Flint (the second within a fortnight, on Monday 6th April, 1913, of which there was a good attendance, and the Flintshire Observer of 10th April reported the event:

Messrs A J Mothersole and George Clews acted as masters of ceremonies, whilst Messrs A R Hughes (Swan Hotel) and W H Bennett (Shotton) were the referees in the various contests. Mr W Jones (Sydney Street) was timekeeper, and the usual seconders. Mr Ted Carroll acted as ring manager.

The opening contest was a 10-round fight between Reuben Stacey (Flint), the cup winner of the last competition, and Archie Gunther (Flint), the runner-up for the cup in the same competition. The rounds were of two minutes' duration. Mr Bennett refereed. At the outset the contest was very keen. Gunther seemed to be heavier than his opponent, but the latter had a longer reach. In the second round Stacey rained a shower of hits on his opponent, including a severe blow on the mouth. Gunther guarded off several would-be hits by cleverly ducking.

The third round took a different course. Gunther boxed well and drove home a series of blows. In the fourth round, Stacey regained the lead, and before the expiration of the two minutes Gunther surrendered. Stacey was awarded a silver cup, which was given by Mr A R Hughes.

Mr Mothersole then announced that for the local lads' competition between 8 and 9 stones, 10 entries had been received, but only two turned up, viz., Jack Bithell and D Jones.
The winner in six rounds would be awarded the cup. We may mention that the cup was given by Mr Mothersole. Jones put up a good fight, but the tactics of Bithell quite mystified him, and in the third round he was beaten.

Afterwards an interesting exhibition was given by Charlie Milestone, light-weight champion of Cheshire, and Young Macfarlane of Mold, who challenges Flintshire at 10st. 4. Mr A R Hughes was the referee. During the four rounds – each of three minutes' duration – Macfarlane showed skill in the defensive, whilst Milestone was very scientific. A very amusing three-round match was witnessed when H Pierson (Connah's Quay) met Sam Grant (a negro) of Bagillt.

The most exciting event of the evening was the fight between Jack Doyle (Flint), runner-up Army and Navy Championship, and Battling Vernon (Moss), known as the "fighting collier" – a winner of over 40 contests. Mr Hughes was the referee. The announced 15 rounds were reduced to 10 rounds. The first round was rather equal. Doyle was tricky, whilst Vernon exhibited fine defensive work. The second and third rounds were of a similar character, but the fourth round saw a slackness on Vernon's part. He acknowledged defeat shortly afterwards, having injured his thumb. Syd Hunt and Ned Peck gave a capital exhibition.

The last contest was between Dan Sullivan (London) and Harry Phillips (Flint). Phillips gave a good account of himself, but was inferior to Sullivan. In the second round Sullivan drove home a hit under the jaw, and the bout went in favour of Sullivan. The proceedings terminated with the awarding of the prizes.

Archie left the army and was employed at the Hawarden Bridge Ironworks, Shotton and in 1914 married Elizabeth Foster. They set up home at 7, Castle Street and in 1914 had a son named John, who married Eileen McKeown, in 1935, and had at least three children.

He re-enlisted in Flint in 1914 and landed at Gallipoli on 8th August, 1915.

In an interview with a County Herald representative on Wednesday, 7th October, 1914 Mrs Mary Gunther proudly stated she had five sons and a son-in-law now serving under the British Colours. She said that three of her sons were serving with the Flintshire Territorials: Gunner John Gunther, who served in the South African Campaign, was a member of the Royal Field Artillery, at the Front; another son was on His Majesty's Ship Brilliant, and a son-in-law was in Kitchener's Army. Apparently, Mrs Gunther's family had been connected with the army for generations. She said that her grandfather "was one of Sir Watkin Wynne's men in Ireland, about one hundred years ago". Her father, John Gittins, had served 21 years in the Royal Welsh Fusiliers, and her husband was a member of the Prince Consort's Own Rifle Brigade for 11 years. Mrs Gunther stated that another of her sons was anticipating joining the Colours, and that she had a brother who was in the RWF Regiment, and where he has been some years. He was also at the Front, she said, and another brother was believed to be invalided from the Front, and was in hospital in Southampton.

Archie was killed at Suvla Bay, Gallipoli on 14th September, 1915, and was buried in the Hill 10 Cemetery, Turkey (Plot I, Row D, Grave 19).

Private Archibald Gunther

Archie and Elizabeth

A friend of Archie, who was with him when he died, related the circumstances surrounding his death to Mrs Gunther, whose granddaughter from her second marriage passed on to the author. He said that someone had to fetch water for the men and a 16-year-old soldier was nominated. Archie had said he was too young and that he would go instead; when he got there he was shot in the head by a sniper.

He is remembered on two war memorials: Flint Town and St Mary's Catholic Church, Flint, and was awarded the 1914–15 Star, British War Medal and Victory Medal. He is also commemorated on the North Wales Heroes' Memorial Arch, Bangor.

In early October, 1915, an intimation reached the Borough that Archie Gunther had been seriously wounded, but the source of the information was not divulged definitely, and, therefore, further news was awaited anxiously. The official news from the Records Office, Shrewsbury, was delivered at the house of his mother, on Monday the 4th October stating that Private A Gunther was dead, and that his death had occurred in the field on the 14th September, followed by the words "Died of wounds." A story transpired that Archie, together with his brothers, Ned and David, landed at Suvla Bay, Gallipoli on the 8th August, 1915. Two days later they went into action, and the battalion was cut to pieces, losing its commander and a good few officers. They made a second attack on the 14th, but didn't succeed.

Archie's brother Private Edward, who was with the Flintshire Territorials at the Dardanelles, had forwarded a letter to his mother, having a remarkable reference to his brother. He wrote under date of September 19th, just five days later than the intimation of his brother's death from the Military Authorities:

> I am sorry that I have got some bad news for you, and the news is that Archie has been wounded. He was wounded last Tuesday, September 14th. I am glad to say that he is going on very nicely, and I expect he will be well on his way to England by the time you get this letter from me. David also got hurt, but it was an accident. He fell in what we call the dug out, and he is in hospital.

Mrs Gunther received an anonymous letter of condolence from a 'friend' in Holywell, regarding the loss she had sustained by the death of Archie. The letter stated that the deceased was a generous young man and made many friends in Holywell when he used to go to that town. The writer felt sure that he was greatly missed by all his friends in Flint, and he asked to be allowed to express his deepest sympathy with Mrs Gunther in her saddest hour, for she had lost a noble son in this Great War. He was liked by all who knew him; and they all who knew him in Holywell keenly regretted the loss.

'Archie Gunther,' as he was familiarly termed amongst his friends in Flint, was very popular. When the 1/5th Battalion left Flint and proceeded to Northampton, Royston and Higham Ferrers, he earned the esteem of the people where he was billeted. Those people were made acquainted of Archie's death, and did not lose any time in communicating with his widow.

Mr and Mrs Croxford, of 2, Abington Place, York Road, Northampton, expressed their sorrow at the sad news. They received a letter from him when he landed at the Dardanelles. They saw him before he left England, and were hoping to see him again had he been spared to return.

Mrs Emily M Abbott, of 40, York Road, Northampton, writing to Mrs Gunther, said she was grieved at hearing that her husband had been killed in action. She could imagine what a shock it must have been to her. It seemed sad that brave men should lose their lives; but she would have the satisfaction of knowing he died for his King and Country.

> It was indeed hard for wives and children . . . and just now I am sure everything seems very dark for you; but I pray that our Heavenly Father may comfort you and give you strength to bear this heavy trial, and I trust that your future may be blessed in some way; and also that your little child will grow up to be a comfort to you. I shall always be glad to have known your husband, and that he was in our home. Some day later on you will feel proud that he did his duty so bravely. There must be many sorrowful hearts and homes in Flint, and many men we have known here will never return. We can only hope that this dreadful war may soon come to an end. My sister joins me in kind remembrance.

Mrs Goodbody, of Moreton Street, Royston, Herts, wrote:

> I am so sorry to hear the sad news of poor Archie. You have our deepest sympathy. I am sure it is a dreadful blow to you all, and I hope God will give you health and strength to bear your terrible loss of one who was so dear to you and your dear little son. I hope he will grow up and be a little comforter to you, as his poor dada was so good and kind.

Writing from 68, High Street, Higham Ferrers, Mrs Willmott expressed her surprise at the sad news, and her sympathy with Mrs Gunther. She said it seemed such a short time since he was there full of life and strength, because he was so lively. Everyone knew him – soldiers and civilians, and all the neighbours. He was a good soldier and a good friend to them all; and they were very pleased that they knew him, if only for such a short time.

Mrs J H Williams, of St Mary's Mount, Church Street, interested herself in the fine family record of military and naval careers which the Gunther's possessed. She communicated with the Government Authorities on the subject, believing that the record was worthy of some recognition.

Mrs Williams, on Tuesday 19th October, 1915, was the recipient of an official letter from the Keeper of the Privy Purse, Buckingham Palace, in acknowledgement of her letter, and at the same time informing her that Mrs Gunther had been favoured by a letter as follows:

>Privy Purse Office,
>Buckingham Palace
>15th October, 1915
>
>MADAM,– I am commanded by the King to convey to you an expression of His Majesty's appreciation of the patriotic spirit which has prompted your six sons to give their services to His Majesty's Forces. The King was much gratified to hear the manner in which they have so readily responded to the call of their Sovereign and their Country; and I am to express to you and to them His Majesty's congratulations on having contributed in so full a measure to the great cause for which all the people of the British Empire are so bravely fighting.
>
>I have the honour to be, Madam,
>Your obedient servant,
>F M Ponsonby,
>Keeper of the Privy Purse.

The following are the names, etc., of the six sons: Private John Gunther, of the Royal Field Artillery; Private Idwal Gunther, 2/5th Battalion of the Royal Welsh Fusiliers; Private Archie Gunther, 1/5th Battalion of the Royal Welsh Fusiliers; Private Edward Gunther, and Private David Gunther, 1/5th Battalion of the RWF; and Seaman Robert Henry Gunther, in the Royal Navy. Note: Private William Samuel Gunther, who enlisted after the above letter from Buckingham Palace, became the seventh son in the armed forces. He served with the 14th Mobile Veterinary Detachment.

Archie's widow, Elizabeth, re-married in 1919 to Thomas Campbell, and they resided at 17, Maesydre Avenue, Flint. She died on 3rd June, 1975, aged 79, and was buried with her husband, Thomas, in Pantasaph Cemetery.

Mary Ann Gunther was born at Henllan Street, Denbigh and died of a stroke at 29, Castle Street on 23rd September, 1923, aged 71, and was buried with her husband. After her husband's death she had carried on the greengrocer's shop in Castle Street.

†
THOMAS CAMPBELL
1891 – 1972
ELIZABETH CAMPBELL
1896 – 1975
FLINT

Edward - Archibald - David.
Idwal Howell

Four of the Gunther brothers

IN MEMORIAM

The fairest flower, the first to fall,
A son true and brave,
The dearest, fondest, best of all,
Has found a hero's grave.
Too far away your grave to see,
But not too far to think of thee.
Sadly mourned by his sorrowing Mother,
Brothers and Sisters.
(County Herald, 14th September, 1917)

We loved him in life he is dear to us still,
But in grief we must bend in God's holy will,
Our sorrow is great, our loss hard to bear,
But angels, dear brother, will tend you with care.
Sadly missed by his
Sister and Brother-in-law
and children, Sarah and Jack.
Castle Street, Flint.
(County Herald, 14th September, 1917)

DONKEYMAN
ROBERT HENRY GUNTHER

Mercantile Marines

Robert Henry Gunther was born in Flint on 5th October, 1877 and baptised on 28th October, 1877 in Denbigh, and was the sixth of 16 children to Charles (Karl) Gunther and Mary Ann (Gittins). He was a brother to Private Archibald Gunther (page 145).

Robert grew up living at 31, Castle Street and attended St Mary's Catholic School, where, on Monday 11th February, 1889, the annual tea party and concert was given to the children of the school and prizes were distributed, which consisted of very handsome bound books on travel and other interesting subjects. Attendance prizes were given to Robert Henry and his brother Thomas. The prizes were donated by Mr Sydney Knowles Muspratt and presented by his wife and daughter.

Sometime in the 1890s Robert Henry enlisted in the Merchant Marines as an able-bodied seaman, so he may never have had a civilian job.

Mary Ann Gunther – drawn from the original by Charles Evans-Gunther

On census night in 1901 Robert was living at 4, Bell Lane, Poole, Dorset with Alice Eliza Perry who was listed as a servant. They married later that year in Poole, the town of her birth.

They were to have seven children, Robert Walter (1903–?), Isabella Sarah (1905–?), John (1907–?), Alice Esther (1910–?), George William Arthur (1911–?), Elizabeth Grace (1912–?) and Harry (1916–1982).

His Majesty's Ship, Brilliant

By 1911 they had set up home at 30, Queen Avenue, Goole, Yorkshire and later moved to 43, Phoenix Street, also in Goole.

Mr and Mrs Eric Gunther (grandson) outside 43, Phoenix Street, Goole (c.2008) where Robert and Alice lived

Robert Henry and Alice with family

Robert probably left the merchant service before WW1 then, when the war began, he joined the Royal Navy. However, nothing is known of his service career from then until his death, whilst serving again with the Mercantile Marines as a Donkeyman (a Rating who tends a donkey boiler, or engine, and assists in the engine-room).

In early November, 1914, Robert forwarded a letter to his mother stating that he was a patient in the Royal Naval Hospital, Chatham and had been suffering from very serious injuries, but there was no intimation where he received them. He was at that time serving on His Majesty's Ship, Brilliant, which was one of the cruisers engaged in bombarding the Germans on the Belgian coast. Brilliant was a light Apollo class cruiser. In 1906 she joined the Newfoundland Fisheries Service and remained on duty in Newfoundland's waters until 1911.

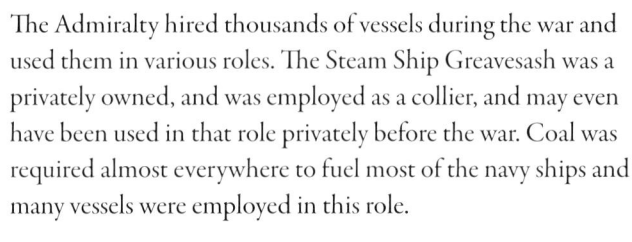

The Admiralty hired thousands of vessels during the war and used them in various roles. The Steam Ship Greavesash was a privately owned, and was employed as a collier, and may even have been used in that role privately before the war. Coal was required almost everywhere to fuel most of the navy ships and many vessels were employed in this role.

Robert was serving on the Greavesash when, on the 26th February, 1918, 10 miles northeast from Cape Barfleur, France, she was torpedoed without warning by German submarine UB 74. She sunk en route from Le Havre for Barry Roads, which was a stretch of navigable waters that ships used to enter Barry docks. Robert was one of the eight lives lost.

Robert Henry Gunther is commemorated on the Tower Hill Memorial, London, on Panel 8

His body was not recovered but he is commemorated on the Tower Hill Memorial, London, on Panel 8. As far as is known he is not remembered on any other war memorial.

He was awarded the Mercantile Marine Medal, British War Medal and was awarded the 1914–15 Star, British War Medal and Victory Medal.

Alice Eliza died at St John's Hospital, Goole, on 2nd December, 1961, and was buried in Hook Road Cemetery, Goole.

Alice Eliza's resting place

PRIVATE
DAVID HAMMOND

45960, 12th Battalion Cheshire Regiment

David Hammond was born in Flint in March, 1892, and was the third of six children to David Hammond and Emma Elizabeth (Jones). The Hammond family resided at 3, The Marsh, Flint for a number of years then by the 1901 census had moved to Cross Town in Knutsford, Cheshire. In 1911 they were living at 1, Armitage Place, Rigby Street, Altrincham.

The war began and David's brothers, James and Robert, enlisted. James was a signaller with the 6th Battalion Loyal North Lancashires and Robert was a bugler with the 11th Service Battalion of the Lancashire Fusiliers.

Mrs Hammond received a letter from James in mid-September, 1915, stating that he was quite well with his regiment at the Dardanelles. He related that he had had a startling experience, and certainly a very narrow escape from death. He was wearing his canteen slung at the back of him when a bullet struck it, and penetrated it. The canteen prevented the missile entering his back, and Hammond, whose regiment had been with the Battalion at the Dardanelles since the previous Christmas, certainly is of opinion that the canteen was the means of his life being saved. He was later admitted into one of the Malta Hospitals suffering from dysentery.

The following month Robert, who had been in France only one month, wrote stating he was an inmate of the Royal Infirmary, Leicester. He had been wounded in the head with a piece of shell and he had also another wound in the arm. He was suffering from an attack of paralysis owing to the injuries. He was wounded again in June 1917.

David senior died on or about the 16th February, 1916, aged 55, and was buried in the Northop Road Cemetery, Flint. He was born in Knutsford, Cheshire and was employed as a chemical labourer and was previously a domestic gardener.

David junior was living at The Green, Partington, Irlam, Lancashire when he enlisted on 26th February, 1916 at Stretford, Manchester, with the 3rd Battalion Cheshire Regiment. On enlistment he was 23 years and 11 months old, 5 ft 5 in, chest 34½ in, had blue eyes, brown hair and a ruddy complexion and his physical development and vision were good. His occupation was given as a labourer.

The Hammond family were living at 45, Chester Street, Flint when David junior married Annie Walters at St Mary's Parish Church on 26th November, 1916. Altrincham born Annie was residing at 2, Upper Queen Street, Flint and was a daughter of William Walters, labourer, and his wife Louisa, of 13, Police Street, Altrincham. David and Annie had no children.

On 27th March Private Hammond was posted to the Army Reserve. On 20th September, 1916, he was mobilised, and next day he was posted to the 3rd Battalion Cheshire Regiment, joining the battalion on the 22nd September. He was posted overseas on 13th January, 1917 and on 3rd May was posted to the 12th Cheshires.

He died on 29th May, 1917, at No. 31, Casualty Clearing Station, Janes, Greece, from a shrapnel wound to the chest received in action at Salonika, and was buried in the Sarigol Military Cemetery, Kriston, Greece (Plot B, Grave 282).

Private Hammond is buried in the Sarigol Military Cemetery, Kriston, Greece (Plot B, Grave 282)

He is remembered on two war memorials: St Mary's Parish Church, Flint, and St Mary's Parish Church, Partington, Manchester, and was awarded the British War Medal and Victory Medal.

Annie was awarded a widow's pension from the army of 13s 9d per week with effect from the 3rd December, 1917. After her husband's death Annie went to live with her in laws, however by October 1919 she was living at 28, York Street, Altrincham. It is not known what became of her after that date.

David junior's Flint-born mother, Emma Elizabeth, died on 4th October, 1926, aged 67, at 8, Princes Street, Flint, as a result of an accident, and was buried with her husband.

The evening following her death Mr F Llewellyn Jones, Coroner for Flintshire, held an inquest at the Town Hall, Flint, and was reported in the County Herald: "Robert Hammond, a silkworker, residing at 8, Princes Street, identified the body as that of his mother, Emma Elizabeth Hammond. He was working nights some time ago when his mother had an accident in the backyard. After the accident she sat on the sofa for a while, and then they took her upstairs. The doctor saw her immediately. Mrs Mary Evans, 10, Princes Street, said she saw the deceased fall. She was crossing the yard about seven weeks ago. She was very feeble, and whilst walking she twisted round and fell on her back, with her leg under her. Dr J Humphry Williams said he was called to the deceased seven weeks last Friday. After examining her he came to the conclusion that she had a fracture of the left hip. He kept her in bed, and there seemed nothing of untoward danger, and she did well for a fortnight. She then had nervous prostration, and later bladder paralysis and bedsores, no doubt accelerated by the accident. He had told the son he could not give a death certificate. The Coroner said this was a case in which Dr Williams could not issue a certificate of death. There was no doubt in his (the Coroner's) mind as to the cause of death, and he recorded a verdict in accordance with the medical evidence."

PRIVATE
THOMAS HARRIS

12823, 9th (Service) Battalion Royal Welsh Fusiliers

Thomas Harris was born in Wolverhampton, Staffordshire c.1883 and was possibly the only child of Henry Thomas Harris and Elizabeth (Harwick). They were living at 12, Bell Street, Wolverhampton in the 1891 census but Mr and Mrs Harris could not be traced after that.

Mr Harris was born in Greenhall, Shropshire c.1860 and was a brewer's drayman.

Mrs Harris was born in Wolverhampton, Staffordshire in c.1861. She was a huckster, who is one who sells wares or provisions in the street; a peddler or hawker.

In the 1911 census Thomas was a lodger at 33, Chapel Street, Flint, the residence of Edward and Harriet R Beck. He was a bachelor and had gained employment as a furnace man at a Galvanized Sheet Works, which was probably the Hawarden Bridge Ironworks, Shotton.

Thomas enlisted in Shotton and landed at Boulogne, France on 19th July, 1915. He was killed in action on 12th May, 1917 and buried in the Vlamertinghe Military Cemetery, Belgium (Plot V, Row M, Grave 3).

He is remembered on the St Mary's Parish Church war memorial, Flint and was awarded the 1914–15 Star, British War Medal and Victory Medal.

PRIVATE
JOHN HAYES

3128, 1st Battalion Welsh Guards

John (Jack) William Hayes was born on 31st December, 1884 at 2, Castle Street, Flint and baptised on 25th January, 1885 at St Mary's Parish Church, Flint. He was the third of seven children to Richard Hayes and Frances Alice (Hartland).

The Hayes family lived at 2, Castle Street for a number of years until moving to Chester Street by 1901.

The 3rd April, 1903 issue of the County Herald reported that Richard Hayes senior, Chester Street, was charged with allowing his pony to stray on the highway on 2nd March. PC Jones, in his evidence, stated he had previously cautioned defendant about it. Hayes pleaded guilty, and stated that as soon as he knew about it, he sold the pony. The Bench fined him 1 shilling and costs, the mayor remarking that it was a great nuisance having those ponies straying about the roads.

The 1911 census found Richard lodging with 10 other men at 4, Evans Court, Flint, the home of a Mr and Mrs William Williams. He was employed as an agricultural labourer. It is not known where Richard's wife Frances was at this time.

John, however, was a boarder at 177, Chester Road, the home of widower Margaret Hughes. He was a bachelor and employed as a furnace man at the ironworks.

He enlisted in Flint c. October 1914 and was killed in action in France on 10th October, 1917. Just a few months previously his mother, Frances, had died in Birmingham, (the place of her birth) aged 53.

Private Hayes has no known grave but is commemorated on the Tyne Cot Memorial, Belgium, on Panel 11.

He is remembered on two war memorials: Flint Town and St Mary's Parish Church, Flint, and was awarded the British War Medal and Victory Medal. He is also commemorated on the North Wales Heroes' Memorial Arch, Bangor.

John's father, Richard, was born in Flint, died on 8th April, 1939, aged 79, at Lluesty Hospital, Holywell, and is buried in the Northop Road Cemetery.

His obituary stated that Mr Hayes, of 2, Fourth Avenue, Flint, was employed for some years by the United Alkali Company Ltd, and afterwards by Hawarden Bridge Ironworks, later being in the yard at Messrs Courtaulds Castle Works. In his younger days he was a keen athlete and a clever high jumper, winning numerous prizes for the high jump at Flint Whitsun sports. He was a member of St Mary's Parish Church.

PRIVATE
THOMAS HEWITT

1377, 1/5th (Flintshire) Battalion
Royal Welsh Fusiliers

Thomas (Tom) Hewitt was born in Flint, in 1895, and baptised on 15th August, 1895 at St Mary's Parish Church, Flint, and was the youngest of six children to Edward (Ned) Hewitt and Margaret (Williams).

In Tom's early years the family were living at Muspratt Terrace, Flint and he attended the National School.

His mother, Margaret, who was born in Bangor, Caernarvonshire, died on 7th December, 1907, aged 48, at 1, Mumforth Street, Flint, and is buried in the Northop Road Cemetery, Flint.

A newspaper photo of Private Hewitt

The 1911 census found Tom living with his sister and her husband, Mr and Mrs James Payton, at 25, Rowsley Street, Gorton, Manchester. Tom's occupation was a trolley boy with the Manchester Tramway.

Tom's father, Edward, re-married to 49-year-old widow Sarah Ann Morris at St Mary's Parish Church, Flint on 5th June, 1911, and they lived for a while at 54, Mount Pleasant, the home of his brother, Lance Sergeant William Hewitt (page 159) and was employed as a steel worker. Edward and Sarah later moved to 45, Mumforth Street, Flint.

Tom returned to Flint and gained employment at the British Glanzstoff Works. He was a single man and a member of the Parish Church.

Tom had been in the Flint Company of the 5th Battalion Royal Welsh Fusiliers for about six months before war broke out. The Battalion landed at Gallipoli in August 1915.

In his last letter home, dated 3rd August, 1915, Tom said: "Probably we shall have seen some fighting by the time you receive this letter." Seven days later, on 10th August, he was killed in action in the first engagement of the 1/5th at Suvla Bay, Gallipoli. He has no known grave but is commemorated on the Helles Memorial, Turkey on Panels 77 to 80.

He is remembered on the St Mary's Parish Church war memorial, Flint, and was awarded the 1914–15 Star, British War Medal and Victory Medal.

In a letter to a friend, dated 21st August, 1915, Sergeant Tom Bithell, of Holywell Road, wrote about his experiences with the 1/5th Battalion of the Royal Welsh Fusiliers. He stated that the Battalion was "still going through it all." They had had a good many losses since they had been there, and he thought they had lost 11 officers. The whole of the men had all had a very narrow escape; but they thanked God they had escaped. When one saw men getting shot it made one feel anxious. The previous week a shell dropped a yard away from him, and killed three and wounded five other men. Three others got away safely. He bandaged two, under heavy fire. That was only one instance of many. One of the men was hit in the shoulder. One was a young lad of Flint, and his father was a Mr Edward Hewitt. At the time Hewitt was just along side of him, and they were all under heavy fire. Sergeant Bithell wrote:

"A bullet just passed my face, and it caught him in the temple, went through his head, and he fell on his face. I dropped down under cover, and put out my hand to turn him over. I saw who it was, and I carried him under heavy fire for about thirty yards. How I got through it I do not know, but one does not know the danger in times like that. I gave him a sip of water and he said he felt a little better. He died a few minutes afterwards. But for all this hardship we are fighting for a good cause, which must be done."

Continuing, he added that after being in the trenches a fortnight one felt like wanting a rest. He had a good chance of getting through the terrible war. They were all getting more used to it. He was just going to have a shot at a sniper. The place was full of them, and every day they "got" some of the men when going for water. He did not think the war would last much longer there. He could not say how many of the Flint men had been wounded until the Battalion were at the base and the roll was called properly, but he could not state when that would take place. The men were not downhearted.

Tom's father, Ned, was born in Flint and died in March, 1923, aged 68, and was buried with his first wife.

IN MEMORIAM

The shock was great, the blow severe,
We little thought that death was near,
Only those that have lost one are able to tell
The grief for the one we loved so well.

He was only a brave young hero,
Longing to do his share,
Only a grave in Gallipoli,
Nameless – who knows where?
Mrs Edward Hewitt,
45, Kirklea, Mumforth Street, Flint.
(County Herald, 18th August, 1916)

I often shed some bitter tears,
When I am all alone,
When I think of my dear son's grave
So very far from home.
From his Father, Mother, Sisters and Brothers,
45, Mumforth Street. Flint.
(County Herald, 16th August, 1918)

Somewhere abroad in a soldier's grave,
Lies our dear son among the brave,
From earthly care to heavenly rest,
Missed by those who loved him best.
Always remembered by Dad,
Mother and all at home,
45, Mumforth Street, Flint.
(County Herald, 15th August, 1919)

A loving birthday remembrance.

Dear brother, how we miss you,
No tongue but ours can tell,
But deep within our hearts
Your memory will always dwell.
(County Herald, 2nd July, 1920)

LANCE SERGEANT
WILLIAM HEWITT

15065, 11th Battalion Royal Welsh Fusiliers

William George Hewitt was born in Flint in 1861 and baptised on 1st January, 1865 at St Mary's Parish Church, Flint, and was the youngest of three children to Hugh Hewitt and Catherine (Edwards).

William's older brother Edward was the father of Private Thomas Hewitt (page 157).

The 1871 census found the Hewitt family living at 38, Chester Street but sadly William's father, Hugh, died in July 1873, aged 49, and was buried in the Old Ground of the Northop Road Cemetery. He was born in Connah's Quay, was a Pilot on the River Dee and came from a well-known family of mariners.

The 1881 census revealed William was a boarder at a lodging house on Chester Road, where widow Elizabeth Williams was the Lodging House Keeper. William was employed as a cooper at the local chemical works.

William married Lucy Evans on 24th April, 1887, at St Mary's Parish Church, Flint. She was born in Flint and was a daughter of William Watkin Evans and his wife Ann of Mount Street. Lucy died in December 1890, aged 20, and lies in an unmarked grave in the Northop Road Cemetery. They had no children.

William married a second time in Chester in 1894 to Margaret (Maggie) Williams. She was born in Flint and was a daughter of John Williams and his wife Jane of Mount Pleasant. They lived for a while at 9, Mill Brow before settling at 54, Mount Pleasant, Northop Road.

His mother, Catherine, was born in Greenfield, and died in January, 1897, aged 76, and is also buried in the Old Ground of the Northop Road Cemetery.

William and Margaret had 13 children: John William (1894–1964); Maud (1896–1915); Hugh (1898–1898); Enoch (1899–1899); Catherine Jane (1900–1900); Elizabeth (1901–?); Enoch (1903–1903); Ada (1904–1977); Edward (1905–1906); Margaret Jane (1907–1907); Albert (1908–1916); Enoch (1909–1909); Margaret Jane (1911–?).

The seven who died in infancy, Hugh, Enoch, Catherine Jane, Enoch, Edward, Margaret Jane and Enoch, were buried with William's first wife Lucy.

By the 1911 census William was employed as a steelworker (gas producer) at the Hawarden Bridge Ironworks and he was also a member of the Flint Castle Lodge of Oddfellows.

Before the war he was with the Flint Company of National Reserves (Flintshire Battalion) when it had headquarters in Mold, and afterwards he became attached to the 2nd Volunteer Battalion of the

Royal Welsh Fusiliers and held a non-commissioned rank.

When the war began he joined the service in response to the appeal for ex-non-commissioned officers and enlisted in Flint on 10th September, 1914. For a long time he was a Sergeant Instructor in the Reserve 3/5th Battalion of the Royal Welsh Fusiliers near Oswestry, and at some point was transferred to the 11th Battalion.

While he was away tragedy was to befall William and his wife Maggie when their 19-year-old daughter, Maud, passed away on 18th December, 1915. Worse was to come the following year when their eight-year-old son Albert accidentally drowned while playing with two friends at the Halkyn Road Brick Works. William was home at the time and was present at the inquest. Albert was buried in the Northop Road Cemetery with his sister Maud.

William's eldest son, John William, served in the war for four years and six months as a Private with the 10th Battalion Royal Welsh Fusiliers, No. 15207. In March, 1916 it was reported that Private Hewitt had been wounded. Private Joseph Frances, of the Manchester Gun Section, connected with the Battalion, writing to Private Hewitt's parents, said he took the liberty of doing so to inform them that Will had been wounded in the leg whilst doing his duty. He and other friends of Private Hewitt, had not heard from him since, and that might probably be due to his having landed in England at one of the hospitals. Before leaving he said that Hewitt left word that if any parcels arrived addressed to him they were to open them and distribute the contents amongst his chums. One parcel had arrived since he was sent away by the hospital authorities, and it was opened in the presence of the remainder of the men of the Gun Section. On behalf of the chums he wrote thanking the senders, and at the same time expressing their sympathy with them, trusting that they would soon hear from their son. They hoped he would be soon all right again.

William was discharged from the army on the 27th March, 1918 and returned to work at the Hawarden Bridge Ironworks.

He died on 29th August, 1921, at Chester Royal Infirmary, of cirrhosis of the liver and heart failure, and was buried four days later in the Northop Road Cemetery (Grave 7, Line 44, South Side).

He is remembered on the St Mary's Parish Church war memorial, Flint. It is not known if he was awarded any medals.

William was not still serving in the army when he died and his death does not appear to be related to his army service, so it is unclear as to why he has a military headstone or why his name is commemorated on the Parish Church war memorial.

William's wife, Margaret, died at 9, Woodfield Avenue, Flint on 23rd June, 1939, aged 70, and was buried in the Northop Road

Cemetery but not with her husband. She was a member of St John's English Congregational Church and Sisterhood.

In WW2 John William's eldest son, Leading Seaman William George Hewitt, was serving on His Majesty's Motor Torpedo Boat No. 2011, and was killed on 19th May, 1945, aged 24. VE Day had passed on the 8th May and they had docked at Lerwick in the Shetland Islands. They were allowed ashore, and whilst he and a comrade, Able Seaman William G Riley, were walking together one of them stepped on a booby-trapped German mine and both were killed instantly. They were buried in Lerwick New Cemetery, overlooking Bressay Sound. William George had completed seven years in the Royal Navy, and was expecting his discharge the following month.

William George's younger brother, Ronald, was a professional footballer who made 26 appearances as an inside-right for Hereford United in the 1963–64 season.

A newspaper photo of Leading Seaman William George Hewitt

Groomed at Wolves by the legendary Stan Cullis, Hewitt went on to win five caps for Wales and was one of the Principality's heroes of the 1958 World Cup. The lively Hewitt made three appearances at the World Cup in Sweden, where Wales reached the quarter-finals, losing only to eventual winners Brazil through a Pele goal. The little Welshman joined Hereford towards the end of an illustrious career in which he also played for Cardiff City, Wrexham, Coventry and Chester. He died in 2001 aged 73.

PRIVATE
JOSEPH WALTER HILL

13459, 9th (Service) Battalion Royal Welsh Fusiliers

Joseph Walter Hill was born in 1888 at Garforth, Leeds, Yorkshire, and was sixth of eight children to William Hill and Ann (Birkin).

Mr Hill was born in Garforth, Yorkshire in 1856 and had worked as a farm labourer and domestic gardener. Mrs Hill was born in Newsam Green, Yorkshire in 1854. Joseph's parents could not be traced after the 1891 census, where they were living at Farm House, West Garforth, Yorkshire, but Joseph's marriage certificate of 1915 stated his father was deceased.

In the 1901 census Joseph was living with his grandparents, Andrew and Martha Hill, at Fernleigh Road, Grange, North Lonsdale, Lancashire, and in 1911 he was listed as an 'assistant' to Chip Potato Dealers George and Hannah Bradley of Calder Vale Road, Burnley, Lancashire.

It is not known how long he was a resident of Oakenholt but he lived for a while with his sister and brother in law, Harriet and Richard Armour, at 5, Gardeners Row, but probably left the area before his marriage.

On 13th July, 1915 he married 50-year-old widow Sarah Jane Gardner, née Thomas, at St John the Baptist Parish Church, Weston-Super-Mare, Somerset. She was first married to painter George Frederick Gardner (1863–1903), and had at least two children named Frederick Charles (1887–1926) and Charles William (1889–?). Joseph's address was given as Perham, Wiltshire, and his occupation was a waiter. They had no children.

Grove Park War Memorial, Weston-Super-Mare where Private Hill is commemorated

He enlisted in Wrexham and landed at Boulogne, France on 19th July, 1915. He was killed in action in France on 25th September, 1915, and has no known grave but is commemorated on the Loos Memorial, France, on Panels 50 to 52.

He is remembered on two war memorials: Flint Town and Grove Park, Weston-Super-Mare, and was awarded the 1914–15 Star, British War Medal and Victory Medal. He is also commemorated on the North Wales Heroes' Memorial Arch, Bangor.

Private Richard Armour was serving with the 9th Battalion of the Royal Welsh Fusiliers in France and in a letter home to his wife, dated 26th September, 1915, he stated: "Thank God, I am able to write once again, but since writing last we have been through hell; but although I am safe, yet there are chums of ours who are lying asleep forever." He also informed his wife that her brother Private Joseph Hill, of the same Battalion, was killed instantaneously in the same battle. Of the platoon he (Armour) was in, several of his chums had either been killed or were in hospital with wounds. George Johnson, Harold Johnson and Johnny Owens were all right; but he was very sorry that his brother-in-law, Private Joseph Hill, was dead. He could not enter into any of the details of the fighting; but what a blessing it would be when the awful slaughter was over, because war it was not.

It was also reported at the same time that Mrs Armour had other brothers who had fallen in battle, and who had been and were still engaged in the present War. Private Andrew Hill, of the 1st West Yorks, was killed in the battle on the Aisne on 20th September, 1914. Private Henry Hill, who was attached to the Canadians, had died of wounds received in France. Private Fred Hill (of Garforth, near Leeds), of the King's Own Regiment, and Private Tom Hill, of the same place and regiment, were prisoners of war in Germany; and Private George Hill, of the 1st West Yorks Regiment, was reported to be missing. Another brother was Gunner William Hill, who was with the Maxim Gun Detachment from the Newcastle district.

In 1916 Sarah Jane, who was born in Cirencester, Gloucester, was living at 10, Longton Grove Road, Weston-Super-Mare. She died on 8th February, 1937, aged 72, and is buried in an unmarked grave at Weston Cemetery, Weston-Super-Mare.

PRIVATE
WILLIAM HODGSON

124459, 15th Battalion Machine Gun Corps (Infantry)

William (Willie) Hodgson was born in Lancaster c.1898 and was one of two children to Martin Hodgson and Elizabeth (Barwise). He had a brother, Joseph, who died in infancy.

The 1901 census found the Hodgsons living at 43, Hulme Street, Coppenhall, Crewe, with Mr Hodgson employed as a brick turner. Born in Arlecdon, Cumbria, Mr Hodgson died on 21st January, 1911 in the Prescot district of Lancashire. He was buried in an unmarked communal grave at St Helens Cemetery, Lancashire.

Mrs Hodgson then took Willie to Flint to live with her widowed mother, Mary, at 1, Halkyn Street, and Willie took a job as an errand boy at a draper's shop. Willie and his mother would eventually settle at 8, Hill Street, and he would change jobs to work as a silkworks labourer. He never married.

Private Hodgson's grave is to be found in the Northop Road Cemetery. In 2014, 94 years after the original burial, a military headstone was placed by the CWGC (left), but mistakenly set over the wrong grave. The original Hodgson headstone is still within the cemetery grounds but has been laid flat and pushed into the hedge and is largely obscured (right)

Willie's service details are unknown but he was gassed in the trenches at some point and, as a consequence, was discharged on 9th January, 1919 after a period of service of three years and 26 days.

He died on 8th March, 1920 at his home, 8, Hill Street, of tuberculosis and buried in the Northop Road Cemetery (Grave 12, Line 40, South Side). His army service would have contributed to his early death, which is why he was commemorated by the Commonwealth War Graves Commission (CWGC).

He is not remembered on any war memorial but he was awarded the British War Medal and Victory Medal.

In 2014, after 94 years, the CWGC decided to place a military headstone over his grave – except it has been placed on Grave 14, Line 39, South Side by mistake (page 163).

Willie's mother, Elizabeth, was born in Little Clifton, Cumberland, and died on 19th September, 1954, aged 90, in a Holywell hospital. She is buried with her son William. She had been confined to her bed for the previous 10 years, but she was only admitted to hospital on the day prior to her death. She had lived in Flint for nearly 50 years, and was a member of the parish church and the Mothers' Union.

IN MEMORIAM

*You are not forgotten, Willie dear,
Nor will you ever be,
As long as life and memory last,
I will remember thee.*
His ever loving Mother.
(County Herald, 11th March, 1921)

*Just when his life seemed brightest,
Just when his day seemed best,
God called him from a world of sorrow
To a home of eternal rest.*
Ever remembered by his loving mother.
(County Herald, 10th March, 1922)

*Torn from my heart, oh how I miss him,
Loving him deeply, his memory I'll keep.
Never while life lasts shall I forget him,
Dear is the grave where my loved one sleeps.*
Fondly remembered by his loving Mother.
(County Herald, 9th March, 1923)

*In the lonely hours of thinking,
Thoughts of him are ever near;
I, who loved him, sadly miss him,
As it dawns another year.*

*God is good: He gave me strength
To bear my heavy cross;
He is the only One who knows
My loneliness and loss.*
From his loving Mother.
(County Herald, 9th March, 1928)

LANCE CORPORAL
EDWARD HUGHES

4829, 1st Battalion Cheshire Regiment

Edward Hughes was born on 18th August, 1874 at Ness, Neston, Wirral, Cheshire, and baptised on 6th September, 1874 at St Mary and St Helen's Parish Church, Neston, Wirral. He was the eldest of two children to Joseph Hughes and Annie (Cottrell).

His father, Joseph, was a farm labourer and was born in Burton, Cheshire. He died at Little Neston on 4th May, 1876, aged 27, as a result of an accident at his place of work. An inquest was held on the 6th May, which returned a verdict of: "Accidentally killed by the falling of two sheer poles." He was buried in St Nicholas' Churchyard, Burton-in-Wirral, Cheshire.

Following Joseph's death, Annie, with sons Edward and George Henry, went to live with her parents, Edward and Mary, in Ness. She met Roger Henry Bellis and they marred in Wirral, Cheshire in 1888. They lived at 26, Duke Street, Flint and had a daughter Mary Elizabeth (1892–1962) and a son Joseph Henry (1899–?).

Edward, however, remained in Ness where he was as farm servant in the employ of Mr Samuel Mealon. He joined the army in October 1894 as a Private with the Cheshire Regiment. He could not be found in the 1901 census so it is quite likely he fought in the Boer War (1899–1902).

The 1911 census found him stationed at Chester Castle and Barracks and when the war began he was one of the first to be posted overseas, landing at Le Havre, France on 16th August, 1914.

He was killed in action at the Battle of Mons, France on 24th August, 1914; he would have completed 20 years with the Colours on 7th October, 1914.

He has no known grave but is commemorated on the La Ferte-sous-Jouarre memorial, France (grave reference not known).

He is remembered on the Flint Town war memorial and his father's headstone, and was awarded the 1914 Star, British War Medal, Victory Medal and Clasp. He is also commemorated on the North Wales Heroes' Memorial Arch, Bangor.

He never married and his home address was 32, Duke Street, Flint, the residence of his mother and stepfather.

Lance Corporal Hughes, it is believed, left with one of the large drafts of regiments for the Front soon after the opening of the War, but up to March 1915 no news had been heard of his whereabouts since August. In October it was said he was numbered amongst the missing after the battle of Mons, where the 1st Cheshires were engaged and suffered loss.

Hughes' mother, Mrs R Bellis, thought he might be interned in one of the prisons. Letters were written addressed to him in the hope they would reach him. On Friday 12th March, Mrs Bellis received through the post a returned letter which was directed to him in October. The envelope bore the name of Zoorrick stamped on it, as well as other words, intimating that probably it had been the rounds via Switzerland to the German prisons, and initialled at more than one bureau. The English Military Authorities were also communicated with some time previously regarding the missing soldier, but the enquiries did not lead to clarity of the position. One soldier, who belonged to Flint, and who was in hospital several months before, had stated that in conversation with one of his fellow patients he was informed Hughes was taken prisoner. But, if that had taken place, and he were alive, he would have had numerous opportunities of writing to his mother and stepfather.

The grave of Joseph Hughes where Lance Corporal Hughes is also remembered

In November 1915, after many months of anxious waiting and persistent enquiries, Mrs Bellis received information from the War Office, dated 3rd November, stating that in reply to her enquiry of the 26th October that the death of Lance Corporal E Hughes, of the 1st Cheshires, was reported in one of the casualty lists.

Edward's mother, Annie, was born in Neston, Cheshire, and died 17th March, 1922, aged 65, at her residence, 32, Duke Street, Flint, and buried in the Northop Road Cemetery (see photo below).

Annie's husband, Roger, died in 1932, aged 79, and was buried with his wife. On leaving school he entered the employment of the United Alkali Company, with whom he served for 40 years, being one of their life pensioners. He was also employed by the North Wales Paper Company, Oakenholt, and later by the Flint Corporation for about five years.

Their daughter, Mary Elizabeth, married Thomas George Lloyd and their son, Gunner Charles Roger Lloyd, died in a Prisoner of War camp in Thailand on 5th October, 1943, aged 22.

IN MEMORIAM

Greater love hath no man than this,
that he laid down his life for those he loved.
Never forgotten by all at home.
32, Duke Street, Flint.
(County Herald, 23rd August, 1918)

PRIVATE
EDWARD THOMAS HUGHES

5815, 1ˢᵗ Battalion Royal Welsh Fusiliers

Edward (Ted) Thomas Hughes was born at 34, Feathers Street, Flint on 8ᵗʰ May, 1886 and baptised on 28ᵗʰ May, 1886 at St Mary's Parish Church, Flint. He was the eldest of nine children to William Hughes and Sarah Ann (Bushell).

The 1891 census found Ted with his grandparents, Thomas and Jane Bushell at Gardeners Row, Oakenholt, but by 1901 he was with his parents at New Western Terrace, Oakenholt and was employed by the North Wales Papermill, Oakenholt.

He married Susannah Andrews at St Mary's Parish Church, Flint on 12ᵗʰ September, 1909, and they set up home at 7, Gardeners Row. By this time, he was a galvanizer at the Shotton Ironworks.

They were to have five children: Sarah Ann (1910–1993); William Edward (1911–1915); Winifred (1912–1912); Lilian (1913–1917); Edward Thomas (1916–1993). Susannah had a son, George, born in 1904, whom Ted adopted.

Ted enlisted in Wrexham on 1ˢᵗ September, 1914 and landed at Le Havre, France on 18ᵗʰ December, 1915.

He died on 9ᵗʰ July, 1916 at No. 36, Casualty Clearing Station, of a wound in his right thigh received on the 5ᵗʰ July at the Battle of the Somme, France. He is buried in the Heilly Station Cemetery, Mericourt L'Abbe, France (Plot II, Row A, Grave 8).

Edward (Ted) Thomas Hughes was the eldest of nine children to Mr William Hughes and Mrs Sarah Ann Hughes (Bushell)

He is remembered on two war memorials: Flint Town and St David's Parish Church, Oakenholt. He is also commemorated on the North Wales Heroes' Memorial Arch, Bangor.

He is also remembered on his wife's headstone in the Northop Road Cemetery (Grave 12, Line 23, South Side). This headstone was actually found lying underneath the stone on Grave 13, Line 24, South Side, and is still there.

He was awarded the 1914–15 Star, British War Medal and Victory Medal.

For his memorial service at St David's Parish Church, Oakenholt (see Corporal John Bellis, page 15).

Ted's father, William, died 30th July, 1934, aged 69, at New Western Terrace, Oakenholt, and was buried in the Northop Road Cemetery. Mr Hughes was a native of Flint Mountain but had lived in Flint for many years, and was well known and highly esteemed in the town. He was one of the oldest members of the Flint Foresters, and was employed as a drayman at the Kelsterton Brewery Company, Connah's Quay.

His mother, Sarah Ann, was born at Bretton, Broughton and died 19th April, 1946, aged 81, at 401, Chester Road, Oakenholt. She is buried with her husband.

Susannah died at her home, 7, Gardeners Row, Oakenholt, after suffering a short illness, on 14th September, 1952, aged 69. She was buried in the Northop Road Cemetery with her children, William, Winifred, Lilian and grandson Barry Hughes, who died in February, 1953, just 5 minutes after his birth. Susannah was a native of Flint and had lived there all her life. She was a member of the Roman Catholic Church and an aunt to Private George Martin (see Volume Two).

Private Hughes is buried in the Heilly Station Cemetery, Mericourt L'Abbe, France

IN MEMORIAM

What happy hours we once enjoyed,
How sweet their memory still;
But they have left some aching hearts
This world can never heal.

Sleep on, dear son, in a soldier's grave,
In a grave we some day hope to see;
And as long as life and memory lasts
We will always remember thee.
From his sorrowing
Father, Mother, Sisters and Brothers.
(County Herald, 20th July, 1917)

A light is from our household gone,
A voice we loved is stilled,
A place is vacant from our home
Which never can be filled.

Never a day but his name is spoken,
Never an hour but he is in our thoughts,
A link in our family chain is broken,
He has gone from our home but not our hearts.
Fondly remembered by his
Father, Mother, Brothers and Sisters.
New Western Terrace, Oakenholt.
(County Herald, 12th July, 1918)

※

Three years have gone, but my heart still sore,
As time rolls on we miss him more,
Only those who have lost one are able to tell
How great is the loss of him we loved so well.
Gone but not forgotten.
Sadly missed by Wife and Family.
7, Gardener's Row, Oakenholt, Flint.
(County Herald, 11th July, 1919)

※

This day brings back the memory
Of one who was called to rest.
And those who think of him to-day
Are those who loved him best.

His heart was good, his spirit brave,
His resting place a soldier's grave;
Without a smile or a shake of the hand,
He left us all for a better land.

We know not where to find his grave,
He died a soldier, true and brave,
On Flintshire's Roll of Honour
You will find our hero's name.
Ever remembered by his
Father, Mother, Brothers and Sisters.
New Western Terrace, Oakenholt, Flint.
(County Herald, 11th July, 1919)

※

To-day recalls sad memories
That time can never heal.
We have lost, Heaven has gained,
One of the best this world contained.
Sadly missed by his
loving Wife and little Children.
Gardener's Row, Oakenholt.
(County Herald, 9th July, 1920)

※

Sleep on, dear son, in a foreign grave,
Your life for your country you nobly gave.
On earth there's strife, in Heaven there's rest,
We miss you most who loved you best.
Never forgotten by his
Mother and Father, Brothers and Sisters.
New Western Terrace, Oakenholt, Flint.
(County Herald, 16th July, 1920)

※

Sleep on, dear Ted, in a far off grave,
A grave we may never see,
But as long as life and memory last,
I will remember thee.
Never forgotten by his loving
Wife and Children, Sarah, Eddie, George.
7, Gardener's Row, Oakenholt, Flint.
(County Herald, 8th July, 1921)

※

The voice we loved is silent,
His fond true heart is still,
His vacant place remains with us
That none can ever fill.

In lonely hours of thinking,
Thoughts of him are always near;
We, who loved him, sadly miss him,
As it dawns another year.

His smiling face and happy ways
Are pleasant to recall;
He was a hero, true and brave,
And died beloved by all.
Ever remembered by his
Mother, Father, Brothers and Sisters.
New Western Terrace, Oakenholt, Flint.
(County Herald, 8th July, 1921)

PRIVATE
JOHN HUGHES

58706, 8th Battalion Welsh Regiment (Pioneers)

John (Johnnie) Hughes was born in Flint in April, 1882 and was the youngest of two children to Thomas Hughes and Catherine (Williams). Johnnie's elder brother, John, died in November, 1881 aged 18 months.

Catherine was previously married to Thomas Davies, who died in 1877, aged 45, and with whom she had five children. She married Thomas Hughes in 1879 and they resided in Mount Street, Flint, and by 1891 they had moved to 30, Earl Street.

When in his late teens Johnnie was employed as a bricksetter, and 10 years later he was still a bachelor living with his parents, at 78, Earl Street, working as a bricklayer's labourer at the Holywell Road Silk Factory, Flint.

On 5th January, 1913 Johnnie's father, Thomas, died at his home and is buried in an unmarked grave in the Northop Road Cemetery.

Mr Hughes was a native of Bagillt and had been in failing health for the last 12 months of his life, death being due to a growth in his lungs. He was a faithful member of the Seion Chapel, and was highly respected by all who knew him. He was also a member of the Ancient Order of Foresters, and was the third oldest member of the Flint Branch, having been in membership altogether over 47 years. He was employed as a chemical labourer at the Alkali Works.

Johnnie married Eleanor (Nellie) Wellings at the Sion Welsh Congregational Chapel, Hill Street, Flint on 13th December, 1916 by special licence. She was born in Leaton, Shropshire, and was a daughter of William Wellings (see Volume Two), licensee of the Windmill Tavern, Nant y Flint, and his wife Elizabeth, and a sister to Private Ernest Price Wellings (see Volume Two).

Nellie's niece, the late Mrs Ethel Salisbury-McLaren, related the story that, when Nellie and Johnnie married, the registrar failed to turn up, so Nellie wouldn't consummate the marriage. Johnnie returned to his regiment and in the early hours of one morning paid Nellie a visit whilst on a 48-hour furlough. Nellie was living with her parents at the Windmill Tavern, Nant y Flint, where she shared a room with her sister. She turned him away and said she would see him the next day, which she did, and they went to the Registrar's Office, for on the marriage certificate is a side note that states: "In entry No 125 Col 2 for Ellen read Eleanor corrected on the 15th January 1917 by me James Jones Registrar in the presence of John Hughes & Eleanor Hughes. The Parties Married." It also states the Registrar was present at the marriage ceremony.

Johnnie's service record confirms that while he was stationed at Kinmel Park Camp, Rhyl, he left the camp at 11:30 pm on 14th January, 1917; except he was AWOL (absent without leave) and not on a furlough. He returned to camp at 8:00pm the following day. Lance Corporal Evans and Sergeant Welch were witnesses and he was "confined to barracks" for two days as punishment.

Mrs Salisbury-McLaren also stated that, as long as she lived, Nellie never felt she and Johnnie were really married. She had a boyfriend, named Jack Griffiths, who had a false leg and owned a shoe shop in the town and whom she courted before her marriage to Johnnie, and after he died, but she refused to marry him.

Service record: enlisted in Flint, 23rd August, 1916, with the 13th Battalion Cheshire Regiment, No. 54667, attached to the 12th Welsh Regiment, and posted to a home base; previously served 36 days with the 9th Battalion Royal Welsh Fusiliers; transferred to the 8th Battalion Welsh Regiment, Indian Expeditionary Force, 12th February, 1917; embarked Devonport, 9th March, 1917; disembarked Bombay, 7th May, 1917; arrived Depot Kirkee, 7th May, 1917; admitted to hospital in Kirkee, 12th July, 1917, suffering from malarial fever with symptoms of vomiting and hallucinating. On enlistment he was 5 ft 6¾ in, chest 39½ in, weight 156lb, had flat feet, and his physical development was good; his wife, Eleanor, was awarded a widow's pension of 13s 9d per week with effect from 28th January, 1918.

Private Hughes died on 20th July, 1917, at 10pm, at the Deccan British War Hospital, Poona, India, of Malaria.

He has no known grave but is commemorated on the Kirkee Memorial, Poona, India, on Face 6 (see right).

He is remembered on three war memorials: Flint Town, Seion Chapel, Hill Street, Flint and Oddfellows Hall, Flint, and was awarded the British War Medal and Victory Medal. He is also commemorated on the North Wales Heroes' Memorial Arch, Bangor.

Private Hughes' name was engraved twice on the Flint Town memorial because his mother and his wife put his name forward, and since they both gave a different address it wasn't noticed they were one and the same.

Johnnie's mother, Catherine, died on 1st September, 1931 and is buried in the Northop Road Cemetery, but not with either of her husbands.

Mrs Hughes, who was in her 92nd year, claimed to be the oldest inhabitant of the town. A native of Nevin, Anglesey, she had spent most of her life in Flint, having lived in the town for over 70 years. She was well known and highly respected in the town and district, and had been a lifelong member of the Seion Welsh Congregational Chapel, where she took an active part in the work of the cause. She retained all her faculties up to the time of her death, and she was remarkable for an extraordinary and vivid memory of events in the distant past.

Her daughter, Annie Davies, was engaged with the Friends of Armenia Society in the Syrian Mission

Field during WW1 and for many years later. She died in 1958, aged 83, and was buried with her mother.

Nellie died at 11, Cilfan, Flint, in July, 1967, and was buried in the Old London Road Cemetery (see right). She was a member of the Darby and Joan Club and the Parish Church.

IN MEMORIAM

*Not now, but in the coming years,
It may be in the better land.
I'll read the meaning of my tears,
And there some time I'll understand.*
His sorrowing wife, Nellie. Windmill Tavern, Nant, Flint.
(County Herald, 10th August, 1917)

*There is a link one cannot sever;
Fond love and remembrance last forever.*
Gone but not forgotten, by his sorrowing wife Nellie. Windmill Tavern, The Nant.
(County Herald, 19th July, 1918)

PRIVATE
JOHN EDWARD HUGHES

25646, 17th (Service) Battalion Royal Welsh Fusiliers (2nd North Wales)

John Edward Hughes was born 29th May, 1897 at 34, Earl Street, Flint, and baptised 8th November 1898 at St Mary's Parish Church, Flint, and was the only child of Edward Hughes and Annie (Davies).

When John was born the Hughes family were residing at 34, Earl Street and, by the time of the 1911 census, they had settled at 3, Queen Street.

On leaving school he gained employment at the Zinc Department at the United Alkali Company's Works, Flint, and he was never to get married.

John's mother, Annie, a native of Holywell, died at her home on 19th October, 1912, aged 51, and was buried in the Northop Road Cemetery.

Service record: enlisted in Flint, 13th March, 1915; joined regiment at Llandudno, 14th March, 1915; at Llandudno on 28th July, 1915 he was confined to barracks for being absent from 7am parade until 9:30am and not complying with an order; at Winchester on 12th November, 1915 he went absent of Pass and remained absent until reporting himself at 9:40pm on the 14th (45 hours) and forfeited 2 days' pay; embarked from Southampton and landed in France, 4th December, 1915. His medical report stated he was 5 ft 2 in, weighed 9st, chest 33 in and his physical development was good.

Private Hughes died on 20th January, 1916, at No. 7 Hospital Clearing Station, France, of gunshot wounds in the back and chest received in action on the 19th January.

He was buried in the Merville Communal Cemetery, France (in Plot VI, Row G, Grave 7).

He is remembered on two war memorials: Flint Town and St Mary's Parish Church, Flint, and was awarded the 1914–15 Star, British War Medal and Victory Medal. He is also commemorated on the North Wales Heroes' Memorial Arch, Bangor.

The following letter, probably to the War Pensions Department in 1919, suggests the sad plight of Private Hughes' widowed father.

Mr Edward Hughes

3 Queen Street
Flint

2nd Sep 19—

Dear Sir

This statement is as true as I can possibly give it as I was fully depending on my son the soldier there was only me and him and I am 60 years of age. There is only one nephew and he is in France. I could not say what part and I am trying to do a little to help my pension.

I am Sir your obedient servant
E Hughes

John Edward was first cousin to Lance Corporal Henry Weale, of Shotton, Flintshire who, whilst serving with the 14th Battalion Royal Welsh Fusiliers, was awarded the Victoria Cross for action at Bazentin-le-Grand, France on 26th August, 1918.

John's Connah's Quay-born father, Edward, died 28th November, 1932, aged 72, at Lluesty Hospital, Holywell and is buried with his wife in an unmarked grave. He was employed as a labourer at the United Alkali Company's Works, and had previously, for many years, followed a seafaring career, and in that capacity had travelled practically all over the world.

GUNNER
THOMAS HUGHES

258253, 57th Reserve Battery Royal Field Artillery

Thomas (Tommy) Hughes was born in Llanasa 24th July, 1896, and was the second of eight children to William Hughes and Susannah (Williams).

For most of his life Tommy lived at 1, Castle Dyke Street, Flint then moved with the family to 55, Sydney Street, Flint. His occupation is unknown and at the time of his enlistment in the army circa August 1917, he was still a bachelor

He was wounded and gassed in action in France and died 24th November, 1918 at Fargo Hospital, Salisbury Plain, Wiltshire, and the news of his death reached Flint the following day and was reported in the County Herald on the 29th November.

The sad news reached Flint on Monday that Private Hughes had died. It is only a week or two since he was home on Furlough, and he had not been long back at camp, when his father was called away to see him, a telegram informing him that his son was dangerously ill. On Sunday night the gallant soldier passed away, from pneumonia, which followed an attack of the influenza. Widespread regret has been caused by the sad intelligence, for Mr Hughes was well known in Flint, and our readers will sympathise with the parents in their sad bereavement. He was buried five days later, in the grave of his brother William, who died in August 1910 aged 18 months, in the Northop Road Cemetery, Flint, (Grave 7, Line 19, South Side).

He is remembered on three war memorials: Flint Town, St Mary's Parish Church, Flint and Oddfellows Hall, Flint, and was awarded the British War Medal and Victory Medal. He is also commemorated on the North Wales Heroes' Memorial Arch, Bangor.

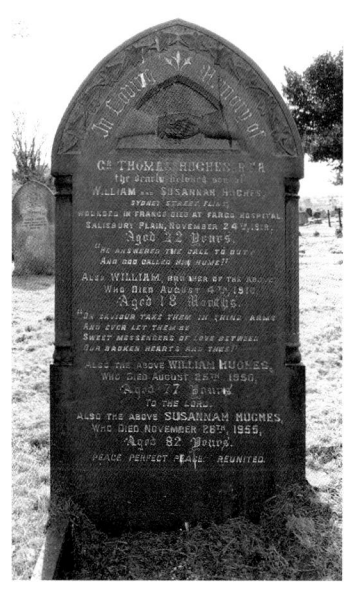

The Hughes family grave

Thomas's father, William, who was a native of Abergele, died 25th August, 1950, aged 77, and is buried with sons William and Thomas. Mr Hughes came to Flint in the late 1890s to join the Flintshire Constabulary. He later became a works policeman for the United Alkali Company. Later still he became a watchman at Castle Works, and though he retired he was recalled to the position at the outbreak of the 1939 war, finally retiring at the age of 75. He was a staunch member of St Catherine's Welsh Church, and was also a member of the Oddfellows' Society and the Borough Workingmen's Club.

William's wife, Susannah, was born in Llanddulas, Denbighshire, and died on 26th November, 1955, aged 82, at her home in 29, Sydney Street, after a long illness, and was buried with her husband. Mrs Hughes came to reside in Flint with her husband and was a member of the Mothers' Union and St Catherine's Welsh Church.

Mr and Mrs Hughes had nine grandchildren, one of whom was killed in WW2.

IN MEMORIAM

In sad but loving 23rd birthday, 24th July, remembrance.

A bitter grief, a shock severe,
To part with one we loved so dear.

We oftimes think of his last words,
The night he passed away,
And those last words in memory
We'll carry to our graves.

We sometimes call his name,
But all that's left to answer now is his
picture in the frame.
So sadly missed by his Father and Mother.

The days may wipe out many things
But this they'll wipe out never,
The memories of those happy days
That we all spent together.

We cannot forget you, nor do we intend,
We think of you daily and will to the end,
We mourn you in silence and sorrow unseen,
And dwell on the memory of days that have been.
Never forgotten by your loving sisters
Louie, Maggie, Susie, Phoebe, Fanny,
and little brother Hughie.
(County Herald, 25th July, 1919)

We sit and think in silence
Till our hearts are sore with pain,
Oh, this world would be a heaven
Could we see our boy again;

We always picture his smiling face,
And we think we can hear him say,
"Don't fret, father and mother dear,
You will come to me some day."

When life's short journey is ended,
When all partings and sorrows are o'er,
We shall know why our loved one was taken
When we meet on that lovely shore.
Sadly missed by Dad and Mam.
(County Herald, 28th November, 1919)

Days of sadness still come o'er us,
Hidden tears do oftimes flow.
Dear memory brings our dear Tom near us,
Though he died one year ago.

Time may heal our broken hearts,
Time may make the wound less sore,

But time can never stop the longing
For our loved ones gone before.

Some day we hope to meet him,
Some day we know not when,
To clasp his hand in the better land,
Never to part again.
Fondly remembered by his loving sisters,
Louie, Maggie, Susie, Phoebe, Fanny
and little brother Hughie.

❧

Deep in my heart you are fondly remembered,
Sweet happy memories cling round your name,
A true heart that loved you with deepest affection,
Always shall love you in death just the same.
Fondly remembered by Eleanor,
Brighton Terrace, Walwen, Bagillt.

The cup was bitter, the loss severe,
To part with one I loved so dear.
Ever remembered by his friend Tom,
6, Coleshill Street, Flint.

❧

Just when his hopes were brightest,
Just when his days were best,
Yet God thought best to call him
To His eternal rest;

His pleasant smile and cheery ways
Are pleasant to recall,
He had a kindly word for each
And died beloved by all.
Ever remembered by Mr. and Mrs. Owens,
Waen Isa, Near Northop.

❧

Long and weary was his illness,
Yet he never did complain,
For he bore it all with meekness,
As his Saviour did the same.
Never to be forgotten by his friend, J Fox, Flint.
(County Herald, 28th November, 1919)

In sad but loving 24th Birthday remembrance.
The voice we loved is silent,
His fond true heart is still,
His vacant place remains with us
That none can ever fill.
Though parted by the hand of God,
In Christ united still,
We'll meet again at the Golden Gate
For Jesus said we will.
Never will he be forgotten by his loving Father,
Mother, Sisters, and only Brother, Hughie.
(County Herald, 23rd July, 1920)

❧

Not dead to those who loved him,
Not lost, but gone before;
He lives with us in memory still,
And will for ever more.

Days of darkness still come o'er us,
Sorrows path we often tread,
But the Saviour still is with us,
By His hand we are safely led.

He will keep us till the river
Rolls the water at our feet,
Then He'll bear us safely over,
Where our dear one we shall meet.
Ever remembered by his Sister Louie and
Brother-in-law Tom. 79, Chester Road, Flint.

❧

So sadly missed by all at home,
He answered the call to duty, and God
called him home.
The Angels of Heaven are guarding his soul,
Till we meet him again at the call of the roll.
Father, Mother, Brother and Sisters. To memory
ever dear. From Elinor. (County Herald,
26th November, 1920)

PRIVATE
THOMAS JOHN HUGHES

6265, 2/19th London Regiment

Thomas (Tom) John Hughes was born on 14th November, 1894 at Bryn y Garreg, Flint Mountain, and was the eldest of three children to Alderman Edward Arthur Hughes and Mary Catherine (Williams).

Living with his family at Bryn y Garreg House, Flint Mountain, Tom was educated at Flint Mountain, Flint Council, and Mold County Schools.

He was employed as a draughtsman with the Flintshire County Council in the County Surveyor's Department, and was previously in the Cost Department of Messrs J Summers and Sons Hawarden Bridge Works Offices.

He was a single man when he enlisted in the army at Flint, circa August 1914, with the Royal Army Medical Corp (RAMC), No. 77404. He was transferred to the London Regiment in May, 1916 and landed at Le Havre, France on 24th June, 1916.

Private Hughes was killed in action on 29th July, 1916 in the Neuville, St Vaast area of Vimy Ridge, France, and was buried in the Ecoivres Military Cemetery, Mont St Eloi, France (Plot II, Row B, Grave 26) along with 31 comrades of his regiment.

He is commemorated on the Flint Town War memorial (as John Thomas Hughes) as well as on the North Wales Heroes' Memorial Arch, Bangor. He is also remembered on his parents' headstone in the Northop Road Cemetery (Grave 8, Line 3, South Side), and was awarded the British War Medal and Victory Medal.

He joined the RAMC with several of his friends, who remained together, being removed from one encampment or depot to another: but eventually they were transferred to one of the London regiments. With that Battalion, they learned the infantry duties proper. They were only there a comparatively brief period before being drafted to France, and from thence to the trenches, where, after a short time Private Hughes was a victim of the enemy. There were reports that since the men became involved in trench work Private Hughes always exhibited a most cheerful disposition, and together with his bonhomie and kindliness of demeanour, all of which were youthful

Mary Catherine Hughes with son Harold

characteristic traits in him when at home, he was literally 'the life and soul' of those near him.

It was reported that Tom was well respected at his places of employment before his enlistment, and his death was lamented likewise by his former co-workers.

With his parents, he was associated with the Welsh Wesleyan Methodist Causes at Flint Mountain and Peniel (Flint), and the whole of the members of the congregations of these places of worship, as well as members of other immediate branches of the denomination, offered their sympathies to Mr and Mrs Hughes and members of their family.

The following two letters, which are respectively from the Reverend J E Reilly, Wesleyan Chaplain of the Division, and Private John Tegid Williams, son of Mr and Mrs John Williams, Riverslea, Flint, speak volumes, and are eloquent tributes to the deceased and his heroic attempted rescuer:

July 31, 1916.

DEAR MR HUGHES,

I suppose you have had word from the War Office regarding your son. You are called on like many more parents to pay the great price and offer of your best at this time. I was called on to conduct the last rites for your boy yesterday. He was badly wounded on Friday and passed away on Saturday whilst being brought down to the dressing station. All was done for him that could be done. It may be some comfort to you to know that we have the exact place marked and there will be a neat wooden cross, with name and date on it, erected within a few days, and later on you will be acquainted with the exact locality. We got the body brought back to a proper Cemetery, which will be kept in order by the Government after we leave the country.

Your son is all right; he died trying to stem back the torrent of cruelty and wrong that might have spread over the world. No man can die a nobler death. It is well with him today, but you are called on to bear the loss and to go through the world without seeing him again. I pray that the God of all Comfort will strengthen and console you in the loss you are called on to bear.

I try to get into touch with all these boys, but as I am the only Wesleyan Chaplain for the whole Division, it is impossible to know them all. Probably his Company Officer will give you more information. I was in another part at the time, and gleaned a little about him from others.

I am, Yours sincerely,

J. E. REILLY, C.F

DEAR MR AND MRS HUGHES,

I really don't know how to begin this letter, as it is the saddest day in my life. Poor Tom has been killed on Saturday morning, July 29th at 5 a.m. by a sniper. As far as I can gather, his death was practically instantaneous, and he was shot, I think, somewhere in the groin or stomach. Poor Tom, he did not suffer much agony, thank God. The rest of the Flint boys, except Jack Edwards, were in another part of the line when this terrible event occurred. Jack was a good distance away, too, when it happened, but a great chum of ours, Ernie Crellin, and he was a great chum of Tom's, too, leapt over the parapet immediately to try and rescue him, but alas! Poor Tom was gone. Tom was fixing a barbed wire in front of the trench with another man whom I don't know, when he got hit. Ernie and this man brought him in. The thing that grieves us Flint boys is that we were nowhere near him, and did not ever see him after his death. Oh, if only I could have tried to save him! Ernie risked his life to try and save him, but nothing could be done absolutely, as he died in a few seconds.

I was out on a similar job to Tom on the night but one previous to this, and another man next to me was shot almost in the same place as Tom, i.e., in the thigh or thereabouts, and three of us dragged him in, but he died of wounds the following morning. We boys are absolutely stunned by the blow. We have lost a brother, and more than a comrade, who was one of the bravest and cheeriest soldiers in the Battalion. The Colonel said he had lost one of his best men, and so he had. It is awful really. I shall go and seek his grave when I get out of the trenches.

All that could be done to save poor Tom was done. I could not believe it when Idwal told me of it, about a couple of hours after; I could not really at all. So sudden it seemed, and without a parting word. Oh, my God, how cruel! May his soul rest in peace.

I wish to convey the deepest sympathy of all the Flint boys, and also the man who attempted to save him, in your sad bereavement.

Yours very sincerely,

Tegid

Note: Ernest Crellin was killed on 22nd March, 1918 and is buried in Jerusalem.

Writing to his father and mother, who received the letter on Saturday afternoon, Private John Tegid Williams says: "Poor Tom! He was a soldier and a man. May his soul rest in peace. It is a terrible blow to us, and will be to his family, I know. But, when you know the history of his death and of the attempt to save his life you will consider it one of the bravest deeds in this war. Give my deepest sympathy to his father and mother. He was a lad to be proud of; and we deeply mourn his loss."

Note: Tegid Williams survived the war with the 2/19th, though was wounded in Palestine in the Spring of 1918.

Mr and Mrs Hughes received a number of letters of condolence; and it is believed another letter from one of the Flint youths was received bearing kindly references to the late Private Hughes

His commanding officer also wrote a letter of condolence:

> B.E.F., France,
>
> 4th August, 1916
>
> DEAR MR AND MRS HUGHES,
>
> I expect that you have already received the sad news of your son's death, and as the officer who witnessed his death, and as a friend of Tom, I am writing to you personally to give you the circumstances leading up to it.
>
> On Friday last the Germans blew up a mine just in front of our line, and, as is usual on these occasions, we worked all night to consolidate the crater. Your son worked at the top of the crater all night, and by his courage and bravery in the face of many dangers set a magnificent example to the rest of the men during that very trying period. Towards morning a volunteer was called for to put up wire entanglements, and your son immediately volunteered. It was whilst doing this work that he was shot by a sniper – death being instantaneous. We all, both officers and men, deplored his loss. He was a splendid type of British manhood, and his unfailing cheerfulness and bravery in many dangers was most marked.
>
> I know your grief is great, and words seem hard to find with which to express one's sorrow; but this I do feel – that your grief will be mingled with pride in that he died so nobly for England.
>
> I brought down 12 men from the trenches yesterday – men who have spent a very strenuous time on that crater and are down for 3 days rest, and we all went this afternoon to see Tom's grave in the British Cemetery here. He is buried side by side with the other brave lads who have given their lives for England.
>
> Doubtless the other Flint boys have written concerning the arrival of parcels, etc., and I am returning letters which have recently arrived. The Flint boys are much esteemed in our Battalion, and especially the D company, to which they all belong – fine lads.
>
> If there is any further information I can give you, do please write to me.

> With profound sympathy,
>
> Yours sincerely,
>
> CHAS. F. ASHDOWN,
> 2nd Lieut.

Further communications were received from the Front concerning the death of Private Hughes and all conveyed additional testimony to the excellent soldierly qualities he possessed. The letters were couched in the most touching terms. Private Hughes was undoubtedly exceedingly popular amongst all his comrades, and his courage and bravery, combined with his self-sacrifice in strict attention to duty, have earned for him the undying fame that he died the noblest of deaths after performing a duty of great danger.

The following letter was from the Captain of his Company, of one of the London Regiments:

> DEAR SIR,
>
> Please allow me to offer you my very sincere sympathy in the loss you have suffered in the death of your son. In the couple of months he had been with us I had come to know him not only as a good soldier, but as a fine fellow as well. You may well be proud of your son's end, for he died very gallantly, performing a duty of great danger, and it was satisfactorily completed before he was shot through the body. It will, I hope, be some consolation to you and Mrs Hughes to feel that his life was not given in vain, but that the task we were engaged upon was brought to a successful end. He only lived a few seconds after being hit, and it was one of his own pals, I think, who brought him back to the trench. If it is allowed, I will let you know particulars of his place of burial, and his personal effects and correspondence shall be returned to you. In conclusion, let me assure you again of my sympathy with you both, and my personal sorrow at the loss of a gallant comrade.
>
> Believe me to be,
>
> Yours sincerely,
>
> F. W. EAMES,
> Capt.

Alderman Edward Arthur Hughes, who was born in Ffynnongroyw, died at his home at Bryn y Garreg

House on 1st December, 1918, aged 51, after a long and painful illness. His obituary, as reported in the County Herald, makes interesting reading and is as follows:

"He had been in failing health for the greater part of a year, but with characteristic grit and perseverance he stuck to work as long as possible. For the past two or three months, however, he had been compelled to relinquish his various activities, under the advice of his medical attendant, Dr J H Williams. For some time he was a patient at the Royal Infirmary, Liverpool, but he returned home, and, gradually weakening, died as stated, to the great grief of his family, relatives and friends.

Alderman Hughes was the son of the late Mr Thomas Hughes, underground manager of a colliery in the Mostyn district. While he was still a boy, the family came to live in Flint, his father having received an appointment as underground manager at the Red Pits Colliery. Upon completing his education at the Flint Church of England School, young Hughes became an assistant to an ironmonger named Caparoni, who then carried on business in Chester Street. After remaining there for some time, he obtained employment at the Red Pits, under Mr Dawes, who was at that time the manager. He remained there for a number of years, rising to the position of cashier and secretary. Eventually the colliery was closed, and Mr Hughes then took up a position as traveller for a Leeds firm of colliery rope manufacturers, covering the Yorkshire, Lancashire, and North Wales district. After being engaged in this work for two or three years, and on the death of the late John Morgan, succeeded that gentleman as secretary and organising agent of the Flintshire Liberal Association. In that important office he displayed great industry and ability, and was for some years a prominent figure in the Registration Courts in the county. Upon the outbreak of war in 1914, his sphere of activity was transferred to the

Private Hughes is buried in the Ecoivres Military Cemetery, Mont St Eloi, France

IN MEMORIAM

In loving memory of my
dear friend Geoffrey.

*In the bloom of life death claimed him,
In the pride of his manhood days,
None knew him but to love him,
None mentioned his name but with praise.
There is a link death cannot sever,
Fond remembrance last for ever.*
From his dear friend Tom Hughes,
12, Mumforth Street, Flint.
(County Herald, 7th March, 1919)

County Recruiting Committee, and in this capacity his services were of great value to the county.

In the Borough of Flint, the late Alderman Hughes was a very familiar figure for the past twenty years. He entered the Town Council in November 1899 as a councillor, and speedily came to the front as a member of that body. His special forte lay in the financial business of the council, and as chairman of the Financial Committee for many years he displayed great skill and resourcefulness in managing the borough's finances. Two years ago, upon the resignation of Alderman S K Muspratt, he succeeded that gentleman as an alderman of the council. On July 27th last occurred the death of Alderman C E Dyson, the Mayor of Flint, and on August 6th Alderman Hughes was, by the unanimous vote of the council, elected as Mayor in his stead. It was observed at the time, by those who were present at the Council meeting, that his physical powers were waning. After his election to the Mayoralty he was only able to make one of two more appearances in that capacity, and his last was on Remembrance Day, when he gave an address from the balcony of the Oddfellows' Hall.

Alderman Hughes had filled a number of public positions apart from his connection with the Town Council. He was secretary of the Flint Liberal Club for some time, secretary of the Flintshire Branch of the Welsh Heroes' Association, and chairman of the Borough Food Committee. He was at one time a keen cricketer, and president of the Flint Cricket Club, and he also played a first class game of billiards.

Alderman Hughes was well known in religious circles, as a prominent member of the Welsh Wesleyan denomination, and was one of the leaders of the Bethel Chapel at Flint Mountain, as well as a local preacher connected with the Flint Circuit.

The deceased gentleman leaves a widow, one son, and one daughter to mourn his loss. His eldest son, Tom, who was in the army, was killed in action last year, a bereavement which was a great blow to his father. General sympathy will be felt with the family in their grief, while it is recognised Flint has lost one of its most prominent and useful public men.

Alderman Edward Arthur Hughes

At the Borough Sessions yesterday (Wednesday) morning, the Mayor referred to the loss which the Borough had sustained in the death of Alderman Hughes, who, he said, was one of the most useful men they had. They as a Bench tendered to Mrs Hughes and family their sincerest sympathy and condolence in her bereavement– Mr. Matheson (deputy-magistrates' clerk), and Messrs Kerfoot Roberts and Clement Jones (Holywell), on behalf of the solicitors practising in the court, also concurred in the Mayor's remarks.

The funeral of the late Alderman took place on Wednesday afternoon last week, amid general signs of mourning. At 1:45 the cortege left the deceased gentleman's residence at Flint Mountain, and proceeded to the Welsh Wesleyan Chapel, where a service was held, conducted by the Reverend

Gwynfryn Jones. The Reverend T G Ellis read a portion of scripture, and the Reverend D Davies led in prayer. The lesson was read by the Reverend H Evans. The Reverend G Jones then gave an eloquent address to the large assembly. He made a very touching reference to the late Alderman Hughes, and remarked how valuable had been his services to the church, and how faithfully they had been rendered. He was followed by the Right Hon J Herbert Lewis, who also gave a very appreciative address. He spoke of Mr Edward Arthur Hughes, as he had known him personally. The late gentleman was one of the best men he (Mr Lewis) ever wished to meet,– always sympathetic, cheerful, and always ready to lend a helping hand to everybody. Many a time he (Mr Lewis) had gone to Mr Hughes depressed and very worried over some matter, and the sympathy and optimistic cheerfulness with which he was greeted, and with which Mr Hughes conversed, made him go away with a load lifted from his mind. He was a sincere friend, and the personal loss he had sustained was irreparable.– The deceased gentleman's favourite hymn, "Art thou weary, art thou languid?" was touchingly sung, and several other beautiful hymns were also rendered. The cortege then passed down to Flint. It was met half-way by the Mayor and Corporation, who joined in the solemn procession. The funeral procession was a lengthy one, and was joined by parties of sympathisers on the way to the cemetery.

The Hughes family grave in the Northop Road Cemetery

At the next council meeting the Mayor (Councillor Henry Powell) paid the following tribute the late Alderman Hughes: "He was a good and faithful husband and a loving father. Alderman Hughes was a strong personality, and a prominent public man for years. He rose from the ranks, and occupied the highest position the town could offer,–and held the honour with credit to himself and added dignity to the Council. As councillor, alderman and chief magistrate of the ancient borough he attained those high offices by force of character and integrity. He also at different periods was Chairman of the School Attendance Committee, the Fire Brigade, Finance Committee, and Local Food Committee. His motto was "Forward," and he (the speaker) might add, his characteristics were "enthusiasm and perseverance." His life was one strenuous day. His was an example worthy of emulation; his life and work were strongly fixed in the moral, social, religious, and political life of the town. Today they mourned his loss as friend, councillor, and townsman. Might his example in overcoming all obstacles be an incentive to others."

Mrs Hughes was a native of Flint Mountain and died on 23rd May, 1954, aged 80, after a long illness, at 1, Firbank, Caerwys, the home of her son and daughter-in-law, and was buried with her husband.

She was a former Mayoress of Flint and, before leaving for Caerwys in 1940, she was a faithful member of Bethel C M Church, Flint Mountain.

SERGEANT
TREVOR OWEN HUGHES

13633, 9th (Service) Battalion
Royal Welsh Fusiliers

Trevor Owen Hughes was born 11th May, 1893 at 22, Mumforth Street, Flint and baptised on the 5th June, 1893 at St Mary's Parish Church, Flint. He was the eldest of two children to Thomas Hughes and Emma (Jones).

When Thomas and Emma married in St Mary's Parish Church on 22nd June, 1892 Thomas was a widower, his first wife being a Miss Redfern, with whom he had a son in 1875 named Evan Thomas.

In 1895 their daughter Annie Nesta was born while the family were still living at 22, Mumforth Street, however, by the time of the 1901 census they had moved to the Volunteer Arms at 62, Mount Street, which for some unknown reason later became No. 76. On 21st October, 1902 Thomas died at the age of 52 and was buried in the Northop Road Cemetery. He was a native of Halkyn and had been employed as a collier. On her husband's death Emma became licensee of the pub.

A newspaper photo of Sergeant Hughes

Trevor was educated at the Flint National and Holywell County Schools and on leaving became an apprentice joiner with Mr Alfred Bibby Lloyd, builder and contractor, Halkyn Street, Flint.

The 1915 electoral register revealed he was a boarder at the Volunteer Arms sharing a first-floor furnished bedroom and paying a rent of 20 shillings to his mother.

He never married and enlisted in the army at Flint in September 1914. He was promoted to Sergeant, circa June 1915. After a lengthy training, during which Sergeant Hughes applied his abilities when superintending detachments of men in the erection of military huts at Salisbury Plain, he left with the Battalion for the Front in France and landed at Boulogne 19th July, 1915.

He was killed in action on the first day of the Battle of Loos on 25th September, 1915, and the sad news was received by his mother on Saturday 2nd October.

Private Harold Jackson, son of Mrs Jackson, of the Blue Bell Inn, Castle Street, wrote a letter to Mrs Hughes expressing sympathy: "He always led a clean and good life out here, and he met his death doing his duty bravely. We all know what a sacrifice you have made–the same as many more mothers who have lost their sons. We pray to God to give you strength to bear the burden of sorrow."

Private Charles Bennett (page 30), of the same Battalion, and who was near Hughes at the time he received the fatal wound, wrote to inform his friends that Sergeant Hughes died like a hero.

It was reported that Sergeant Hughes was as promising a man in civil life as he was a soldier. He was thorough and straightforward in all things.

As a joinery apprentice he studied for the London Guilds of Arts and Crafts, gaining certificates in various departments. He was an old CLB-ite (probably Church Lad's Brigade), a member of the Church of England Men's Society (CEMS), church choir, and Sunday school, and an active member of the Flint Castle Lodge of Oddfellows. His death was the first of a soldier connected with the Lodge and the flag at the Oddfellows' Hall was hoisted half-mast on hearing the news.

He has no known grave but is commemorated on the Loos Memorial, France on Panels 50 to 52.

He is remembered on three war memorials: Flint Town, St Mary's Parish Church, Flint and Oddfellows Hall, Flint. He is also remembered on his parents' headstone in the Northop Road Cemetery (Grave 4, Line 10, South Side).

He was awarded the 1914–15 Star, British War Medal and Victory Medal and is also commemorated on the North Wales Heroes' Memorial Arch, Bangor.

The Hughes family grave in the Northop Road Cemetery

The Volunteer Arms (centre) is the second house down to the right of the motor car

Sergeant Hughes' medals

IN MEMORIAM

One less at home, the charmed circle broken,
A dear face,
Missed day by day from its accustomed place,
But cleansed, and saved, and perfected by grace,
One more in Heaven.

One less at home, one voice of welcomed hush,
And ever more.
One farewell word unspoken! on the shore
Where parting comes not; one soul landed more,
One more in Heaven.
His sorrowing Mother and Sister.
(County Herald, 29th September, 1916)

❧

Only a step removed,
And that step into bliss!
Our own, our dearly loved,
Whom here on earth we miss.

Only a step removed!
We soon again shall meet,
Our own, our dearly loved,
Around the saviour's feet.
Deeply mourned by his sorrowing
Mother and Sister Nesta.
(County Herald, 28th September, 1917)

❧

A voice from heaven,
I shine in the light of God,
His likeness stamps my brow
Thro' the shadows of death my feet have trod,
But I reign in glory now.

Do I forget! Oh, no,
For memory's golden chain
Still binds my heart to yours below,
Till we meet and touch again.

Do you mourn when another star
Shines out from the glittering sky,
Do ye weep when the raging voice of war
And the storm of conflict die.
His loving Mother and Sister.
(County Herald, 27th September, 1918)

❧

'Tis sweet to know we'll meet again
Where partings are no more,
And that the one we loved so well
Has only gone before.
His loving Mother and Sister.
Volunteer Arms, Flint.
(County Herald, 26th September, 1919)

❧

Time wears off the edge of grief,
But memory turns back every leaf.
From his loving Mother and Sister.
76, Mount Street (late Volunteer Arms), Flint.
(County Herald, 25th September, 1936)

Trevor's mother, Emma, died suddenly on 26th November, 1936 at her residence, 76, Mount Street, which was formerly the Volunteer Arms, but became defunct in 1919.

Mrs Hughes, who was in her 81st year, was making herself ready to go and visit some friends when she complained of feeling unwell. She was ill only a few minutes and died with almost tragic suddenness. Mrs Hughes was a native of Flint and had resided in the town for the greater part of her life. She was well known and held in high regard by all who came in contact with her. She was a faithful member of St Mary's Parish Church and was one of the senior members of the Mothers' Union. The funeral took place the following Monday and she was buried with her husband.

PRIVATE
WILLIAM HUGHES

1151, 1/5th (Flintshire) Battalion Royal Welsh Fusiliers

William (Willie) Jesse Hughes was born in Flint in 1893 and was the eldest of four children to William Henry Hughes and Dorothy (Wynne).

In the 1891 census, Dorothy was living with her mother Mary at 11, Mumforth Street with William listed as a lodger. Mary, who was a midwife, died in April, 1892 and, shortly after, Dorothy and William were married at St David's Parish Church Liverpool, and continued to live in the same house. By 1911 they had moved to No. 12 in the same street and had had their four children, with William working as a stoker at the local chemical works. At this time Willie was employed as a grocer then in about May 1913 he was working as a size maker at the North Wales Paper Company, Ltd, Oakenholt.

Willie was never married and enlisted in the army at Flint in August 1914. He landed in the Dardanelles on the 8th August, 1915.

Private Hughes was killed by a sniper at Suvla Bay, Gallipoli, 18th August, 1915. He has no known grave but is commemorated on the Helles Memorial, Turkey on Panel 70 to 80.

He is remembered on five war memorials: Flint Town, St Mary's Parish Church, Flint, North Wales Paper Company, Ltd, Oakenholt (which is now SCA Hygiene Products UK Ltd), the Royal British Legion Club, Flint (this memorial was originally erected in the Paper Mill), and on the North Wales Heroes' Memorial Arch, Bangor. He was awarded the 1914–15 Star, British War Medal and Victory Medal.

The 17th September, 1915 issue of the County Herald revealed the following:

"One of the saddest stories associated with the present fighting of the Flintshire Territorials at the Dardanelles has just transpired in Flint, where it has aroused feelings of the strongest and the deepest sympathy. At the latter end of last week, Mr and Mrs William Hughes, residing at 12, Mumforth Street, and who had two sons, Privates William and Thomas Hughes, of the 1/5th Battalion of the Royal Welsh Fusiliers, with that Battalion at the Dardanelles, received the official intimation from the Records Office, Shrewsbury, that their son William had been killed in action. His parents were bereaved at the intelligence; and the youth's mother is an invalid. On Saturday afternoon the father, who had been grieving at the loss, left home, stating that he intended walking to Lloc, near Holywell, to make known the sad news to his own brother. At a somewhat later hour in the evening, when he was traversing the main road, presumably walking home to Flint, he came into contact with a motor vehicle, and sustained a very serious injury. As soon as possible Mr Hughes was conveyed to the Holywell Workhouse Hospital. He was unconscious, and not regaining consciousness, he succumbed to his injury about eight o'clock on Sunday morning. On Sunday his wife and daughter were awaiting his return home, and it gradually became known that he had met with a fatality, and this increased the sadness of the household.

On the Tuesday night, at the Workhouse Chapel, the Flintshire Coroner (Mr F Llewellyn Jones) held an enquiry as to the death of William Hughes. The foreman of the jury was Mr T W Sibeon. Mr Clement Jones held a watching brief on behalf of the owner and driver of the motor-van involved in the accident.

Mrs Hannah Turner, of 50, Chester Street, Flint, sister-in-law of the deceased, identified the body of that of her brother-in-law, William Hughes, who was 51 years of age, and a stoker at the Chemical Works. A few days ago he heard that one of his sons had been killed at the Front. She last saw him on the Saturday morning, when he said he was going to Lloc, to see some friends there. He left home at 4 o'clock, intending to walk to Lloc and he appeared to be keeping up pretty well after he heard of his son's death.

William Davies, Glanmorfa Cottages, Bagillt, labourer, stated that on Saturday night at 10.05 he left Holywell, with Edward Williams, to go down to Bagillt. Two motor bread vans passed them just on the turn by the milestone – they were not so close together. They were going at a very modest rate, and had lights. It was a fairly dark night. When they went lower down they saw the cars standing, and he thought something was the matter. Then Fennah called upon him to assist to lift deceased into the car. The driver did not say how the accident happened. When the cars were going down they were on the proper side of the road. When he got on the spot the deceased was on the road, about the middle.

Richard Fennah, Queensferry, said he was a motor driver in the employ of Mr Thomas, The Bakery. He had driven a motor since January 1st. He had been in Mr Thomas's employment a little over three months. On Saturday last he had been to Kinmel Park, and he left there on his return journey about half past eight, coming back through St Asaph and Holywell. He was alone in the van. There were two vans, and Mr Thomas was driving the first van. As they were going from Holywell, witness went slowly, as he knew what sort of a hill it was, and he put his clutch out and applied the brakes. He was going about five to ten miles an hour. Mr Thomas was 100 to 200 yards in front of him. He saw a man on the right side of the road and he sounded his horn. The man was in the middle of the road, and when he was close to him the man turned round and ran into his mudguard, which must have struck him. He pulled up at once. He shouted to two men who were coming up, and they came to his assistance, and pushed the car back from the deceased, and they lifted deceased into the van. He asked the men where was the best place to take the man, and they said Holywell, so he turned round and took him to the Police Station and from there to the Hospital. It was this side of the Twll Farm where the accident happened, on the straight road. At that time he could see the light of the first car going round the turn in front. The man must have heard him, as he sounded the horn. He had his lights obscured.– By the foreman: The van did not go over deceased, but just touched his thigh. Deceased's head went against the mudguard, and that knocked him on his back.

Samuel Blythin, New Brighton Terrace, Bagillt, collier, stated that on Saturday night he was coming from Bagillt up to Holywell, and when near the Twll Farm, Fennah shouted for help. Witness went to him straight. The car was close to the body of the deceased, pointing slightly down the road. Deceased was by the right hand front wheel. When he got there he pushed the car back. Deceased was unconscious. He helped get the deceased in the car. Another car had previously passed them on the road about three minutes before the other side of the Twll, travelling at a moderate rate. He did not see the second car until he got near to it and heard Fennah calling to him.

Dr C E Morris (Dr Jones & Morris) stated that shortly after eleven o'clock on Saturday night he saw deceased in the car at the Police Station, and ordered his removal to the Workhouse Infirmary, and came up to see him. He had a fracture on the right side of the skull, bruised back and legs, and was quite unconscious. He did not recover consciousness, and died on the Sunday morning. The fracture would be the result of the fall, there was nothing to show he had been run over, and appearances were quite consistent with the evidence of the driver of the car.– By Mr Clement Jones: If the driver had not been driving carefully he would have gone over the deceased.

The Coroner, in summing up, said from the evidence he thought the jury could not arrive at any other verdict but that the deceased was accidentally killed. Deceased might have got out of the way of the first motor, and then got back to the middle of the road, and not heard the second motor. It was possible he got confused, and got struck by the motor before he could get out of the way. There was nothing to show but that the driver was driving at a most reasonable rate.

The jury at once returned a verdict of "Accidental Death," and exonerated the driver from blame.– The Coroner agreed, remarking the evidence showed he must have been driving very slowly.– The Jury passed a vote of sympathy with the relatives of the deceased."

Willie's brother, Private Thomas Hughes, who was with the Flintshire Territorials at the Dardanelles, wrote the following letter to his mother dated 24th August:

> Dear Mother,– I am very sorry to send the news of Will's death. He got killed on August 18th. Herbert Price (Swan Street) was with him. I hope you will keep up after this sad news, for you have still another one to try and do his best. I cannot say much. He was buried very decently . . . I shall come back.

Private W G Davies, of Flint, and of the Machine Gun Section of the 1/5th Battalion of the Royal Welsh Fusiliers, wrote a letter on Monday, 23rd August, to Mr Robert Cartwright, of 87, Swan Street, Flint. The letter, which was received on Friday afternoon, stated that Herbert Price and himself were at the time in the best of health. Continuing, he wrote:

> But this is a very sad letter for me to write. Poor Bill Hughes has been killed. He was killed last Wednesday morning by a bullet through the head. He lived for about 40 minutes. Herbert was with him at the time, and had just told him to keep his head down. A few seconds afterwards he was shot. He was buried that night a few yards from the trench. Herbert George, and a few more men of Flint buried him. Jack Price, of the Gate House, made a cross and wrote on it, and Herbert put it on his grave. I could not go there myself. We had a lot of work to do to make ourselves

> safe. I expect by the time you get this letter you will have heard that Arthur Jones has been wounded in the side and shoulder. Sheady was wounded in the arm, but not serious. Poor Povey has been sent to hospital. He was struck deaf and dumb the first day that we went into action. He is being sent to England, home again. I think he will recover his hearing and speech in a few weeks' time. I hope he does. Bert George was hit in the arm last Friday and has gone to hospital . . . We are at the base for a few hours rest."

Private Herbert Price, of 65, Swan Street, Flint, who was with the 1/5th Battalion of the Royal Welsh Fusiliers at the Dardanelles, wrote to his parents informing them that he was alongside of Private Will Hughes when he was shot. He stated that the body was buried not far from where they were in the trenches.

Dorothy, who was a native of Flint, and was an invalid, died in August 1919, aged about 57, and buried with her husband in the Northop Road Cemetery.

IN MEMORIAM

Our loss Heaven has gained
One of the best the world contained.
From Mother,
Phil and Molly, and Tom,
in Egypt.
(County Herald, 17th August, 1917)

❧

In the bloom of life death claimed him,
In the pride of his manhood days,
None knew him but to love him,
None mentioned his name but with praise.

There is a link death cannot sever,
Fond remembrance lasts forever.
From all his beloved mates,
also his brother.
Sergt W G Davies,
Feathers Street, Flint.
(County Herald, 17th August, 1917)

In loving memory of William Hughes,
the dearly beloved husband of
Dorothy Hughes,
who died September 12th, 1915.

❧

There is no death, thank God for that,
He's safe within His care,
And with his thoughts to comfort us,
We can all sorrow bear.
From his Wife and Children.
(County Herald, 14th September, 1917)

❧

From my heart, Oh, how I miss you,
My loving son so kind and true,
In all my sorrow and silent suffering,
The Lord alone has helped me through.
Sadly missed by his Mother
and Brothers and Sister.
(County Herald, 16th August, 1918)

W T HUGHES

This person could not be identified but is remembered on the war memorial in St Mary's Parish Church, Flint.

PRIVATE
JOSEPH ALBERT HULLEY

61275, 40th Company Machine Gun Corps (Infantry)

Joseph (Joe) Albert Hulley was born on 8th January, 1884 at Tavern Houses, Wepre, Northop, and baptised on 10th February, 1884 at St Mark's Parish Church, Connah's Quay. He was the ninth of 11 children to William Hulley and Mary (Berry).

The Hulley family were living at Vine Cottages, Connah's Quay in 1891, and 10 years later at 1, Red House Cottages, Connah's Quay and Joseph was employed as an ironworks labourer, a position he held throughout his civilian life.

On 17th October, 1903 Joe married Elizabeth (Bessie) Cartwright at St John's Parish Church, Chester and lived with Bessie's parents at 299, West View, Oakenholt. Their son, William George, was born in 1904, daughter Beatrice Louisa in 1906, and son Albert Cecil in 1908.

Joe's father William died on 7th July, 1913 at his residence in High Street, Connah's Quay, aged 73, and was buried in Connah's Quay Town Cemetery. He was a native of the district, of which he was one of the oldest inhabitants, and was well respected. He had been employed as a foreman at the old chemical works, which were then at Wepre, and after fulfilling duties in Scotland he returned to Connah's Quay, where he held a position as foreman at the old Borax Works.

Joe and Bessie had the last of their children with the birth of their son, John Harold in December, 1913, and by this time they were living at 4, Gardeners Row, Oakenholt.

Joe enlisted in Wrexham on 31st August, 1914 with the 8th (Service) Battalion Royal Welsh Fusiliers, No. 12578. He landed at the Balkans on 6th July, 1915 and his Battalion were connected for a time with the Australians' contingent, which he praised for splendid work. Sometime after July, 1916 he was transferred to the Machine Gun Corps.

He died of wounds in Mesopotamia on 11th April, 1917. He has no known grave but is commemorated on the Basra Memorial, Iraq on Panel 41. He is remembered on three war memorials: Flint Town, St David's Parish Church, Oakenholt and the North Wales Heroes' Memorial Arch, Bangor. He was awarded the 1914–15 Star, British War Medal and Victory Medal.

Private Hulley, who was with the Battalion on the Peninsular of Gallipoli, forwarded a letter, dated 29th September, 1915, to Mr J Cartwright, of 168, Chester Road, Flint.

He referred to the fighting with the Turks and stated that on the night of the 28th September they "had a — of a night of it." The Turks made an attack upon the Battalions' trenches and they gave them something to go on with. They allowed the Turks to get right up to the British trenches. Then the order was given to the lads to charge, "and you should hear them shout when they saw the bayonet. You would stare to see some of the fellows about the size of me chasing some about 6 feet. They would have been beaten a long time ago only for the Germans who are with them. We have met Joyce and the rest of the Flint boys. I expect you will have heard all the news by now . . . It's queer how pals should meet together out here. We had a lovely voyage out here. We were on the boat 14 days, and we landed under heavy fire. We all thought our number was up; but we are here yet ... all the Pentre boys are well, excepting W. Wright. He is in a hospital, with a slight wound . . . We are amongst the hills . . . Well, now I must ring off now as old Jack, the Turk, is dropping a few shells over us, but he is getting a few back."

In a letter received two weeks later he said:

> . . . they were still pegging away at the Turks, and doing their little bit. The 8th Battalion were much in evidence. Some people thought it was a bit of a picnic out there; but if the men went for a rest they were under shellfire all the time. He did not think the 'black swine' the Turks, would hold out much longer; they would have given up long before then but for the Germans who were with them. He believed Ernest Joyce was to get the DCM; and he deserved it.

The following letter, dated 29th November, was sent to a friend, probably in 1916.

> Dear Old Sport
>
> Just a line in answer to your letter which I have received & glad to hear you where all in the pink as it leaves me at present. I believe Ben & Forrester is down the line somewhere & are going on alright as far as I know I have received a letter from G. Hooson I should just like you to read it he dose'nt (sic) half call them some names. Square heads & B- B- & B. Swines of all sorts, I can see by the reports their as been H-ll to go in France & our lads as done well Hooson was saying their prisoner's say we have to many big guns but the

swines did not say that in 1914. Well old cock their does not seem no sign of homeward bound yet & expect we will have to finish these B-----s up here first, the weather up here is a lot cooler here now but it as been H-ll up here, we are expecting the rain here any time now but I don't want another summer out here I had enough of the last one, you want to keep T Lloyd & D. Evans in good trim & I wonder what sort of a breed Bob will throw, Well Joe I must ring off now Remember me to Mr & Mrs Bellis & Ned Evans tell him to keep on the steady till me & Hooson drops on him & hoping you have had a good Xmas & wishing you all the best of luck & a Happy New Year from your Pal J. Hulley

Remember me to Gert & Willie & hurry up with the family

Right Da

How is Mash getting on with is better half.
If you know of anyone writing tell them this address

Pte J. A. Hulley
C/o Advance Base
Mac. Gun. Depot
Mes. Exp. Force

The grave of Joe's parents in Connah's Quay Cemetery (left) and Joe's wife Elizabeth's last resting place (right)

Joe's mother Mary, who was a native of Manchester, died 27th November, 1923, aged 81, and was buried with her husband and their son Frank, who died on 4th February 1915, aged 22.

His Flint-born wife, Bessie, never remarried and died on 30th October, 1954 following an illness covering some years and is buried in the Old London Road Cemetery, with her daughter and son-in-law Beatrice Louisa and Joseph H Watton. She was a member of St David's Parish Church, Oakenholt.

> **IN MEMORIAM**
>
> *Not dead to us, we loved him dear,
> Not lost but gone before,
> He lives with us in memory still,
> And will forever more.*
> Sadly missed by his loving
> Wife and Children, Mrs E Hulley.
> (County Herald, 11th April, 1919)

PRIVATE
THOMAS HUMPHREYS

76087, 9th (Service) Battalion Royal Welsh Fusiliers

Thomas (Tom) Humphreys was born in Flint in 1892 and baptised 30th November, 1892 in St Mary's Parish Church, Flint. He was the second of 11 children to Robert Humphreys and Miriam (Smith), and was a first cousin to Private William Thomas Humphreys (page 198).

For a number of years the Humphreys family were residents of the Yacht Inn, Evans Street, where Robert was the licensee and who also had a job as a general labourer.

The 1911 census found the family living at 1, New Western Terrace, Oakenholt and Robert was now working as a boiler fireman at the Shotton ironworks. Tom was also employed at the ironworks working as a galvanizer. He was also a single man and remained so. The Humphreys family were to move once more to 297, Chester Road, Oakenholt where they settled.

Tom enlisted in Wrexham in August, 1914 and landed at Boulogne on 19th July, 1915.

He was killed in action on 7th November, 1918 in Courtrai, France. He has no known grave but is commemorated on the Vis-en-Artois Memorial, France on Panel 6. He is remembered on three memorials: Flint Town, St David's Parish Church, Oakenholt and the North Wales Heroes' Memorial Arch, Bangor. He is also remembered on his parents' headstone in the Northop Road Cemetery, Flint (Grave 12, Line 38, South Side).

He was awarded the British War Medal and Victory Medal.

Writing to his parents, his officer said: "I am writing to you to extend my sincere sympathy to you and yours, at the great loss of your son, Private Humphreys, killed in action November 7th. Your son was in my platoon. He always was a good boy, and his death is felt as much by myself as by my platoon. He was unhappily killed by a shell, and it was a comfort to know he died a painless death. Assuring you of my heartfelt sympathy."

Tom's father, Robert, died 10th August, 1933, aged 65, at his home, 297, West View, Oakenholt. His obituary stated he was employed at the North Wales Paper Mill, Oakenholt for many years (which must have been during the latter part of his working life); also, as well as the Yacht Inn, at some time he held the licence of the Miners' Arms, Flint. He was a native of Flint and was very well known and highly respected. He was a member of the St Catherine's Welsh Church, where for many years he was a chorister. He was also a member of the Flint Borough Workingmen's Club.

A young Miriam Humphreys

Mrs Humphreys was born in Kelloe, Durham and died in Flint on 7th November, 1929, aged 61, after a severe illness. She was buried with her husband and their son, Edwin Smith, who died of tuberculosis on 21st April, 1919, aged 12. Before her marriage she was employed as a domestic servant for Mr Thomas J Grierson, a land agent, of Bryntirion, Bagillt.

It was reported the news of her death cast a gloom over the whole district, where she was greatly esteemed as a neighbour and friend whose kindness was always to be depended upon. She was a lifelong and staunch churchwoman, and St David's Church, Oakenholt would miss one of its most faithful members and devoted workers. She was a prominent member of the Mothers' Union attached to the church.

Robert Humphreys in his later years

An older Miriam Humphreys

The Humphreys' family grave

IN MEMORIAM

Days of sadness still come o'er us,
Hidden tears do often flow,
Dear memory keeps our loved one near us
Though he died a year ago.
Time may heal a broken heart,
Time may make the wound less sore,
But time can never stop the longing
For our loved one gone before.
Sadly missed by his
Mother, Father, Brothers and Sisters.

❧

Far away in a distant land,
Suddenly struck by death's strong hand,
A brother most dear, a hero brave,
Now lies within a soldier's grave.
Somewhere in France he is sleeping,
One of the bravest and best,
And the stars in the heavens are keeping
A watch over his lonely place of rest.
Sadly missed by his sister and
brother-in-law Sarah and George Evans.
8, Gardener's Row, Oakenholt, near Flint.

❧

Softly at night the stars are gleaming,
On a distant lonely grave,
Where our dear Tom lies sleeping,
One we loved but could not save.
Never forgotten by his loving sister Lil, and
brother-in-law Davy.
Wern House, Bagillt.
(County Herald, 7th November, 1919)

❧

In loving remembrance of our dear son, Edwin
Smith Humphreys.

Gentle in manner, patient in pain,
Our dear one's left us, heaven to gain;
With a nature so gentle, and actions so kind,
Hard in this world in his equal to find.

Links are snapped beyond repairing,
And the firmest chains are riven,
None can fill the void created,
But the gentle hands of heaven.
Sadly missed by his sorrowing Father, Mother,
Brothers and Sisters.

❧

In loving remembrance of our dear brother,
Edwin Smith Humphreys.

Dear is the grave where our brother is laid,
Sweet is his memory that will never fade.
We do not forget him, nor do we intend,
For dearly we love him and will to the end.
Fondly we love him; he is dear to us still,
But in grief we must bend to God's holy will.
Our sorrow is great, our loss hard to bear,
But angels, dear brother, will guard you with care.
Sadly missed by his loving Sister Sarah, and
Brother-in-law, George.
(County Herald, 30th April, 1920)

❧

For Memory
Oh God, how mysterious are Thy ways,
To take our boy in the best of his days;
Forgotten by some in this world he may be,
But never one moment forgotten by his
Father, Mother, Brothers and Sisters.
(County Herald, 5th November, 1920)

❧

Sleep on, dear one, in your far-off grave,
Your life for your country you nobly gave;
No one was near you to say good-bye.
But in God's keeping you safely lie.
In life we loved you dearly,
In death we do the same.
Fondly remembered by his Father, Mother,
Brothers and Sisters.
(County Herald, 11th November, 1921)

PRIVATE
WILLIAM THOMAS HUMPHREYS

105299, 2ⁿᵈ Squadron Machine Gun Corps (Cavalry)

William Thomas Humphreys was born in Flint in 1886 and was the eldest of three children to Evan Humphreys and Jane (Evans). He was a first cousin to Private Thomas Humphreys (page 195).

In 1891 the Humphreys family were living at 40, Mount Street but by the turn of the century had moved to 81, Swan Street, by which time William was employed as a labourer.

His father Evan died on 7th February, 1907 after an illness of 13 years, and was buried in the Northop Road Cemetery. He was born in Flint and was a chemical labourer. He had been a member of the Ancient Order of Foresters for many years, and was accorded a Forester's funeral.

By 1911 William was working as a packer at the ironworks in Shotton and was unmarried. He was also connected with the Welsh Wesleyan denomination of the Borough.

He enlisted at Dunwick, East Sussex in about December, 1914. He had served with the 2nd Welsh Horse Yeomanry, No. 1523, and the East Surrey Regiment, No. 28439, before transferring to the Machine Gun Corps.

In early April 1918 it was reported that Private Humphreys had been home on leave of absence from the Front in November, 1917. Soon after, he returned and the intelligence reached Flint that he was missing and that no news of his whereabouts was obtainable.

In mid-April, 1918 news reached the Borough that he had been killed in action at the Battle of Cambrai, France on 3rd December, 1917. He has no known grave but is commemorated on the Cambrai Memorial, Louverval, France on Panel 13. He is remembered on the Flint Town war memorial, the North Wales Heroes' Memorial Arch, Bangor and his parents' headstone in the Northop Road Cemetery, Flint (Grave 8, Line 14, South Side).

He was awarded the British War Medal and Victory Medal.

The Humphrey's family grave

William's mother, Jane, was born in Bagillt and died on 6th

January, 1927, aged 64, and buried with her husband and daughter Mary Elizabeth.

Mary Elizabeth died on the 21st November, 1930 at her home, 81, Swan Street, Flint. She had been ailing for about two years, but her death came suddenly, passing away in her chair while having tea. She was 40 years of age, and was very well known and highly respected in the town, and was a faithful member of the Peniel Welsh Wesleyan Church. For four years prior to her death she had occupied the position of cashier at the Empire Picture Theatre, Flint.

GUNNER
WILLIAM HUNT

199306, 32nd Siege Battery Royal Garrison Artillery

William Henry Hunt was born on 22nd May, 1887 at Llantwit Fardre, Llantrisaint, Glamorganshire. He was the eighth of 12, children to Henry Hunt and Elizabeth (Rullins).

Henry was born in Misterton, Somerset in c.1840 and was employed as a navvy, engaged in railway construction, and his work took him to various parts of the country.

His 'wife' Elizabeth (Lizzie) was born in Penryn, Cornwall c.1844, but no record of this marriage could be found. In the book The Railway Navvies by Terry Coleman, it seems that many of these communities lived by their own rules. If there was ever a marriage it might have been an informal affair. There are, however, ample records of baptisms of their many children.

At the time of the 1891 census the Hunt family were living at Machen Upper, Newport, Monmouthshire.

Henry died of tuberculosis at the Huts, Cwm yr Aber, Eglwysilan, Glamorgan on 24th January, 1892, aged about 52. After Henry's death (Lizzie) later married, or lived with, John Brown, a dock contractor's labourer, of Basingstoke, Hants, but no record of this marriage could be found either. At the time of the 1911 census they were living at 37, Spring Street, Landport, Portsmouth.

After his father's death, William was adopted by a Mr Samuel Cottle, a foreman ganger (navvy) and his wife Charlotte who resided in South Shields, Durham. The 1901 census revealed they were living at 87, Denmark Street, Durham, and William was aged 13 and employed as a general labourer. By the 1911 census William had moved to Flint and was a lodger at 44, Mount Street, the home of Mr and Mrs Edward John Bellis, and was employed as a labourer at the local chemical works.

On 4th December, 1911 William married Phoebe Catherine Jones at the Register Office, Birkenhead. William's occupation was given as dock labourer, but eight months later the couple had moved back to Flint, and were living at 4, Johnson Street, the home of her parents Joseph and Catherine, where Phoebe was born. Before the marriage Phoebe was employed as a servant to a provision merchant in Liscard, Wallasey.

William and Phoebe had a son named Samuel George Cottle Hunt (1912–1981). They also adopted the natural daughter of Phoebe's sister Maria, also named Phoebe Catherine Jones, who was born in 1904.

William had been working as a labourer when he enlisted in Wrexham on 25th March, 1918 and his medical report stated he was 5 ft 8 in, 140lb, a chest measurement of 37 in and his physical development was good. He had a fresh complexion, grey eyes and brown hair.

His service record is as follows: posted to Derby, 27th March, 1918; posted to 3rd SA Brigade at Prees Heath, Shropshire, 10th April, 1918; posted to France, 4th June, 1918; joined 32nd Siege Battery, 9th July, 1918.

Gunner Hunt was wounded in action resulting in his death on 26th August, 1918 at the 88th Field Ambulance, France.

He was buried in the La Kreule Military Cemetery, Hazebrouck, France (Plot III, Row C, Grave 3).

William's mother Elizabeth (Lizzie) Hunt

He is remembered on the Flint Town war memorial and the North Wales Heroes' Memorial Arch, Bangor. He was awarded the British War Medal and Victory Medal.

Phoebe was awarded a widow's pension of 25s 5d per week for herself and her two children, with effect from the 10th March, 1919.

William's mother, Lizzie, died in Port Talbot in the early 1930s, and would have been well into her 80s.

Phoebe was residing at 159, Prince of Wales Avenue, Flint, when she died on 15th June, 1948, aged 69. She is buried in the Old London Road Cemetery with her son Samuel and his wife Doris.

The final resting place of William's wife Phoebe

CORPORAL
JOHN ANDREW HYDE

12453, 8th (Service) Battalion Royal Welsh Fusiliers

John Andrew Hyde was born in 1888, in Red Lake, Shropshire and was the eldest of 10 surviving children (three others died in infancy) to William Henry Hyde and Elizabeth (Jones).

The Hyde family lived for many years at Red Lake, Wellington, Shropshire but by 1911 had moved to Flint and were living at 113, Chester Road. John was now employed as an ironworker and was unmarried. By 1915 they had moved again to 72, Swan Street.

He enlisted in Shotton in about August, 1914 and landed at the Balkans on 28th June, 1915.

The Flint Petty Sessions, reported in the 5th November, 1915 edition of the County Herald, revealed: "An elderly man named William Hyde, of 72, Swan Street, was summonsed for having assaulted a neighbour named Thomas Wedge. The evidence of the complainant was to the effect that they were in the "Hawarden Castle" Inn one evening, when without the slightest provocation defendant made use of some language and struck him on the face. Mr W Hughes, who was for the defence, cross-examined complainant with a view to showing that an argument had arisen as to the defendant's men serving with the RWF at the Dardanelles, and that the complainant having a son would not allow him to enlist; but the complainant denied there had been any such discussion. Mr Hughes said they did not deny the assault, and said there was some provocation, owing to the argument, which he had mentioned. Defendant was fined 10s."

In late 1916 Corporal Hyde had not been heard from for some time and there was clearly some confusion as to his whereabouts, for the 24th November edition of the County Herald reported that he was missing and the 6th July, 1917 edition stated that information had reached the Borough that he was a prisoner of war. It must have been a shock to learn that he had actually been killed in action in Mesopotamia on the 9th April, 1916.

He has no known grave but is commemorated on the Basra Memorial, Iraq on Panel 15.

He is remembered on three war memorials: Flint Town, St Mary's Parish Church, Flint and the North Wales Heroes' Memorial Arch, Bangor. He was awarded the 1914–15 Star, British War Medal and Victory Medal.

John's father, William Henry, was born in Snedshill, Shropshire and died in June, 1933, aged 76, and is buried in an unmarked grave in the Northop Road Cemetery. He was employed as an ironworker.

His mother, Elizabeth (Lizzie), was born in Red Lake, Shropshire and died at 46, Jubilee Street, Shotton in October, 1940 aged 75. She is buried with her husband and their son, Joseph Henry, who died in December, 1947 aged 42.

FIRST WORLD WAR MEMORIALS IN FLINT

The Cenotaph, Chapel Street (121 names). There are two John Hughes's listed who were one and the same. Apparently, his wife and his widowed mother both put his name forward. There are also two errors: 'K Bellis' should read 'H Bellis', and 'George E Roberts' should read 'Edward George Roberts'

St Mary's Parish Church, Church Street (78 names). There are two errors – 'W C Wheeler' should be 'W E Wheeler' and 'G E Kerfoot' should be 'J E Kerfoot'

Caersalem Chapel, Chapel Street (two names)

Seion Chapel, Hill Street (four names) – this building was demolished in the 1960s but fortunately the memorial was rescued and is now in safe keeping in someone's garage in Flint Mountain

The Bryn Mission, Bryn Road (two names) closed many years ago and was converted into a house. The memorial is now held at the Caersalem Chapel

The Royal British Legion Club has a memorial that was originally erected in the North Wales Paper Company, Oakenholt, in memory of two of their employees

XXII

The Cottage Hospital, Old London Road (one name)

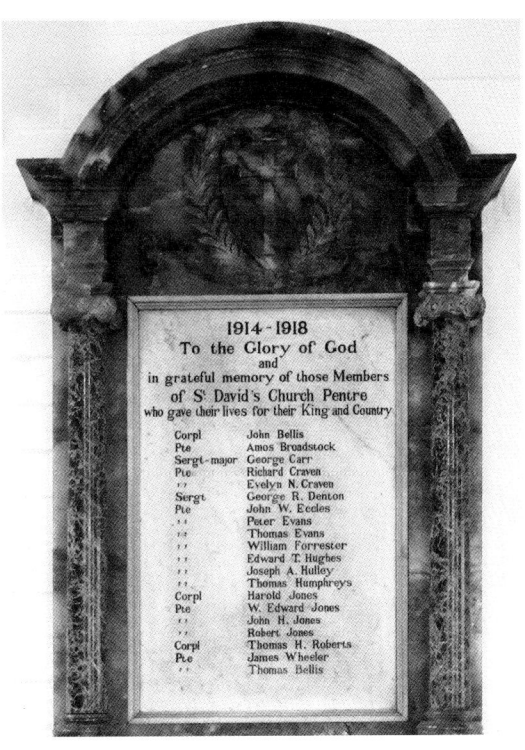

St David's Parish Church memorial:

1914-1918
To the Glory of God
and
in grateful memory of those Members
of St David's Church Pentre
who gave their lives for their King and Country

Corpl	John Bellis
Pte	Amos Broadstock
Sergt-major	George Carr
Pte	Richard Craven
"	Evelyn N. Craven
Sergt	George R. Denton
Pte	John W. Eccles
"	Peter Evans
"	Thomas Evans
"	William Forrester
"	Edward T. Hughes
"	Joseph A. Hulley
"	Thomas Humphreys
Corpl	Harold Jones
Pte	W. Edward Jones
"	John H. Jones
"	Robert Jones
Corpl	Thomas H. Roberts
Pte	James Wheeler
"	Thomas Bellis

St David's Parish Church, Oakenholt (20 names) has recently closed. The memorial was moved to St Mary's Parish Church

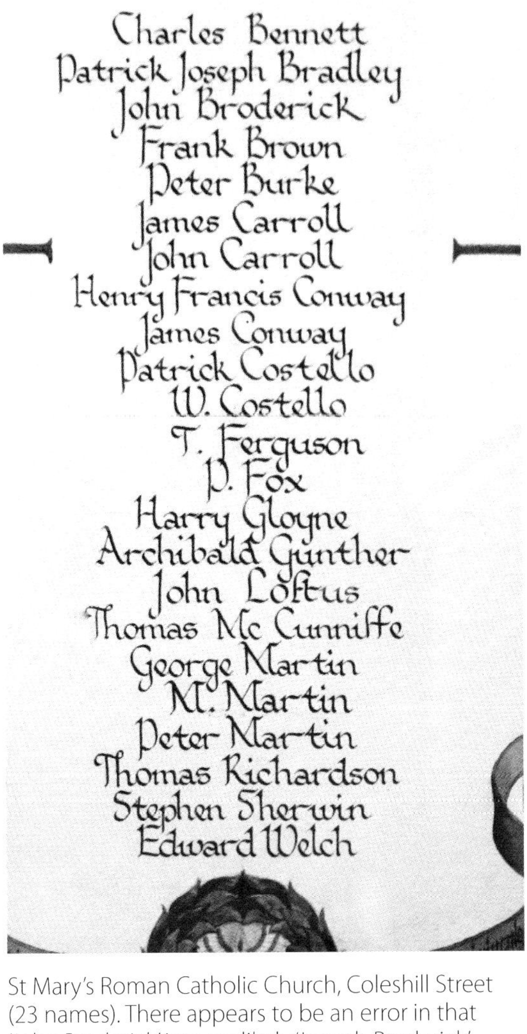

St Mary's Roman Catholic Church memorial:

Charles Bennett
Patrick Joseph Bradley
John Broderick
Frank Brown
Peter Burke
James Carroll
John Carroll
Henry Francis Conway
James Conway
Patrick Costello
W. Costello
T. Ferguson
P. Fox
Harry Gloyne
Archibald Gunther
John Loftus
Thomas Mc Cunniffe
George Martin
M. Martin
Peter Martin
Thomas Richardson
Stephen Sherwin
Edward Welch

St Mary's Roman Catholic Church, Coleshill Street (23 names). There appears to be an error in that 'John Broderick' is most likely 'Joseph Broderick'

North Wales Paper Company memorial:

FOR GOD KING AND COUNTRY LIBERTY
HONOUR
ROLL OF HONOUR — ROLL OF HONOUR

TO
COMMEMORATE
OUR GALLANT
STAFF AND WORKMEN
WHO FOUGHT FOR
OUR JUST CAUSE
IN THE
WORLD WAR
1914 - 1918

Pte Jones, R.W.
Sr Jones, S.
Dr Jones, S.S.
LCp Joyce, E. DCM
Sr Joyce, S.
McMenicall, E.
A Moulton, J.
Price, W.
Price, H.
Rogers, J.
Roberts, T.
Rush, M.
Rush, W.
Smith
Stanley, J.R.
Stevenson, W.A.
Wheeler
Williams, J.

The North Wales Paper Company Ltd (two names) is now owned by SCA Hygiene Products UK Ltd but they still have the Roll of Honour commemorating all their employees who served in the war. It includes the names of the same two soldiers as appear on the Royal British Legion memorial

The North Wales Heroes' Memorial Arch, Deiniol Road, Bangor (114 names) contains the names of over 8,500 soldiers, sailors and airmen from the counties of North Wales, who fell in the First World War. The interior of the first floor is lined with oak panels inscribed with the names of the fallen, arranged by parish and county

In addition to those illustrated, Oddfellows Hall, Trelawny Square (19 names) is believed to have disappeared when the inside of the building was renovated in the early 1990s.

Presbyterian Chapel, Chester Road, with four names, also disappeared when the chapel closed some years ago.

CAMPAIGN MEDALS MENTIONED IN THIS BOOK

The **1914 Star** sometimes (unofficially) called the Mons Star, was awarded for service under fire in France and Belgium, 5th August–22nd November, 1914. This included sailors serving ashore

The **1914–15** Star was awarded for service in all other theatres of war: 5th August, 1914–31st December, 1915; and for service in France and Belgium, 23rd November, 1914–31st December, 1915

The **British War Medal** was approved in 1919, for issue to officers and men of British and Imperial forces who had rendered service overseas 5th August, 1914–11th November, 1918

The **Victory Medal** (also called the Allied Victory Medal) was issued to all those who received the 1914 Star or the 1914–15 Star, and to most of those who were awarded the British War Medal. It was never awarded singularly.

The combination of a Star, Victory Medal and British War Medal was fairly commonplace and earned for itself the nickname 'Pip, Squeak and Wilfred', who were cartoon characters in the Daily Mirror.

The pair of the Victory Medal and British War Medal, however, is seen more often simply because more men and women began service overseas after 1st January, 1916 than before. This combination was often called 'Mutt and Jeff', after the popular cartoon characters of the day in the San Francisco Chronicle

The **Silver War Badge** was issued in the United Kingdom to service personnel who had been honourably discharged due to wounds or sickness during World War I. The badge, sometimes known as the Discharge Badge, Wound Badge or Services Rendered Badge, was first issued in September, 1916, along with an official certificate of entitlement. The sterling silver lapel badge was intended to be worn on civilian clothes. It had been the practice of some women to present white feathers to apparently able-bodied young men who were not wearing the King's uniform. The badge was to be worn on the right breast while in civilian dress; it was forbidden to wear it on a military uniform

The **Territorial Force War Medal** was awarded to members of the British Territorial Force who joined before 30th September, 1914 and served in a theatre of war between 5th August, 1914 and 11th November, 1918

Mentioned in Despatches (MiD). A soldier mentioned in dispatches is one whose name appears in an official report written by a superior officer and sent to the high command, in which is described the soldier's gallant or meritorious action in the face of the enemy. For 1914–1918, and up to 10th August, 1920 the decoration consisted of a spray of oak leaves in bronze

The **Distinguished Conduct Medal (DCM)** was instituted by the British during the Crimean War (from 4th December, 1854) as a means of recognising acts of gallantry performed by 'other ranks' (i.e. non-commissioned officers). Until 1993, the DCM was an extremely high-level award for bravery, second only to the **Victoria Cross** in prestige

The **Distinguished Service Medal** was established on 14th October, 1914. It was awarded to personnel of the Royal Navy and of other Commonwealth countries – up to, and including, the rank of Chief Petty Officer – for bravery and resourcefulness on active service overseas

The **Military Medal (MM)** was established by King George V on 25th March, 1916 and was intended to meet the enormous demand for medals during the First World War. It was the other ranks' equivalent to the Military Cross (MC) and was awarded to the non-commissioned personnel of the British Army, and other Commonwealth countries, for bravery in battle on land

The **Mercantile Marine War Medal** was awarded by the British government (the Board of Trade). It was given to prior recipients of the British War Medal who had served at sea during the First World War and had sailed through dangerous waters

The **China War Medal (1900)** was a British Campaign medal approved in 1901 for issue to British and Imperial land and sea troops who fought during the Boxer Rebellion of 1900

The **Croix de Guerre** is a French military decoration, similar to the British 'Mentioned in Dispatches'. It was created to recognise French and Allied soldiers who were cited for their service in the war

The **Memorial Plaque** (popularly known as the 'Dead Man's Penny') was issued after the First World War to the next-of-kin of all British and Empire service personnel who were killed as a result of the war. The one above was commemorated to Sergeant George Robert Denton

WAR POETRY

The following three poems and song appeared in the local newspapers during the war years.

FALL IN
by Harold Begbie
(Flintshire Observer, 3rd September, 1914)

What will you lack, sonny, what will you lack
When the girls line up the street,
Shouting their love to the lads come back
From the foe they rushed to beat?
Will you send a strangled cheer to the sky
And grin till your cheeks are red
But what will you lack when your mate goes by
With a girl who cuts you dead?

Where will you look, sonny, where will you look
When your children yet to be
Clamour to learn of the part you took
In the war that kept men free?
Will you say it was naught to you if France
Stood up to her foe or bunked?
But where will you look when they give the glance
That tells you they know you flunked?

How will you fare, sonny, how will you fare
In the far-off winter night,
When you sit by the fire in an old man's chair
And your neighbours talk of the fight?
Will you slink away, as it were from the blow,
Your old head shamed and bent?
Or say – I was not with the first to go,
But I went, thank God, I went?

Why do they call, sonny, why do they call
For men who are brave and strong?
Is it naught to you if your country fall,
And Right is smashed by Wrong?
Is it football still and the picture show,
The pub and the betting odds,
When your brothers stand by the tyrant's blow
And England's call is God's.

PRO PATRIA
by Kathleen M Barrow
(Evening Standard, 29th August, 1914)

Listen, oh women of England!
Hark to a sound you know,
Calling your men to honour
Bidding them rise and go.

Here in the hush of waiting,
Harder than grief to bear;
When every thought is a yearning,
And ev'ry hope is a prayer.

Never a word must hinder,
Never a hand must stay,
Never a voice must falter
That cheers them upon their way.

Mothers, whose hearts are breaking,
Who sorrow and pain have known,
How would you answer England,
If you gave not England her own?

Sisters and wives and sweethearts,
Have you not urged them yet?
Yours is to point to duty,
Yours is to pay the debt.

Hark to the call of England!
Clear as a twilight bell.
Listen, O wives and mothers,
Listen. And heed it well!

A ROYAL WELSH FUSILIER RECRUITING SONG
(Tune: "Tramp, Tramp, Tramp, the Boys are Marching")
by a Captain
(Flintshire Observer, 1st October, 1914

Don't you hear your Country calling
All her sons to join the fray?
They have got a job on hand,
Just to smash a German band,
And to push Kaiser Wilhelm off the sea.

Come, boys, can't you hear them calling,
Aren't you going to lend a hand?
'Tis for freedom that you fight,
And to help maintain the right
Of the little Belgian heroes to their land.

Don't forget your King is looking
To you all to play the man;
Won't you join that noble throng
Just until they right the wrong
Of the Kaiser and his Huns near Waterloo.

Come, boys, join the Fifth Battalion,
They're just the crowd to see you through;
Men of Flintshire to the bone,
And "Men of Flint" 'twill soon be shown
They have proved themselves to be near Waterloo.

THE LANDING OF THE 1/5TH ROYAL WELSH FUSILIERS IN THE BALKANS
by Jack Hughes
(Flintshire Observer, 2nd December, 1915)

If after reading these few lines
they make you feel quite shirky,
Just join us in the trenches, boys, and help us capture Turkey.

The following poem was published 11 years after the war ended, and gives us some idea of how those that survived were treated in peace time.

LEST WE FORGET
"They died that we might live"
by Dick Thomas
Penyball, Holywell
(County Herald, 22nd November, 1929)

Sleep, brave warriors, in your bed of clay
Until Reveille sounds, on that Great Day,
When we shall meet again to part no more
With our Heavenly Father on that golden shore.

Eleven years have passed, yet still we don't forget
To honour you, who helped to pay that debt

XXX

Of Sacrifice, so that we all should live
Unfettered, free, what more, then, could you give?

Fear not, your names will never be forgot,
Nor deeds of valour on some foreign spot,
You gave your life, your all, without regret,
God bless you, lads! We shan't forget;

When duty called, you gave up home and love
To serve your King and Country and your "King above,"
You nobly did your duty, while others calmly slept,
You gave your all – we don't forget.

'Tis well perhaps you died, not lived to see
Your comrades, some in dire poverty;
For work and promises they ended all in smoke,
And now they're homeless, destitute, and broke.

'Twas not for this you fought and nobly died,
And when in danger oft your foes defied;
The honour of your flag you bravely kept
You did your duty – we must not forget.

Sleep on, old comrades, you are safe at last,
All your troubles over, and your dangers past;
Again we hope that some day we may meet you yet,
Farewell, dear comrades – God does not forget.

REFERENCES

Birkenhead Library
Cheshire Births, Marriages and Deaths Indexes (www.cheshirebmd.org.uk)
Cheshire Record Office
Colwyn Bay Cemetery
Colwyn Bay Library
Commonwealth War Graves Commission (www.CWGC.org)
Find a soldier's will (www.probatesearch.service.gov.uk)
Flintshire County Council (Connah's Quay Town Cemetery burial register)
Flintshire County Council (Northop Road Cemetery, Flint burial register)
Flintshire County Herald
Flintshire Observer
Flintshire Record Office
Flintshire War Memorials (www.flinshirewarmemorials.com)
Goole Council Offices, Goole, Yorkshire (Hook Road Cemetery burial registers)
Lancashire Births, Marriages and Deaths Indexes (www.lancashirebmd.org.uk)
The Long, Long Trail (www.1914-1918.net)
The National Archives, Kew, Richmond, Surrey
   (references: ADM/188/226; BT 351; WO 363; WO 364; WO 372; WO 374)
North Wales Births, Marriages and Deaths Indexes (www.northwalesbmd.org.uk)
Prisoners of the First World War, the ICRC archives (www.grandeguerre.icrc.org)
Republic of Ireland 1911 census and Births Index
Soldiers Died in the Great War Index (SDGW)
St Helens Cemetery burial register
St Mary's Parish Church, Bagillt parish registers
St Mary's Parish Church, Flint parish registers
St James's Parish Church, Holywell parish registers
St Mark's Parish Church, Connah's Quay parish registers
St Mary's Roman Catholic Church parish registers
The Pioneer, Colwyn Bay
The Wigan Observer and District Advertiser
UK Births, Marriages and Deaths Indexes (www.ukbmd.org.uk)
UK Census Returns
University of Wales, Bangor Archives Department
Wigan Record Office and Library
Wirral County Council (Bebington Cemetery burial register)